JAPANESE SOCIETY AND HISTORY

by John McKinstry and Harold Kerbo
California Polytechnic State University–San Luis Obispo

cognella
San Diego, CA

First published in the United States of America in 2011 by Cognella, a division of University Readers, Inc.

Trademark Notice: Product or corporate names may be trademarks or registered trademarks, and are used only for identification and explanation without intent to infringe.

15 14 13 12 11   1 2 3 4 5

Printed in the United States of America

ISBN: 978-1-60927-885-4

www.cognella.com 800.200.3908

Contents

Preface

In one sense, human societies are like individual human beings: Individuals are influenced by their environments and by events which happen in their lives. But while it is often possible to perceive and even to predict the effects of these factors, individuals who are subject to identical environmental and historical conditioning—siblings, for example—often end up with completely different personalities. And so it is with societies. Effects of some environmental factors are fairly obvious to see. For example, the Japanese have a healthy curiosity about the non-Japanese world, but at the same time, they tend to harbor attitudes that make it difficult for them to open up to a wider social reality. The United States, in turn, is a place where people become intimate very quickly, using first names almost at once and visiting the interior of homes of people they have just met. Both these traits have been forged to a great extent by geography. In Japan, people's attitudes were formed by the relative isolation of their homeland before the modern period; in the United States, they were formed by the broad expanses of territory, which dictated that people were often set down among strangers and had to learn to interact quickly in order to survive.

However, no amount of information about geography, or history, or physical characteristics, or anything else, can ever give us a complete explanation of why a particular society is the way it is. The best we can do is to learn about these things and use them as a framework to slowly fill in a more complete picture, the only way we can—by examining the important features of a society, one by one.

The American view of the world is what could be called "Eurocentric." We study mainly European languages, travel to Europe, and tend to know about the history, geography and cultural traditions of that area of the world more than any other. If we were to ask a reader of this page to name three cities in Italy, it is likely that, with a brief moment for reflection, he or she could do so. How many average U.S. citizens can name three cities in Japan or China?

That kind of Eurocentrism is understandable. North America was populated by Europeans more than by people from any other place. Many of our institutions are modeled on European prototypes. We share a spoken tongue with a European nation. Europe is part of our history.

Knowing something about Europe, or for that matter knowing something about any foreign place, certainly adds to our level of sophistication. However, it turns out that many people in this country, although we refer to them as Eurocentric, really don't know that much about *any* other place. Recently, the United Nations surveyed randomly selected people in eight countries, asking a few questions about current events in areas around the world. Americans didn't do so well, coming in at 6th place, trailing people from Canada, Australia, Germany, England, France and Spain, and barely coming in ahead of respondents from the Philippines and Algeria. More bad news came in the annual report published by the Swiss World Economic Forum, which ranked Americans quite low in their international experience and understanding. Such ignorance harms American competitiveness in the world economy in many ways. But there is further damage. An inward-looking view of the world inhibits us from grasping important truths about our own society. Seymore Martin Lipset put in nicely in one of his recent books: "Those who know only one country know no country."

This book is, in part, a second edition of an early book, *Modern Japan* (McGraw-Hill, 1998). It has been updated throughout, and several new chapters on earlier Japanese history have been added. As before, this book focuses on Japan, not because it is necessarily more important to be aware of that place than any other, but because it may help to make comparisons with ourselves and to broaden our understanding of how other people deal with the unavoidable tasks facing us all. As we say above, Europe is part of our history, but how about the present? The world is constantly changing. It is likely that some who read this have names emanating from some version of the Italian language, but in terms of such things as economic transactions and the exchange of technology, we have far more interaction with Japan and the rest of Asia than we do with Italy or any other place in Europe. It would be a good idea for Americans to begin to catch up with the reality of what places in the world are actually more strategic for our future, and to learn more about those places.

This writing is an attempt to give some basic orientation to Japan in a simple, non-scholarly way. We have avoided using citations whenever possible to make it as smooth a read as we can. You may be a little distracted by so many Japanese terms followed by the words in their native script. Most of you do not read Japanese, so simply ignore the Japanese writing. It is included for those students studying the language, who may wish to know how those specific vocabulary items are written in their native form. We should add here that all Japanese names are written Japanese-style, family name first. You may know him as Hideki Matsui, but in Japan, and in this book, he is Matsui Hideki.

We begin our exposition in the following pages with basic elements: The geography and physical characteristics of the Japanese and their homeland, a brief outline of Japanese history, and an examination of specific cultural features. We continue our foray into Japan with a look at Japan's economy and governmental structure, finally ending by exploring some social problems and commenting on possible future paths for that nation.

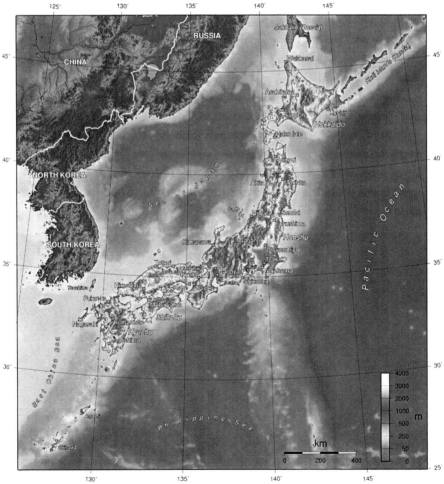

Chapter 1
The Place

Environment plays a significant role in the evolution of any culture. It provides challenges, creates restrictions, provides various degrees of access or isolation in regard to other peoples, and prior to modern technology, it determined when and how work could be done. Culture has to adjust to these realities, and in doing so, formulates, to a degree, the character of a given social tradition.

Consider the American prairie: Pioneers went to live there in comparatively small numbers, in comparison with the huge expanses of territory. American pioneers, as they moved into the wilderness, did not as often form village life as is the norm for other agrarian peoples; they tended more often to live in isolated households, often miles from their nearest neighbors. There were market settlements with stores and churches, but those places could not be traveled to easily or often. Most of the time, those people who settled the Midwest were on their own. The isolation of those people formulated, or at least helped to formulate, many of the characteristics so stereotypical of North American culture. These would include, among others, the famous pioneer self-reliance, an egalitarian view of society, an almost exaggerated sense of hospitality, independence, the unusually strong role of women in family life, and an indifference to, and even distrust of, distant governmental authority.

The Japanese have experienced a different physical and social environment altogether and have dealt with their own surroundings, and so completely different types of social themes evolved. Geography provided Japan with excellent furnishings for wet-rice agriculture, and after it arrived in ancient times from the Asian mainland, a great deal of social tradition has been influenced by that system. Throughout history, Asians have lived in villages. Maintaining the irrigation ditches for village rice production requires group effort and cooperation. Strong individualism doesn't work so well in that kind of setting. We will take a look at that environment, and before discussing anything else, consider Japan as a physical entity.

Japan consists of a series of four large islands together with many smaller ones. The largest is the main island of Honshū 本州, which would constitute a fairly large country if that's all there was to Japan. Over eighty percent of the Japanese population lives on that single island. Kyūshū 九州, in the south, was the route of ancient migrations and remained important historically, while Hokkaidō 北海道, in the north, has only been completely integrated into Japanese society for about 150 years. It is in many ways the most expansive and open part of the country, with some wide prairies and pasture land. The smallest of the four main islands, Shikoku 四国, is located off the southwestern coast of Honshū. The four islands extend between latitudes 30 and 45 degrees north.

While, as you can see from the map, the whole of Japan is made up of rather long narrow stretches of land—no place in the entire nation is more than seventy miles from the sea—the Japanese archipelago runs quite far from northeast to southwest, with a range of about seventeen hundred miles. In climate, the long series of islands that constitute Japan is similar to the east coast of the United States, with Japan's northernmost island of Hokkaido comparable to New England. Summers in Hokkaido are shorter and milder than further south, and winters are long and cold; there is even glacial ice in the ocean off the north coast of the island in the winter months.

The large middle island of Honshu and the smallest of all the larger islands, Shikoku, have a climate something like the area from New York to Washington, with four full seasons, including some hot summer days and perhaps a little snow in winter. Further south, Kyushu is somewhat similar to North and South Carolina, and finally, a few hundred miles further to the south, Okinawa 沖縄 is reminiscent of southern Florida, with the same kind of beaches beckoning northern tourists from November through March.

Something which greatly distinguishes Japan from the U.S. east coast, however, is terrain. As a string of mountain ranges pushed up above sea level by volcanic activity, Japan is in a geological sense very young. The rough mountainous terrain of Japan has not had enough time to wear down, and so there is comparatively little flat land anywhere. In fact, the country is so mountainous that wheeled vehicles were never widely used in Japan until the railway system made it there barely a hundred and fifty years ago; there was simply not enough level land to develop a road system suitable for carriages.

The Japanese customarily think of their nation as a small place, and in comparison with the United States, which including Alaska is about twenty-six times larger, it does seem small. But Japan, with 124,000 square miles of territory, is larger than the average nation. It is larger, for example, in land mass than Italy or Germany, and larger than the entire British Isles, including Ireland. However, in spite of its relatively large map size, Japan in anthropological terms is much smaller than it first appears. For the people who live there, Japan certainly suffers from a shortage of arable land.

Even if the nation were not so mountainous, with a population of a little over 127,000,000, only a little less than forty percent of the population of the huge United States and twice the population of Britain, Japan would have less land to go around than most other countries. What makes the situation of crowding so much more critical is that most of the population has to be packed together in small coastal plains; the interior of the country is simply too rugged for large-scale urban development or even for extensive agriculture.

Some parts of northern Honshu are actually under-populated, with quite sparse people-to-land ratios. Other parts of the nation are crammed with people; the two metropolitan regions centered around Tokyo and Osaka are areas of enormous population density in which over thirty percent of the Japanese reside. The metropolitan area around Tokyo, usually called *kantō chihō* 関東地方 or the Kanto region, smaller than the Los Angeles basin, has a population of around 23,000,000, just under five times the population of the Los Angeles basin.

While short on flat land, and lacking the resources of many other nations, one thing that Japan has plenty of is coastline. With more access to the ocean than many larger nations such as the United States, the sea has been and continues to be extremely important in the lives of the Japanese people. Coastal boats were for a long time a major form of transportation in such a mountainous country, and the Japanese take more food from the sea than any other people.

The four islands of Japan used to be separated by water. Today, all of the four islands are connected by land transportation with a long tunnel connecting Honshu and Hokkaiko, and a vast bridge network which now spans the distance between Honshu and the island of Shikoku. Kyushu and Honshu were tied together in this way early in the twentieth century. The famous bullet train system, the *shinkansen* 新幹線, which spans the entire rib of Japan from the top of Honshu to northern Kyushu, reaches speeds of 140 mph. The French super express can go faster, but covers less than one seventh the total rail distance of the total *shinkansen* system.

Japan lies on the western edge of the so-called "ring of fire," the arc of seismic action ranging from Southeast Asia up through Taiwan and

Japan, and across to the Aleutian Islands and down the west coast of North and South America. More so than for California, the ground under Japan is alive. One cannot stay in most parts of Japan for more than a few weeks without experiencing a minor earthquake. They usually don't cause serious damage—glasses rattle, light fixtures sway, everyone stiffens up in a kind of nervous reaction. And of course, we hear of far more serious quakes from time to time, which bring heavy damage and loss of life.

Japan suffered one of the most severe natural catastrophes in history in 1923. At slightly after 9AM on September 1, a devastating earthquake struck the Kanto region, the area of Tokyo and its surroundings. It was "The Great Kanto Earthquake Disaster," *Kantō Dai Shinsai* 関東大震災 in Japanese. The quake itself damaged over half of the city, but as in the Great San Francisco quake two decades earlier, most of the disaster was caused by the fire storm that followed. Over forty percent of the area's residences were completely destroyed. More than 130,000 people lost their lives, about six percent of Tokyo's population at the time of some 2.2 million.

As modern and economically developed as Japan has become since the 1960s, it was forced to delay the construction of very tall buildings in its major cities by several decades. Even today the skyline of Tokyo is much less impressive than that of New York City, built as that city is on solid granite, with no area history of earthquakes. It is a tribute to Japanese engineers that a few buildings of over seventy floors in height now exist in Tokyo, considering the stringent regulations inherent in the building code. All steel and concrete buildings in Japan are required to be anchored at least as deeply into the ground as their planned height above ground. This leads to slower and much more expensive construction than in many other places.

Another element of nature the Japanese have to live with is the yearly cycle of storms which sweep up from the south. They are called *taifū* 台風 in Japanese, or "typhoons." They arrive in late summer and early autumn; in some years not much more than just heavy storms with strong winds. But just as our own hurricanes and tornadoes, they can be deadly. In 1959 a typhoon destroyed the entire Nagoya harbor, killing more than 700 people. In the following chapter, you will read about the great typhoon of 1284, which saved Japan from a Mongol/Chinese invasion.

FOOD PRODUCTION

It follows that with so much population density in major urban areas, residential units tend to be smaller than in most nations, and the Japanese have had to learn to use land with great care. Farms in most parts of Japan are only a few acres in size and seem more like large gardens to foreigners. They are intensively worked, and in spite of their small size, they are among the most productive per acre in the world.

Japan does have one resource important for producing food—water. Sufficient water for agriculture was always a problem for the large populations of north China, resulting in diversion of rivers and other huge irrigation projects. This required powerful central authority, a condition which characterized all Chinese Dynasties, at least during their robust periods. Until just a little over a century ago, Japan was subdivided into smaller political units which later became feudal states. Japan, with from 50 to 120 inches in most places, has always had so much rainfall that the kind of central concentration of power characteristic of China throughout history has not always been needed.

As in other Asian societies, the traditional food staple in Japan was, and still is to a considerable extent, rice. It is grown in flooded rice paddies; one cannot travel very far in Japan without noticing the square pieces of land, which, early in the spring, look like small swimming pools, before the rice stalks peek up above the water level. A full forty percent of all cultivated land area is devoted to rice cultivation.

Until the opening of Japan late in the 19th century, a typical Japanese meal consisted of rice plus broiled fish and a small amount of vegetables. With the exception of sushi, which was developed by professional cooks in Tokyo around 1740, the famous Japanese cuisine served in restaurants all over the world today is made up mainly of dishes influenced by foreigners who came to Japan after 1870: Such things as *tempura, sukiyaki, shabu-shabu, tonkatsu*, etc.

The percentage of full time farmers in the Japanese population is only a little larger than that of the U.S., about four percent. That small percentage has played a much more powerful role in Japanese policy making than farmers have in the U.S. Food prices in Japan are surprisingly high. Rice, for example, costs close to three times what it costs in American supermarkets. Most other food products hover around twice the U.S. price, with Japanese average incomes barely above those of the U.S. What is the reason for this? Part of it is the effective pressure put on the government by the Japanese farm cooperatives. But even if this were not the case, it is likely that Japanese consumers would be willing to pay higher prices for raw food products than would seem to be justified.

Japan urbanized later than did North America. A fairly large portion of the Japanese population has parents, or at least grandparents, who were born and raised on farms. When Japanese think of farmers, they often think about their own relatives, who still live on farms and work at least part of the year as food producers. The *o-bon* お盆 festival, held each autumn, a kind of all-souls festival, is a time when many Japanese return to their ancestral roots, that is to say, to the farms where their parents or grandparents grew up. Japanese people are perhaps more sympathetic than Americans to the argument that food prices must stay high enough to support the agriculture segment of the population. The farmers who would suffer disadvantage if prices would fall drastically are often people they share some personal identity with. This sentiment seems to be weakening somewhat as some chain stores in Japan now offer food at more bargain prices.

Japan now imports far more of its food supplies than do the U.S. and most other industrial nations. Soy, for example, is fundamental to a great deal of Japanese food preparation. Over ninety percent of the soy beans used in making Japanese tofu is now imported. This makes the Japanese uneasy because if those supplies were ever cut off, Japan would be in a difficult situation. This is one reason Japan has been so stubborn about keeping out foreign rice and has dragged its fee in opening up Japanese agricultural markets.

JAPANESE CITIES

The Japanese have for a very long time been especially attracted to urban life. Although it could be said that Japan got a rather late start in having cities—Nara, the first urban center, did not begin to take shape until the middle of the eighth century—during most of recorded history, the Japanese have strongly preferred urban over rural life; as mentioned in the next chapter, for a long time, for the elite Kyoto-based population, banishment from the capital was among the severest of punishments.

Even today, the term *inaka* 田舎, "country" or "countryside," draws up images in the Japanese mind of crudeness, backwardness, and simplicity in a distinctly negative sense. *Inakappei* 田舎っぺい, "bumpkin," is a person of the country, someone ignorant of the finer nuances of cultivated living. Of course, bumpkin is an English word, and it is occasionally still used in much that same way wherever English is spoken. However, in the English-speaking world, an image of the countryside as outside the boundaries of true civilization has been countered somewhat by other images—the image of the gentleman farmer, for example, and the country residence of the British aristocracy. In the new world, men like Washington and Jefferson considered their true residence to be the country, not the city.

As you will learn, in the 12th century, Japan fell into widespread civil war. The areas around castles were the only places secure enough for sustained market activity, and for that reason all castles developed towns around them, the largest and most important ones eventually growing into true cities. European castles sometimes forged the same pattern, but in most cases, castles in Europe and elsewhere did not form the nucleus of urban life.

SOME FEATURES OF MODERN JAPANESE CITIES

A visitor to Japan could not be blamed for puzzling over such a strong preference for city living. Except for just a few places such as parts of downtown Yokohama and some new towns like Tsukuba (a kind of upscale industrial park northeast of Tokyo), Japanese cities and towns don't usually strike non-Japanese as being very attractive. While some of the recent architecture in the central parts of Japanese cities is exciting, there is rarely a sense of continuity in the Japanese urban landscape. Zoning has usually been avoided in Japan in order to support and encourage small businesses, resulting in what may be good for business, but not very good for creating a pleasant visual environment. Because Japan is so land poor, plots of land are sometimes unbelievably tiny; the buildings that end up on them are packed together with neighboring buildings of divergent sizes, styles and ages in a visually dizzying mess.

For a nation with 127 million people, as we have seen, the geographic area of Japan is not very big to begin with. To make matters worse, the country is very mountainous, as pointed out above, so that the actual area available for urban development is less than one seventh the total landmass. On top of this, Japanese tax laws encourage people with a little extra space to keep plots of land as food-producing gardens. Even though they may live only minutes from the centers of large cities, and are in every sense city dwellers, they are officially classified as farmers and pay almost no real estate taxes on their entire adjoining property. This of course adds to the shortage of land the rest of the people have left over for adequate housing.

It is hardly surprising then to learn that urban Japan is a very crowded place with space a highly valued luxury. Living accommodations are compact, and roads and highways are narrow even by the standards of the smaller European countries. Public park space in Japan is less available than in most other nations; in fact, almost everything that requires a place for it to exist is in short supply, or at least downsized compared to its counterpart elsewhere. Garbage trucks are a perfect example of downsizing. From a distance, garbage trucks in Tokyo and other cities of Japan look exactly like the ones developed for use in American cities. They have the same hydraulic arms that extend the garbage bucket to the back of the truck and all the way in front over the cab and the same stuffer which compacts the load into the truck. On closer approach, a visitor from abroad suddenly realizes that they are in a sense scale models, about one-half the size of trucks in the U.S. They have to be this size in order to squeeze through some of the tiny residential lanes in Japanese urban space.

HOUSING

One piece of evidence suggesting that the current racial makeup of Japan includes some ancient immigration from the southwest Pacific region is the nature of traditional housing. Up to the modern period, Japanese houses were made of wood, almost never of brick or stone as in China and Korea. Part of the reason for this was undoubtedly because that material can be made to withstand earthquakes better, but when we examine Japanese traditional domestic architecture, we see things reminiscent of coastal south Asia and the Pacific Basin that have little to do with earthquakes. Japanese straw mat flooring, for example, is not seen in other north Asian societies, being more like mat flooring in more southern climes.

The mat flooring is called *tatami* 畳 in Japanese, and traditional houses, still the abode of most wealthy Japanese, have floors of these mats throughout. They are like very hard hospital mattresses, covered with a polished straw material, and the covering needs to be replaced every few years. Even small modern apartments usually have one *tatami* room, and local *tatami* shops, places where the mats are made and repaired, continue to do brisk business.

Japanese share one cultural characteristic with Americans: The desire to live in a privately owned detached house is widespread and quite strong. For reasons pointed out above, this is less possible than in the U.S. People in Japan often have to make a choice between two alternatives: To live in a house located far away from the business district of an urban area and endure a long, exhausting commute to work, or to live in one of the hundreds, or in some cases thousands, of little apartment-like cells in a *danchi* 団地, the condominium complexes which dot the urban landscape usually a little closer in than the single home residential areas. The reason for the dilemma is that land prices are almost perfectly correlated with distance from the central parts of cities; the closer to the center, the more expensive, and the further out, the more affordable.

Danchi life often (but not always) offers escape from the grueling trip back and forth to work (ninety minutes or more each way is not unusual), but it is not a very attractive compromise. A family of three or four people supported by an adequate income, but with no more than five or six hundred square feet between them—roughly the area of a small one-bedroom apartment in the U.S.—is not the kind of life one would expect in a country with one of the highest per capita GNPs in the world. On the other hand, a ninety-minute train ride to work is not exactly luxury living either.

Not all Japanese have to make a choice between these two less than ideal alternatives. Some lucky people inherit a house close in to the urban core. Such property will probably stay in the family for the foreseeable future, because to sell it would be to turn over a very high percentage of the sale price in taxes, typically around forty percent, but to keep it requires only a comparatively modest annual property tax. But even these fortunate few must make some sacrifices. If people who manage to live in crowded neighborhoods close to the business district want to own and operate an automobile, municipal regulations require that they park it off the street overnight. In Tokyo, in fact, proof of a parking space is required by the city government before one can even register ownership of a car. Only rarely is there room on the property for a private garage; typically, car owners have to rent space in a parking facility, which can cost several hundred dollars per month.

Another way some people who live in crowded urban Japan avoid at least the stress of commuting to work is by living at their work. Merchants in Europe and the U.S. normally close down a small business enterprise after a day's operation and travel back to a separate residence. In Japan, with property values comparatively higher on average than in Europe and the United States, small business owners find it is simply too expensive to maintain two properties, one for business and one for residence. The most common practice is to operate the business out of the ground floor of a small building, and for the owner and his family to use the second and other floors as residential area. Until a hundred and fifty years ago, cottage industry was the only type of business in Japan, and today merchants are still referred to as family units: *honya-san* 本屋 さん, "the book house family," *nikuya-san* 肉屋さん, "the butcher house family," *denkiya-san* 電気屋さん, "the electric utensils house family," etc.

URBAN LIFE

When they talk about city life, most Japanese do the same thing we have been doing up to this point—they focus on the bothersome nature of urban environment. Japanese people often refer to their homes as "rabbit hutches." People tend to be more conscious of what is wrong with any social arrangement than with what works well. Crowded, yes. Beautiful, not usually. But neither is urban Japan a place of teeming masses miserably unhappy and poorly served. A more balanced view reveals that Japanese towns and cities are in some ways models of civility, with excellent facilities and a successful strategy in the face of difficult circumstances.

Public transportation is one of those impressive aspects of modern urban Japan. Hundreds of miles of inter-urban train tracks crisscross the urban landscape of the largest cities; trains leaving heavily populated suburbs to carry passengers to their work in downtown areas arrive at stations every few minutes during commute hours.

These trains are very crowded during rush hours, but the service is dependable, with train personnel as courteous and helpful as situations allow. Eight Japanese cities have subway systems; the network under the streets of Tokyo recently passed New York City as having the most subway miles of any city in the world.

The lack of urban zoning, although contributing to visual messiness as mentioned above, does have a positive side. For people who live in the built-up parts of towns and cities, shopping is much more convenient than the typical situation in the United States. Very few places in Japan are zoned for residential use only, with merchants prohibited from running businesses from their property. As neighborhoods develop, consumer businesses sprout up and develop along with them, so that most people can shop for food or other things needed for daily life with only a short few-minute walk, instead of having to drive, park and go through all the fuss required of most Americans.

Urban anonymity and indifference to shared communal interests has always been a drawback to city life everywhere. It is common for next door neighbors not to really know each other in modern urban residence areas all over the world, especially in large apartment complexes. The Japanese have some of this problem too, and in fact, in some ways the

Japanese are more indifferent to strangers in public than are Europeans and Americans. Japanese urban communities, on the other hand, try to work against that kind of disunity with all sorts of communal organizations, some of which work very well and have the effect of bringing a bit of village communalism to life in the faceless city. Many urban communities have neighborhood cleanup days for which a member of each residence unit contributes a few hours to tidying up the area.

It is not uncommon for older neighbors in Japanese cities and towns to form tour groups, traveling to hot springs resorts, and even taking trips to foreign countries together. Where one would expect the most facelessness of all, the large *danchi* complexes, there are usually various kinds of organized activities, including shared child care and different kinds of hobby groups.

So while it is not usually possible for the Japanese urban population to avoid conditions of crowdedness, people there bring considerable resourcefulness to the problems they have to face.

THE KANTO REGION

It is helpful in trying to understand urban Japan to take a closer look into the character of some of the largest and most important Japanese metropolitan areas. At the center of the Kanto region, a large plain along the pacific coast in the center of Honshu, lies Tokyo 東京, the nation's capital city, and just a few miles south of Tokyo lies the great port city of Yokohama 横浜. The meaning of the two Chinese characters used in writing *Kanto* 関東 is "east of the gate," originally referring to the area to the east of an important check point used to monitor movement of people back and forth between Edo and Kyoto by the Tokugawa regime in the Edo Period (1600–1868). Today it is used to mean the huge metropolitan area around the capital including Tokyo and several hundred square miles of satellite cities and suburbs. It is the place where decisions are made which affect the economies of nations all across the globe.

With around twenty-two million inhabitants, the Kanto region is the largest metropolitan area by far in Japan, and second in Asia only to Shanghai. French, Russians, and Mexicans can easily understand the central place of Tokyo in Japanese life. In their countries as well as in Japan, so much is both drawn to, and emanates from, a dominating capital city. Americans might have a harder time with this concept because American culture derives out of many regional urban areas, some which have traditionally played a dominant role in a particular industry: Detroit in the automotive industry, Pittsburgh in the steel industry, Southern California in the movie industry, etc. No one city in the U.S. is at the heart of all facets of national life. In Japan, Tokyo does indeed dominate virtually every aspect of that society; it is the political center, the nucleus of business and financial life, the entertainment center, the hub of national rail and air travel, the center of national and international communications, and the place where five of the top ten universities are located.

Except for a very few corporations such as the Toyota Motor Company centered near Nagoya, large Japanese enterprises have their main offices in the Tokyo area even if they manufacture most of their products elsewhere. Many Japanese complain that the nation is far too centered around the capital and its surrounding area, causing everything—government, businesses, services of all kinds, and above all, people—to try squeeze into that one place of a few hundred square miles, smaller, as mentioned above, than the urban area around Los Angeles. In a nation without much land for urban space, the area around Tokyo is the most crowded of all.

The Kanto region is the place where more opportunities exist for high-paying jobs than in any other part of Japan. It is also the center of higher education and certainly the center of political influence for the nation as a whole. This creates an artificially high value of real estate and also contributes to more crowding than would be the case if these things were more spread out over the nation. Although a lot of people who live in the Tokyo-Yokohama area would actually prefer to live in a smaller city and find life in the Kanto region a bit overwhelming, most Japanese are proud of their capital city. School children take group tours during their tenures as both junior high school and senior high school students, and at least one of those trips for schools in the provinces will be to Tokyo.

They visit the Imperial Palace, the National Diet building which houses both houses of the Japanese legislature; Meiji Shrine, the large park dedicated to the first emperor of the modern period; and the Tokyo tower, modeled after, but slightly taller than the Eiffel tower in Paris. We have lived most of our lives in California, in places like Los Angeles and San Luis Obispo. When people mention specific places in New York City in conversation, on occasion we will not be able to come up with any mental images of what they are talking about. Probably most of you have that same problem. But wherever we go in Japan, from the most remote areas of Hokkaido or Kyushu, if some place in Tokyo is mentioned, almost everyone knows about it because they have been there and seen it. A large percentage of adult Americans, certainly more than half, have never visited New York City or Washington D.C. To meet a Japanese adult, even an older and not so educated one, who has never been to Tokyo is quite a rare experience.

THE KANSAI REGION

Some three hundred miles to the southwest of the Kanto region is the second largest metropolitan area in Japan, the Kansai 関西 region, "west of the gate." In current usage, Kansai refers to the area around the city of Osaka 大坂 and includes the cities of Kobe 神戸 (where a calamitous earthquake did billions of dollars of damage and caused the deaths of more than 6,000 people in 1995), and Kyoto, the official capital city of Japan for over a thousand years until the middle of the last century.

With somewhere between eight and ten million people, the area has less than half the population of the area around Tokyo, and today it is not the center of very much of national life. But the history of the Kansai region goes back much further than that of Tokyo, and many people who live there are convinced that their area, Kansai, and not Kanto, is the real heart of Japanese culture.

The Tokugawa Shoguns, the regime which reigned over Japan from 1600 to 1868, in a real sense stole the center of Japanese life from Kansai and moved it to Kanto. True sons and daughters of Kansai have never quite forgiven this theft, and though most important institutions were eventually drawn to the new *de facto* capital, in their hearts they consider Tokyo an upstart region full of displaced farmers. An interesting symbol of this pride is the way media personalities in Kansai, for example people who read the news on local television, continue to speak Japanese with a distinctive local rhythm and accent, while television news in the rest of the nation has succumbed to imitating the speech patterns of Tokyo.

Osaka itself had its origins as a commercial center and even now still has the reputation of a place where business interests take center stage. This is one of the reasons that among large cities of the developed world, it has a notoriously small amount of public park space. Osaka merchant families were the first to develop modern capitalism in Japan; some of the most famous names in Japanese business history—Mitsui, Sumitomo, Nomura, Matsushita—originate from Osaka; a few of them were famous even before the modern period in Japan began in 1868.

American military commanders were ordered not to bomb the city of Kyoto during the war with Japan, and so it escaped the destruction rained down on most of the other urban centers. It exists today, as it has for centuries, as an architectural record of Japanese civilization. There are over 500 temples of historical significance in Kyoto, some dating back to the ninth century. Those, together with some of the most famous gardens in the world, as well as the old imperial palace, draw more tourists than any other place in the country, both foreign and native. If one were limited to just a single place to see as a tourist in Japan, Kyoto would probably be the best choice.

SAPPORO

The northernmost and second largest island of the Japanese archipelago, Hokkaido, was the last area to be brought into the sociological and economic orbit of Japanese life. As late as 1910, less than two percent of the Japanese population lived there, and its capital, Sapporo 札幌, was little more than a military post near the middle of the island surrounded by a town of hardy pioneers. A Japanese Rip Van Winkle from that time would not have believed what he would see a scant 100 years later. For decades it has been the fastest growing urban area in Japan, recently passing Nagoya as the nation's third largest city, with a population of close to four million.

Together with Kyoto, which lies next to a large lake, Sapporo is the only other large Japanese city which is not a seaport, and it is located about fifty miles inland from the nearest port of Otaru 小樽. Most of Sapporo's growth has taken place since the 1950s, and being so young, it has had a distinct advantage over older Japanese Cities in that as it grew, it was able to better accommodate modern street planning and the motorcar.

We mentioned above that Japanese cities usually do not appear very attractive to outsiders. Sapporo comes closer than most to avoiding that characterization, and in fact, some parts of the urban area are rather handsome. Most streets in residential areas are laid out in straight lines and cross each other at right angles, a rarity in the rest of Japan. Street numbering in Sapporo is consecutive, as in most of the rest of the world, and does not follow the maddening chronological numbering system of the rest of Japan.* The downtown area, while perhaps not to the extent of a San Francisco or a Seattle, has a certain functional attractiveness to it. One notable feature is the underground city, a shopping area one story under the surface of the central part of downtown that stretches for many blocks—a convenience for shoppers on cold Hokkaido winter days.

The development of the area around Sapporo during the second half of the twentieth century was quite extraordinary. The city itself had a population of around 250,000 immediately after the war. By 1980, it had grown to almost two million! Wheat and dairy products began to catch on in Japan in the 1950s, and because Sapporo is too far north for successful rice production, the several thousand square miles of rich soil surrounding Sapporo was available and quickly became the source of two new massive industries—wheat products, especially wheat noodles, and a wide range of dairy products. A second source of growth is a tourist

---

* It may be hard to believe, but the normal way of numbering properties in Japan is according to the date of their development within a relatively small demographic area, so that property number 5 may be next to number 18, etc.

industry which has put the area second only to Kyoto as a destination for tourists.

As Japan joined the ranks of affluent populations of the world, skiing became a popular recreation. With long winters and situated as it is close to mountains perfect as ski slopes, Sapporo rapidly grew into the winter sports and recreation capital of Japan, and not just as a winter destination for Japanese travelers. Hokkaido has a climate unlike that of any other part of the nation. It is outside the range of rain clouds which cover Japan for most of the spring and early summer, which make a sunny day during those months a rare treat. It is also far enough north to escape the scorching heat and humidity of Japanese summers, making Sapporo an attractive year-round tourist destination.

So then we can see that just as in the United States, geography, weather, population density, agricultural practices—all these things— have worked to help create definitive themes in Japanese life. Japanese are more community oriented than are Americans; this is true even for those Japanese who live in very large cities. This is no doubt due to the long historical period when close-knit village life and close cooperation in the agricultural cycle was the norm for all but a very small minority of aristocrats and townspeople. The group, especially the work group, has long been noticed as far more central to Japanese life than in most other places. Historically the Japanese have had an unusual curiosity and respect for cultural elements which come to Japan from the outside. This is easier to understand when we contemplate how recent it has been that these people could escape the bounds of their island isolation.

This then has been a discussion of the physical aspect of the Japanese nation. Next we will take a look at the people who lived and adjusted to those circumstances.

NAGOYA

Some geographers rank the third largest metropolitan area in Japan a place called Kita Kyushu 北九州, but all you have to do is go there and you will discover that the place has no actual core city, it's just a bunch of large towns all bunched together and counted as an urban area. The real third largest, and certainly historically a far more important urban area is Nagoya 名古屋, center of a region usually labeled Chubu 中部 or *middle area,* signifying its important location. Nagoya lies on the old tōkaidō 東海道, the road linking the two great historical power centers of Japanese life—Kyoto and Edo (which later became Tokyo).The population of Nagoya proper is only a little over 2 million, but the metropolitan area surrounding it contains over 5 million inhabitants, about the same as its sister city of Los Angeles, California.

Nagoya has a fine deep water port and was significant as a shipping area as far back as Japanese history goes. During the Edo Period, which you will read about later, Nagoya was administered directly as a fief of the ruling Tokugawa clan. They built a castle there, completed in 1612, which was destroyed in the war but rebuilt exactly to its original dimensions in 1959. It has been turned into a very interesting museum. Atsuta Shrine 熱田神宮 is in the Nagoya area, the second most venerated holy place in Japan, next to Ise 伊勢 further to the south.

In modern times, Nagoya has been one of Japan's chief export centers (nearly 40% of Japan's exports ship from its port), as well as one of its main manufacturing hubs. Before the end of World War II, Nagoya was home to the Japanese aircraft industry, one reason why the city and surroundings were so heavily bombed by the U.S. Air Force. Although not targeted for nuclear weapons, destruction brought about by standard bombs was in many ways as great as for Hiroshima and Nagasaki.

Over time it made a complete recovery and came eventually to be home to the largest vehicle manufacturing center in the world. One of Nagoya's suburbs changed its name a few years ago to reflect the importance of the largest single employer in the area. The suburb is now officially known as Toyota City.

The Toyota plant covers several square miles, and although as you know they have been having some very serious quality control problems recently, Toyota was established over a decade ago as the world's largest producer of cars and trucks. The importance of the company to the economy of the Nagoya area can hardly be exaggerated: Over 30,000 workers are employed directly at the plant and another 20,000 work for suppliers located nearby.

The physical features of a nation and a culture can be important, as suggested earlier, in the way people live their lives. Human culture, however, has a reality of its own, and societies that share the same physical environment often turn out to be quite different. At this point, we leave geography, topography, the nature of the urban landscape, etc. and concentrate on the people who inhabit the Japanese islands; who they are, what they do, and how they live.

Chapter 2
The People

As strong as the feeling of nationalism often is among Americans and Canadians with all that diversity, imagine if, save for very small segments of the population, the U.S. had only one religion for almost the entire nation, one race, one ethnic background, and all names emanating from a single language. And imagine if we shared almost no local history with any other society. That is exactly how it is to be Japanese.

As we have seen, compared with some of its neighbors, Japan does not cover a particularly large land area. However, with about 127,000,000 residents, Japan until quite recently was still one of the ten most populous nations of the world. No European nation save Russia has as many people, and no large nation on earth has a population which is as homogeneous as that of Japan. How does this homogeneity set Japan apart from almost all other nations? Consider this: Over ninety-five percent of the residents of Japan are of the same race, have family names emanating from a single language, relate to the same religious orientation, and trace their ancestry back as far as historical records go to the area of their present country. *Over ninety-five percent!* The only other nations that can even come close to that kind of homogeneity are places like Norway and the two Koreas. But Norway has less than one fourth the population of the single city of Tokyo, and both Koreas together make up only about half the population of Japan. North China is as homogeneous as Japan and has more people, but of course North China is not a nation.

In the modern world, several nations—for example Britain, Denmark, and Malaysia—have retained constitutional monarchies, symbolic holdovers from a previous time in history before more representative forms of governments were developed. The Japanese have a symbolic constitutional monarch as well. However, in a historic and psychological sense, there is a basic difference between the Japanese emperor and all the rest of the royal and imperial families. The Japanese emperor traditionally was defined as a connection with divinity and with the gods of Japanese mythology, the theoretical ancestors of the Japanese people. Of course virtually no one in Japan today carries those kinds of notions, but there is still the feeling among many Japanese, perhaps the bulk of the population, that the Emperor is something more than simply a traditional role. It is a little difficult to pinpoint just how the Japanese feel about the Emperor, and there is a range of attitudes on the subject, but however people consider his role, it is at the heart of Japanese identity.

Other kings and emperors have intermarried with foreign royal families, but it would be inconceivable for a member of the Japanese Imperial family to marry anyone but another Japanese. In a way, Japan is a family, with the Emperor as its head. He is more than the symbolic head of a nation; for many in Japan, he is a kind of spiritual father. Because of that feeling of kindred connection to the nation (quite unconscious in most cases), one can live *in* Japan, but one cannot be actually *of* Japan without a specific combination of genetics and geography.

JAPANESE IDENTITY

The issue of "what a person is," that is to say, who he/she is and to which of the various categories available does one belong, or belongs partially, can be a complicated question in many societies. People in places like the United States and Canada most likely carry strong feelings of national pride characteristic of people all over the world. But they share that identity with all sorts of sub-identities: Identities of ethnic heritage, identities of race, identities of religious affiliation. With many religions, several races, and all kinds of separate ethnic history, the *nation* is the only thing all Americans and Canadians share. If the U.S. Olympic basketball team plays a team representing another country, there almost surely will be some young people in the audience shouting "U-S-A, U-S-A"! at the top of their lungs.

For those of you who grew up in the United States, a place where people of divergent races and ethnic heritages identify as members of the same nation, it is probably difficult to conceptualize Japanese attitudes about their own society. Although Japanese today travel a great deal in the world and have superficial contact with different kinds of people, the great bulk of the Japanese population has never really interacted with anyone but other Japanese. People who are not of the Japanese race and who have not grown up in Japan are given labels. The most common of these labels is *gaijin* 外人, which means "non-Japanese" or foreigner. This is used to label non-Japanese of European and African racial characteristics. Other Asians, together with people of the Japanese race who have grown up elsewhere and are not Japanese citizens, are given different labels. These labels are never outgrown, no matter how long one lives in Japan or how well one speaks Japanese.

While it is often annoying to foreign residents in Japan to be labeled as *gaijin*, the label does not necessarily have a negative meaning associated with it. Foreigners who come to Japan as adults to work, study, and teach, provided they are "respectable," i.e. reasonably well educated with a middle class lifestyle, are usually treated with courtesy and respect. They usually do not stay for more than a few years and are considered to be guests in the country.

There are a few exceptions to the temporariness of *gaijin*. For example, David Spector, an American who originally came to Japan as a student, has lived in Japan since 1983. He has become a kind of "professional American." Fluent in the language, with an engaging and amusing personality, he writes columns for two Japanese magazines and often appears on Japanese talk shows, explaining the American perspective on some issue or other, or simply being the affable and likeable American he is. His face, often used in advertising, is as well known to every Japanese beyond infancy as their own popular media stars.

David Spector is a *gaijin*; neither he nor anyone else would ever attempt to deny that. His popular position in Japanese society certainly proves that the *gaijin* label does not necessarily incite rejection or a negative reaction. David lives a comfortable life in Japan and is perfectly acceptable to the population. But he is and will always be an outsider. The boundary between Japanese and non-Japanese is as fundamental as it is durable.

For the Japanese population, except for two rather small minority groups we will explore later in the chapter, there is hardly any possibility of a basic, ascribed secondary identity. With that in mind, it is easier to understand the depth of feeling of being Japanese. It is not that Japanese are so overtly patriotic; only rarely does one see Japanese shouting the equivalent of U-S-A in public. It is that there is an intense feeling among Japanese that they belong to a special breed, completely unlike any other. This can be seen rather clearly in the way they follow the exploits of Japanese in other parts of the world. It might surprise an American visitor to a Japanese home to turn on local television in the morning and suddenly be confronted by a baseball game broadcast from a foreign country, several thousand miles across the Pacific Ocean. Most people are at work at that time, but there is still a fairly large viewing audience for the game. It all began with the exploits of one man.

Suzuki Ichiro is a wonderful athlete, a star player for the Seattle Mariners baseball team. His contract was purchased by Seattle following a stellar baseball career of more than ten years in Japan. After moving to the United States, for several years running he had more base hits than any other player in the American major leagues. Even though his team does not always have a successful season, as long as he continues to play, every single game of the Seattle Mariners will continue to be broadcast on Japanese television.

Other Japanese baseball stars playing in the United States have had almost as much media coverage. If Matsui Hideki, the star outfielder recently traded to the Los Angeles Angels, hits a home run, the story is sure to receive more print space in Japan than in Los Angeles. Nomo Hideo was the first Japanese player to reach authentic star status in the United States. He pitched for the Los Angeles Dodgers from 1995 through 1998 and was named rookie of the year in his first year with the Dodgers, striking out more hitters than any pitcher in the National League for two seasons running. During the 1995 and 1996 seasons, each time Nomo pitched, the game was broadcast on huge screens on the sides of buildings in downtown Tokyo. Compare that with the coverage of Warren Cromartie, who, following a successful career with the Montreal Expose, was purchased by the Tokyo Giants of Japan's Central League. He played for the Giants for four years, leading the league in hitting in his first year (1992), and in home runs for two other years. Perhaps a whopping one percent or less of American sports fans even knew that he ever played in Japan.

THE JAPANESE RACE

The Japanese consider themselves to be a separate race. Exactly what constitutes a human race is a controversial subject among scholars. Whether or not the Japanese constitute a race, it certainly is true that the majority of Japanese people, present and past, have been interbreeding for thousands of years, evolving physical characteristics that are different on average in some small respects from other north Asians such as the Koreans or Mongolians.

Although the Japanese are quite conscious of their homogeneity, in some ways thinking of themselves almost as one big racial family, scholars who study the subject have solid evidence that the Japanese are made up of a mixture of racial ingredients. It is quite obvious that the bulk of the population is basically of East Asian origin, with most of the genetic inheritance coming from north Asia, probably by waves of tribal people who came to the Japanese islands through the Korean peninsula. These tribal people seemed to have arrived sometime between three to four thousand years ago. There is general agreement, however, that the Japanese are not pure East Asian, but actually a mixture of mainly East Asian with at least two other racial types.

At least a thousand years before the large infusion of population from north Asia, people similar in racial type and culture to present-day Pacific Island people such as Micronesians and original Taiwanese, people of darker skin and wavier hair than north Asians and without the characteristic Asian eye shape, drifted into the islands. As mentioned in the previous chapter, remnants of this part of Japan's prehistory can still be seen in domestic architecture, with light wooden prototypes not seen anywhere else in the northern part of the Asian region. And of course, they left some of their genes as well; the range of physical appearance in Japan, more than in China or Korea, includes many people who could fit unnoticed with a group of Pacific Islanders.

The third and smallest of the mixture of three racial types is with what is usually considered to be the aboriginal population of the islands. Not very much is known about where this group originally came from or even when they arrived, but it is believed that they predate the two larger waves of immigration by several thousand years. They were short in stature, did not have the typical Asian epicanthic eye shape, and had much more body and facial hair than East Asians.

The aboriginal population did not practice agriculture, although some of them did have a form of gardening. They lived mostly by hunting and fishing, and just as other hunting and gathering people in other parts of the world, they were "in the way" in the minds of the more sophisticated newer arrivals. When the Asiatic Japanese began to spread over the islands in the first millennium BC, a slow process of removal, cultural dominance, and even occasional genocide reduced the aborigines to marginal status.

The survivors of this race of original inhabitants of the Japanese islands are known today as the *Ainu* アイヌ. In previous times, the people we now call Japanese had other names for them. They called the largest group of aborigines *Ezo* 蝦夷, and *Emishi* (written with the same two characters), something like "wild barbarians." For the last 100 years or so, the aborigines are most associated with the Ainu, people who still live mainly in the southern part of Hokkaido. The fact that Japanese today on average have more body hair than other north Asians and men in Japan have the ability to grow fuller beards than most of their neighbors is usually attributed to a small strain of aboriginal admixture in the Japanese gene pool.

Early records of Chinese who made contact with people in Japan during the first couple of centuries of the Christian era describe them as being a race of physically small people. Until well into the twentieth century, very few Japanese consumed meat or dairy products, both good sources of protein aiding in full development of potential stature. Added to this was the fact that Japanese traditionally sat on the floor, either cross-legged, or more formally sitting directly over their lower legs. That habit can hinder development of leg length. These circumstances produced a population shorter on average than, for example, the Chinese.

Your first author remembers riding the subway in Tokyo back in the 1970s and at 5' 11" being often the tallest person of the fifty or so people in the car. But that changed as Japan began to prosper and expand its tastes for a wider variety of foods. Japanese architecture still provides for traditional sitting arrangements, but at school, work, and even at home, fewer Japanese sit in the traditional fashion for much of the time. Japanese are now about average in bodily displacement in the world. A few years ago the Kabuki theater in downtown Tokyo had to replace its seats because many young Japanese could not fit in ones designed back in the 1930s.

The racial mixture discussed above is the stuff of scholars, completely lost on the great bulk of the contemporary population of Japan. They certainly do not consider themselves any kind of mixture. The people who lived in that country were cut off from other cultural systems for several thousand years. Of course, there has always been some internal diversity among people who came to think of themselves as Japanese. But what has really impressed them has always been the contrast between their own identity and all others in Asia, or in the world for that matter.

Some Japanese theorists, in their enthusiasm to honor and give credence to the unique way of life that developed there, have tended to interpret Japanese uniqueness in terms of race. Since the 1920s there has been a genre of writing in Japan called *Nihonjin-ron* (日本人論) which is a kind of popular anthropology of the Japanese people. Some of it is academically legitimate, but it can degenerate into all kinds of silly discourse concerning the racial basis for Japanese cultural features, with no scientific validity at all. Unfortunately, people who should know better are sometimes influenced by that kind of theorizing. The Japanese pharmaceutical industry still uses this kind of argument to keep out foreign competition. A few years back, Japan was being pressured to open import markets to more U.S. and Australian beef. At that time a Japanese government spokesman, apparently in complete seriousness, claimed that it would not be possible for Japanese people to include large amounts of beef in their diet due to the unique way the Japanese digestive system functioned.

Perhaps the best way to dismiss this kind of nonsense is to point out how people of the Japanese race have adopted as easily as anyone else to various lifestyles all over the world. Third and fourth generation Japanese Americans, Japanese-Peruvians, Japanese-Brazilians, or the descendents of Japanese living anywhere outside Japan, even when they are of purely Japanese racial stock, usually have diets and lifestyles indistinguishable from the other people they live around.

Thousands of Japanese-Brazilians have returned in recent years to Japan in search of employment. For a time, the Japanese government actually encouraged the trend, perhaps influenced by the ideas of *Nihonjin-ron*, that all people of the Japanese race have some sort of invisible bond. Some have gotten on well, but the bulk of the Brazilian returnees, most of them carrying a complete set of Japanese genes, have had difficulty adjusting to life in Japan. They, of course, speak Portuguese, and most have remained illiterate in the language of their new host country. They congregate together during their leisure time doing the things which were familiar to them back in Brazil.

It would not be unfair to suggest that the current wave of Japanese-Brazilian immigrants to Japan have created considerable friction between themselves and their local non-Brazilian neighbors. They were given special immigration privileges unavailable to people of any other nation; the plan was to use them to fill the worker gap in needed occupations. However, after a few years, many employers refused to hire Japanese-Brazilians. They were considered on average to be sloppy workers, often tardy and difficult to communicate with; so much for the invisible bond.

For all their remarkable homogeneity, the Japanese do have social cleavages. Surprisingly, given the historical division of people into almost caste-like categories during the eighteenth and nineteenth centuries, which you will read about later, social class division is not very pronounced. Unlike western Europe and to a lesser extent North America, where speech patterns, dress and life style distinguish people of varying social levels, the Japanese are more egalitarian in those regards. There is, for example, no "society page" in Japanese newspapers.

But one way the adult population is separated into disparate groups as much as other nations, certainly more so than the United States, is politics. Japanese politics extends further to the right and further to the left than is the case in North America. There is a viable communist party, and together with the socialist party, which is further to the left than socialist parties in the West, they together can claim nearly twenty percent of the Japanese electorate. The ultra right in Japan is not very much a part of the formal government scene, but they are hard to ignore due their constant public demonstrations. The two extremes hate each other and make no bones about it.

LIFE IN A DEVELOPED NATION

There are, of course, several different ways nations can be compared and classified. There are currently about 200 societies in the world which are sufficiently large enough and autonomous enough to qualify as nations. If we examine these 200 nations carefully, we uncover many social and cultural aspects that cause them to be different from each other, and we see other aspects that cause each of them to be similar to other societies. In comparing Japan with other industrial nations of the modern world, we can see how societies can be both very different and quite similar at the same time.

The level of economic development of societies by itself is a powerful determinant of the way people live their lives. The overwhelming majority of the nearly 200 nations of the world are poor in economic terms, and while all of them include people with advanced education and high standards of living, those kinds of people are part of a small elite sector of the population, not representative of average citizens. There are relatively few nations in which ordinary people enjoy high standards of living. Japan is one of them, along with a couple of dozen other societies such as the United States.

In a sociological sense, a list of the ways the vast majority of Americans and the vast majority of Japanese are similar is a fairly long one. To begin with, both societies have a large middle class. By world standards, average people in both places eat well, dress well, know a lot, travel a great deal both within and outside their nations, and share, along with the rest of the economically advanced nations, the fruits of a highly developed and widely dispersed technology. An average Japanese person might well find it easier to stay for a time in a rural American household than in, for example, a typical rural Chinese household. The modern world of advanced nations has to a considerable degree produced a common culture, at least on a superficial level, sharing much of the same hardware and spending time doing many of the same things.

Both Japanese and Americans give more than a third of their young people some kind of formal education beyond high school, the highest of any two large nations in the world. Both complain about government a lot, but people in neither society need live in fear of it, and both receive expansive and expert services from all levels of government, which they both tend to take for granted. Survey research reveals that most people in both societies, while recognizing that their nation has difficult problems, consider it the best place to live of any place in the world.

But of course, there are significant ways in which Japanese and Americans are different, and in fact, Japan stands alone in certain cultural and social features, somewhat set apart from all the other nations of the economically developed world.

The Industrial Revolution was the starting point of modern economic development, and the nations earliest to be effected by that historical phenomenon are still among the leading economic powers. The modern economic system began in Europe, and for more than a hundred years, only European societies and their offshoots were part of it.

Europeans saw themselves as leaders of a new world order based on economic power, which ultimately translated into military power. This was the mentality which produced the system of European colonialism; the characteristics of European-based culture and history were often widely assumed to be necessary for joining the club of rich and powerful nations.

Japan destroyed those notions forever. For the first time in history, a nation traveled a completely different route into the top level of industrial powers. Japan proved to the world that a nation need not be European, trace its civilized roots from classical Greece or Rome, or have any significant connection to Christianity, in order to become a fully developed industrial society. The significance of all this will be stressed a bit more in later chapters on the political and economic institutions of Japan.

MINORITY POPULATIONS

In Japan, people tend to take for granted that the people they deal with in everyday life will be very much like themselves. Their culture is comparatively intricate, full of subtle nuances. Foreigners are cut a little slack; Japanese don't expect them to understand just how everything should be done, and even if they stay a long time in the country, they are usually given some reprieve from all the little details of etiquette adult Japanese have to pay attention to. But for people who are defined as part of the Japanese population, Asian people who look like Japanese, but are in some way different, there has been an unfortunate tendency to shut them out and to put them in special categories with all kinds of resulting discrimination. In other words, except for racially distinct foreigners, Asians residing in Japan who are not biologically Japanese tend not to be included as part of the big family suggested above.

For all their real and imagined homogeneity, the Japanese do have minority populations that don't fit the "one big family" ideal. These minority populations aren't very large in comparison to minority populations in many other societies; otherwise, we couldn't count the Japanese as so homogeneous.

The two minority populations described below have been the target of prejudice and discrimination, as have minority populations in many other parts of the world, including the United States. Unfortunately, in the history of the human race, the urge to feel superior to others and to act upon that urge to keep certain people in a vulnerable position is not often avoided. What you read in the next section can make the Japanese appear to be heartless villains. But imagine how the story of slavery and racial exploitation in the U.S. must sound to the Japanese. In both cases, the situation, negative as the story is, has improved markedly in recent years. There has not been anything akin to a full-fledged civil rights movement in Japan, but both groups described here are in a much better position in the society than ever before.

THE DŌWA

The largest minority group in Japan is a subdivision of the Japanese population, historically just as Japanese as anyone, but traditionally considered by ordinary Japanese to be outcasts, somehow not a legitimate part of the "big family" concept. The label given to this group changes over time: Until around the end of World War II, they were usually labeled *Eta* 穢多, "unclean;" then, the term *Burakumin* 部落民, "people of *that* district" became their standard label; more recently, at their own urging, people in Japan have referred to the group as *Dōwa* 同和, "equal Japanese."

Dōwa do not look on average any different from other Japanese. They have ordinary Japanese names; in fact, there is nothing to distinguish them other than their historic identity as *Dōwa*. Some Japanese, even today, are always on the lookout for *Dōwa* trying to pass as non-*Dōwa*, and extensive family background searches are sometimes still carried out (almost like security clearances for sensitive State Department jobs in the United States) by prospective employers and by families interested in the background of people they might consider as marriage partners for young members of their own families. Estimates of how many people live in this predicament range between two and three million, or between 1.5 and 2.5 percent of the total Japanese population.

It is always rather difficult to explain the *Dōwa* phenomenon, especially their origins, without making the whole nation appear to suffer from some kind of ghastly neurosis. It is a bit hard to believe, but in spite of the fact that the *Dōwa* population is regarded by many Japanese to be somehow fundamentally different from everybody else, no one knows for sure exactly how they got to be identified as an outcast group. The most widely believed explanation is that they were people who were engaged in slaughtering animals and working with hides at a time when a very strict version of Buddhism spread over the land, which considered such occupations defiling.

There are fundamental weaknesses to this explanation, such as the fact that many families not identified as *Dōwa* have histories of working with hides far back into the past, together with the fact that evidence of *Dōwa* populations seems to stretch back beyond the time when Buddhism became a truly popular religion in Japan. But whether their origins are clear or not, there has been nothing unclear about the result of being born into a *Dōwa* family.

During the pre-modern period of Japanese history, *Eta* were officially registered as a separate population. Late in the nineteenth century, the category was officially abolished, and a few decades later, in the 1920s, it was declared illegal to discriminate against what the government con- sidered "former Burakumin." However, they continued to be treated as outcasts by many Japanese. *Dōwa* even today tend to live in segregated neighborhoods, and the discrimination, while not as widespread or severe as it once was, continues.

Since many Japanese do not like to work with *Dōwa*, some feel compelled to reject known *Dōwa* as employees, while never admitting that *Dōwa* status is the real reason. Even the most educated and liberal- minded Japanese normally would not consent to marriage between their own children and children of people known to be *Dōwa*. They know that, although they may not approve of discrimination against *Dōwa* themselves, others will not likely share their tolerant views, and they would be subjecting their own offspring to a life of subtle and sometimes not so subtle rejection.

As with many social groups which suffer from discrimination else- where, all sorts of stereotypes and rumors characterize the image of *Dōwa*. They are widely believed to practice sexual deviancies such as incest and promiscuity. It will not surprise you to learn that *Dōwa* have lower incomes than the average Japanese and that their educational achievements are well below average.

One of the most conspicuous aspects to the *Dōwa* phenomenon is its lack of conspicuousness. One can live for several years in Japan without ever hearing or seeing any reference to the problem in the Japanese media. Part of this is due to the reluctance of Japanese to confront controversial social issues in public, but another major reason for the conspiracy of silence concerning the *Dōwa* stems from their own organizations. Like minority populations in other places, *Dōwa* have formed organizations which represent their interests to the society in general. Unlike similar organizations in the United States, who for example in representing interests of Black America brought intense focus on their problems to the media, *Dōwa* organizations have decided that silence is the best policy. Any mention of *Dōwa* by print or electronic media not officially approved by *Dōwa* spokesmen in advance can bring ugly sit-ins and other demonstrations by highly organized groups of *Dōwa*. Since these are seen as bad for the image of the publishers or broadcasters, they simply avoid the subject whenever possible.

In past years, we used to think young Japanese were simply lying to us when they declared nearly complete ignorance of the whole issue of identity and treatment of *Dōwa*. But over time we began to realize that it is not hard to believe that many Japanese only become familiar with the actual situation when *Dōwa* actually touch their lives in some way. One might imagine that this kind of widespread ignorance of the problem would cause it to gradually disappear. But in spite of the fact that the existence of *Dōwa* has become something of a national secret, there always seem to be enough people around who know how it is supposed to operate to keep the pattern of discrimination very much in place.

THE KOREANS OF JAPAN

There are about half a million residents of Japan who are defined by themselves and by other Japanese as belonging to what the Japanese consider the *Korean race*. They are people who live in Japan but whose parents, grandparents or great grandparents came from Korea. Almost all of these Koreans of Japan trace their decent through families that have lived in Japan for at least three generations. In most other countries—the U.S., Germany, Britain—they all would have long ago become citizens, and since they are not physically distinguishable, they would have blended into the social fabric of the surrounding society. But Japan is not just any other country. The Japanese have always had a difficult time with the concept of outsiders becoming a part of their nation. Although they have been assimilated in almost every sense, most Koreans of Japan still today live in the country as residents, but officially as foreigners, citizens of one of the two Koreas.

People of Korean ancestry live in several nations outside the two Koreas. Northeast China has a sizeable Korean population as well as extreme eastern Russia, and there are now more people of Korean ancestry in the United States than in Japan. In the United States, Koreans and their descendants have tended to blend in with an overall Asian-American category, and after a generation or two have done well in areas such as income and education attainment.

How there came to be so many people of Korean ancestry in Japan is a long and complicated story that we can only touch upon briefly here. It is a result of Japan's imperial period, roughly from 1890 until Japan's defeat in World War II in 1945. Japan wanted to expand its influence in Asia and put together an economic and political empire with Japan as the center. The Korean peninsula at that time was controlled by China, but China was in one of its down periods. During the late Ching 清 and early Republican periods, the roughly one hundred years prior to the 1950s, China was weak and divided.

In 1895, the Japanese prompted a war with China, essentially over control of the Korean peninsula. Japan was quite far along in its program of industrialization by that time, but China was technologically still quite backward. The imperial forces of China were easily routed by Japan, and the Japanese military virtually took over control of all of Korean territory.

Japanese leaders had for some time been interested in Korea for at least two important reasons. They coveted Korea's resources—its rice, its coal, and other minerals. But another reason had to do with Russia, which was at that time moving into East Asia in what the Japanese considered a menacing way. Japanese military and economic elite were afraid that if it was Russia who pushed China aside and gained control of the peninsula, they would own, as some Japanese at the time put it, "a dagger pointed to the heart of Japan." That competition over control of Korea was an important reason for Japan's attack against Russian forces in 1905, initiating what is called in the West the Russo-Japanese War. Again, Japan was victorious, consolidating its hegemony over both Korea and Manchuria.

Japan began a process of developing Korea economically for its own use shortly before the beginning of the twentieth century, building railroads, ports, electric facilities, etc. Finally, in 1910, Japan formally annexed Korea as a colonial possession. The Korean king was kept on his throne for a time, but every aspect of governmental control was firmly in the hands of the Japanese. Koreans from that time until the end of World War II in 1945 were colonial subjects of Japan.

This initiated significant immigration of Koreans into Japan. As Japanese subjects, Koreans could come to Japan as laborers with no documentation, and thousands did just that. Koreans were useful as a source of cheap labor for Japan's continuing economic development. They lived and worked in Japan at the bottom of the social and economic stratum.

Korean labor was particularly needed later, when in 1937 Japan went to war again with China. When the war in China was followed by the outbreak of World War II, Japan simply ran out of workers as more and more young Japanese men were drafted into military service. Not enough Koreans would come to work the mines and factories on their own, so the Japanese turned to a more drastic tactic; they simply arrested young Korean men and shipped them to Japan and elsewhere to work as virtual slave labor. At war's end, there were almost three million Koreans living in Japan out of a total population of about 45 million.

At the end of the war, most Koreans wanted to return to Korea, and the U.S. Navy obliged by transporting them back to their home country, now a free and independent nation. About half a million Koreans decided to stay in Japan, mostly ones who had been in Japan for many years. Most of them had small businesses or jobs, spoke little or no Korean, and could see no way of making a living in Korea.

The Japanese allowed them to stay but refused to grant them Japanese citizenship. It remained almost impossible for Koreans to become citizens of Japan for a long time, but it has become much easier in recent years. But even when Koreans of Japan do become Japanese citizens, some maintain membership in Korean organizations and identify strongly as Koreans of Japan; others do not wish to be so identified.

It is not easy to precisely determine how many people are in this category in Japan because of increasing intermarriage and because of vagueness surrounding the way they define themselves. About the best we can do is to declare that there are over a half-million Koreans of Japan, but somewhat less than one million. Sort of splitting the difference, many students of Japan put the figure at three-quarters of a million. As minority populations go, it is only a very small segment of a country with a population of 127,000,000.

The Koreans of Japan, although they have been there longer on average than Korean-Americans have been in the United States, have had a much more difficult time. Discrimination against people of Korean ancestry in Japan is not simply something in the minds of Koreans; it can be documented by a long list of social results: Koreans of Japan earn significantly less money on average than other Japanese, and even when they do well financially, it is rarely in the kinds of employment that carry high prestige. The ideal in Japan for many men is to be a salaried employee with a large corporation. Koreans of Japan are less likely to be found among the ranks of those kinds of workers. In a nation where nearly forty percent of the people currently graduate from college, and where a university degree is unusually important for middle class status, less than twenty percent of Koreans of Japan attain that goal.

We mentioned at the beginning of the section about minority populations that the situation is improving. For example, *Dōwa* intermarriage with non-*Dōwa* has been increasing rather impressively. In some areas, nearly half of *Dōwa* now marry ordinary Japanese. Anti-*Dōwa* graffiti, once common around *Dōwa* residence areas, has become a rarity. As with minority groups in other societies, *Dōwa* have created their own organizations, which have been quite effective in keeping negative references to themselves out of public media. Some observers consider this development self-defeating because it allows the whole issue of attitudes toward the *Dōwa* to remain hidden from open discussion.

As for the Koreans of Japan, improvement in their place in Japanese society is easier to see and document. Two factors have contributed to this: First of all, there are now lawyers in Japan who are Koreans of Japan, people who are capable of using the Japanese legal system to fight against discrimination. Becoming a lawyer in Japan is quite different from the situation in most other societies. One must be admitted to the government-run lawyer academy which is the only route to law practice. For a long time Koreans, whatever their citizenship, were kept out of the academy. In the 1980s, that policy began to change, and now there are several dozen lawyers who are both Koreans of Japan and members of the legal community.

Secondly, the image of "Koreanness" has undergone a complete refurbishing as South Korea morphed into an industrial power fully in competition with Japan. Recall how the initial entry of large numbers of Koreans into the country was from a poor agricultural society which the Japanese controlled. Most of the Koreans the Japanese got used to being around were illiterate farm boys working in the least prestigious jobs. No one in Japan today is obtuse enough not to recognize that South Korea is home to a modern, well-educated, relatively prosperous brand of Koreans. Korea has finally become a popular tourist destination for Japanese, and certain Korean popular media has recently been very well accepted by the Japanese public. This, of course, will cause, and is causing, the negative stereotypes surrounding Korean identity to dissipate.

While it is interesting to postulate the Japanese as a physical type, Americans should be especially aware that what makes a society unique does not necessarily have any relationship to what kind of race people belong to. Italian-Americans, certainly after a few generations, don't act very Italian, nor for that matter do Japanese-Americans act very Japanese. It is the behavioral features that make up a way of life, and now in the following chapter, we turn to one of those behavioral features, language.

Chapter 3
The Language

Language is one of the most distinguishing features of Japanese culture. It serves as a communication tool for the Japanese people as well as any other society's language serves that purpose. However, it probably should be pointed out that there are some features of language in Japan that warp back to influence the society in ways which can be seen as detrimental. Language isolation is one of those ways.

People who don't know Japan well often have misunderstandings about the Japanese language. There is, for example, the idea in the minds of many Westerners that Japanese and Chinese are related in the way various European languages are related. The genesis of this error is no doubt rooted in the fact that Japan got its writing system from China. It is a great irony of history, an irony which for the past sixteen or seventeen hundred years or so has been a burden for Japan, that the Japanese and Chinese languages are about as different as it is possible for two languages to be. If some irascible Japanese leader had wanted to scour the earth in a mean-spirited attempt to find the one language, the writing system of which would be absolutely the most difficult to apply to the Japanese language, he/she could not have found a more perfect choice than Chinese.

This lack of fit between a writing system based on the Chinese language, with a spoken language totally different from Chinese, has tended to divide the language into something not so difficult to learn as a spoken tool, but quite difficult to master in its written form.

LINGUISTIC ISOLATION

For several geographical and historical reasons, Japan is more set apart and disconnected in linguistic terms from the rest of the community of industrialized nations than most of the other nations within that community. Australia and New Zealand are just as physically isolated from the core of economically powerful and influential nations as is Japan, but those two countries use English, the international language, and therefore are far more "plugged in" to the what the world is saying and writing.

Japanese grow up to discover themselves speaking and writing in a language that no one else uses. Most places in the world share this problem, but Japan is a world economic power with industrial tentacles stretching to virtually every part of the globe. One could imagine that the enormous Japanese automobile industry, together with its worldwide computer game industry and other aspects of Japanese business, would have spread the language of that nation to far away places. In reality, Japanese has never caught on as an international language, not even in Asia, certainly not commensurate with its economic power in the region.

The first author witnessed an official from the Japanese Ministry of Trade and Industry a few years ago complaining on television about how the other economic powers, especially the U.S., tend to ignore Japan. According to information presented by that official, when trade in annual dollar amounts between Japan and the U.S. is compared with trade between France and the U.S., Japan outstrips France by about 12 to 1. Yet the official estimated that there are more than fifteen times more American high school and university students who study French compared to Japanese. We don't know where the ministry official got his figures, but it sounded about right then, and though he said those things more than ten years in the past, we doubt the ratios have changed very much.

Most of the languages of Europe have linguistic relatives close by. For example, Dutch and German are fairly closely related languages. They have many words with the same root, and the grammar and syntax are only slightly divergent. Spanish and Italian have the same kind of relatedness as do Polish and Russian. Japanese, on the other hand, except for a rather distant historical relationship to Korean, is all by itself. The characteristics of the language are not shared by others, a fact that has worked to isolate Japan much in the same way as geography has isolated it from the Asian mainland. All six of the European languages cited above are in the same language family, the Indo-European family, while Japanese and Chinese are in completely separate families.

THE JAPANESE WRITING SYSTEM

About four thousand years ago, the Chinese began to draw pictures to represent the syllables of their language, each syllable having a kind of base meaning which can be used alone or put together with other syllables to form words. The syllables have tones and inflections which differentiate them from other syllables with the same phoneme. The word pronounced in modern Mandarin as *shin* with a flat inflection has the meaning of *heart* 心. The same phoneme with a downward inflection is the modern verb *to believe* 信.

When Japan's leaders first became aware of China around 400 AD, they were a tribal people. They had wet rice agriculture, but no cities, no real architecture beyond very small wooden structures, no steel, no formal government structure, no theological religion, only the simplest of fabrics, and, of course, no writing system. Many in Japan wanted to learn all about this magical place called China. They must have been overwhelmed by what they found existed on the Asian mainland. Literacy must have seemed like the greatest invention imaginable. The idea of being able to freeze communication, keep it, transport it; it is not difficult at all to imagine how impressed they were and how much they wanted that part of Chinese civilization.

Had the pre-civilized Japanese back in 400 AD had access to Indian or almost any other civilization, they could have adopted a simple phonetic way of writing, and saved their population literally tens of millions of extra hours of study and learning through the ages. But alas, that was not the case. The only civilization they came into contact with was that of close by China. In some ways, having China as teacher was a great benefit, as we will see in a subsequent chapter. But when it came to learning how to write their language, it was not a propitious marriage. As it is, all Japanese school children have to begin the long, arduous task of learning to recognize and write over two thousand Chinese ideographs. Some are relatively simple and quite easy to learn and remember. The Chinese characters for the numbers "one" 一 "two" 二 and "three" 三 are every bit as easy to write as their Arabic counterparts. But most are much more complex, some requiring many brush strokes to write. The three-character Japanese word for "nurse," *kangofu* 看護婦, for example, is written with 39 writing strokes!

At first, the Japanese simply wrote in Chinese while speaking their native language, much as medieval Europeans spoke local languages and wrote (those few who were literate) in the foreign language of Latin. Eventually, some people in Japan began to experiment with a clumsy way of using Chinese ideographs to write their own language, resulting more or less in the way Japanese is written today. Remember how different are the two ways of forming speech. One way of writing with Chinese was to take the Chinese ideographs, even today still called "Chinese letters" (*kanji*) 漢字, and use them to represent similar sounds in the Japanese language. Eventually some of the characters used that way became ab-breviated and were institutionalized into a kind of phonetic alphabet called *kana*. Actually, there are two sets of *kana*, one called *katakana,* a squarish form used mainly for words of foreign origin (the five vowels in Japanese, a, i, u, e, o, written as ア、イ、ウ、エ、オ in *katakana*), and the other more cursive and more commonly used form *hiragana* (あ、い、う、え、お), used for conjunctions, declining verbs, forming negative endings, and words for which *kanji* is no longer used.

Kanji are used for almost all nouns and the base elements of verbs. All that may not sound so messy, except that as the *kanji* were imported, sometimes they were used for Chinese words drafted into the language, while other times they were used to represent native words with similar meaning but with completely different multi-syllable phonetics. So the *kanji* often have multiple readings which take a great deal of time and effort to master.

To make the picture even more confusing, kanji were taken from different parts of China and at different times, so that the Japanese approximation of the original Chinese pronunciation varied widely. For Chinese, each ideograph represents one meaning-syllable, and in any Chinese dialect, except for only a handful of exceptions, each character is read with only one sound. For the same characters used by the Japanese, however, a *kanji* can have two, three, four or more readings, some with completely separate meanings. One of the most egregious examples is the *kanji* 生, most often pronounced *sei,* but with as many as twelve additional readings (*shō, jō, i, u, nama, ki* and, in personal names, sometimes *ari, taka, nari, fu, fuyu, and iku*) along with three or four related but quite distinct meanings!

Surely the Japanese language is the most challenging language in the world to learn to read at an adult level. And this makes the Japanese literacy rate, one of the highest in the world, all the more impressive.

LANGUAGE STRUCTURE

Exactly like English, Chinese grammar is quite simple, with meaning based to a great extent on word order. "The boy chases the dog," "the dog chases the boy." English and Chinese are coincidentally so similar in structure that during the nineteenth century, Chinese merchants who dealt with English and American traders developed a language called "Pigeon English" which simply replaced Chinese words with English ones while keeping the rest of Chinese grammar intact. It may have sounded a bit strange to some people, but it was completely understandable to English speakers. One could never do this with Japanese. That language has a more intricate syntax system in which word order is not as important, and sometimes not important at all. In a simple word-for-word substitution, for example, in Japanese one might very well say, "Chases the dog (object indicator) the boy (subject indicator)." The relationship between subject and object in Japanese is indicated by verbal signposts; therefore, it doesn't always matter which comes first in the sentence.

Japanese is what linguists call an *agglutinative* language. Languages like that form meaning by adding on elements. The gerund "to go" *iku* 行く, for example, can end up as *ikaserarenakattaraba* 行かせられなかったらば, "if (he/she) had not been made to go;" past participle, command, subjective and negative voice simply add on to the gerund to form one long word with a whole sentence of meaning in English. While Chinese sentences tend to be comparatively short with a minimum of grammatical features, Japanese sentences can be very long indeed, especially in formal written form, with all kinds of passive voice, double negative formations and other complicated structure.

Another common error about the Japanese language is that it is somehow vague and less precise than Western languages. In fact, there is often a considerable vagueness in Japanese verbal and written communication, but it is not because of any inherent characteristic of the language. In scientific writing, Japanese is as precise and clear as its counterpart in any language. The vagueness in some forms of Japanese communication is a cultural rather than a linguistic phenomenon.

A major theme of Japanese culture is the protection of the ego and sensibilities of others. Blunt talk, in some situations valued in Chinese and Western societies, is instinctively avoided in Japan outside of very intimate relationships. Japanese are taught from childhood to not, if at all possible, make people feel uncomfortable in any kind of formal or semi-formal setting, and this sometimes has the effect of muting their real intentions in speech. Usually one can grasp exactly what Japanese mean to impart in any kind of business or other dealings—but not always.

It is true that occasionally what to non-Japanese seem to be overly polite and indirect expression can be tricky to interpret, sometimes even by Japanese themselves. In business dealings and other kinds of social intercourse, it is important to the Japanese to continue a pleasant and non-confrontational atmosphere. If any kind of rejection or disagreement needs to be expressed, Japanese will normally use all kinds of verbal gyrations to make it less jarring. Rejection or disagreement may be in there somewhere, and with a little practice it is easier to comprehend such things, but it is often quite camouflaged by politeness.

As many people have heard, there are levels of politeness in Japanese to which speakers have to adjust in different social circumstances. Over time, this feature has dissipated to some degree, but it is still the case that the language one uses to strangers and especially to people of .

superior standing is quite distinct from that used among friends and family. This, of course, is true just about everywhere, such as the difference among English speakers between, "Would you kindly direct me to the nearest restroom," compared with "Where's the nearest toilet." But in Japan, the differences are a little greater and more formal. Even the term for "you" in the above example would vary according to whom one is addressing.

The writing system has in a way been dissected into two quite distinct forms in Japan. Newspapers, most books, magazine articles, personal letters, and various types of written instructions are presented in a language quite close to spoken Japanese. However, there is another type of written language, held over from previous historical periods, that is extremely flowery, full of all kinds of prescribed verbal artifacts, quite distinct from the way anyone talks. For example, if the principal of the school where one's child attends retires and is replaced by another, a printed post card will be sent to all parents. It will begin with a reference in a somewhat poetic fashion to the season in which it is sent. Following that will be a kind of flowery apology for the interruption of one's day in which it is read, and then perhaps after three or four sentences, the message itself, written in language so intricate and formal that it is barely comprehensible.

This is the language of invitations of all kinds, diplomas, honors and awards, announcements of graduations and births, and the accompaniment to many kinds of formal occasions. That kind of writing has its own vocabulary with words and phrases no longer commonly used in other spoken or written forms of the language. Some teenagers have difficulty with that kind of writing, but all Japanese eventually learn to deal with it.

LANGUAGE STANDARDIZATION

Another noticeable feature of language in Japan is its uniformity. Many nations in the world today have a nightmarish mix of languages and dialects. India certainly comes quickly to mind. And even in China, where the government has tried so hard to create a standard spoken language, there are millions of Chinese in the southern part of the country who are at best bi-lingual, using the national language as best they can at school or in other official settings, but speaking a completely different kind of Chinese at home and with friends, a dialect which people who speak only the national language would have great difficulty understanding. There is some degree of regional accent in spoken Japanese as there is in the United States. Many people in the Osaka and Kyoto area take pride in not speaking in the accepted Tokyo way. But overall, Japanese is every bit as standardized as the famously standardized language of France.

Your first author does not speak Chinese very well, but years ago he spoke it a little better. As foreign and clumsy as his Chinese was, he remembers making a telephone call to a small hotel in Taiwan at one point, with the person on the other end not realizing that he was a foreigner until he learned his name after several minutes of talking. She simply assumed that the caller was a Chinese whose first language was not the national language spoken in Taiwan. As suggested above, there are millions of such people.

Such an incident would not likely happen in Japan. Over the past seventy to eighty years, Japanese has been so standardized that people there are masters at picking up any kind of linguistic deviance, no matter how subtle. One can live and work in Japan for years, coming to think that he or she has mastered the nuances of the language, only to have someone over the telephone recognize that he or she is a foreigner within a few seconds.

FOREIGNERS LEARNING JAPANESE, JAPANESE LEARNING FOREIGN LANGUAGES

There are some ways in which the Japanese language is not complicated at all, and in fact is extremely simple. It is very easy to make all the sounds in Japanese. The sound system is quite limited compared to other languages, and although Japanese words are frequently mispronounced by foreigners, anyone without a speech impediment can learn to imitate the sounds of Japanese in very short order.

There are only five vowel sounds, all with long vowel values: *a* as in arm, *i* as in lien, *u* as in lute, *e* as in enter, and *o* as in organ. The three most beloved sounds for Americans, *a* as in ask, *u* as in uncle, and *i* as in it, are not a part of the Japanese sound spectrum, and most Japanese cannot easily reproduce them. Consonants are pretty much the same when written in Roman characters, except that *r*, *l*, and *d* roll into one sound, usually written as *r*, but kind of the middle of all three. (There is also a separate *d* sound which is similar to other languages.)

This poverty of sound turns against the Japanese when, as is so important in the contemporary world, they set out to learn other languages. Japanese is full of words borrowed from Western languages, especially English, but often completely unrecognizable to speakers of those languages. My favorite is the Japanese word written in Roman characters as *ōdoburu* which when spoken by the people there sounds a little like the English word "audible." Believe it or not, it is the Japanese rendering of the French word *hors d'oeuvre*.

Some years back, there was an international swim meet held in Tokyo in which a remarkable Australian swimmer by the name of Ian Thorpe won several medals. The Japanese announcer kept repeating his name, and since we could not see it written anywhere, it was assumed we were witnessing impressing swimming by an athlete with the rather unusual last name of "Soap." With no "th" sound and with no fluid "r" in the language, that is exactly the way the name Thorpe comes out in Japanese.

To somewhat belabor the point, a Japanese professor during a lecture once quoted a line from someone he identified as *Wazuwasu*. Your first author had no idea who he was referring to, but later found out he was quoting the English poet Wadsworth!

Not only are the sounds of words and phrases borrowed from foreign languages somewhat mangled, but the meaning of those foreign elements also are frequently altered. The German word *arbeit*, "to work," pronounced *arubaito* in Japanese, refers there only to work at a part-time job. Japanese borrowed the term "road show," from English, but rather than carrying the meaning of a stage production that moves around from city to city, in Japanese it usually refers to movies, and the meaning has been exactly reversed to refer to a movie playing in only one theater!

Sometimes foreign derivatives are so abbreviated that no non-Japanese could ever figure out what they stand for. For example, *suto*, commonly found in newspaper accounts, is an abbreviation of the word *sutoraiki*, which in turn is from the English word "strike," as in the organized labor action. Can you imagine any native speaker of English who without being told could ever guess what *suto* refers to?

If one were satisfied to learn to speak Japanese without getting involved in the intricate system of reading and writing, in spite of its agglutinate nature and unfamiliar word order, it might well be easier for English speakers to learn Japanese than, say, German or French. There are no German-style cases in Japanese, virtually no plural forms for nouns*, no articles, no gender. There are some irregular verbs, but quite few compared with those other two languages. Even pronouns such as "I" "you" "they" etc. are usually omitted when speaking colloquial Japanese, relying instead more on context to determine things like actor and object. Learning Japanese reveals just how superfluous all that excess grammar is in other languages.

One might suppose that with so many borrowed words from English (and there are hundreds of them used in everyday speech), Japanese people would be quite familiar with the English language and learn it widely as do people in many non-English speaking societies all over the world. It is true that a significantly larger percentage of Japanese can speak passable English now than twenty or thirty years ago, but anyone who spends any amount of time dealing with native Japanese people is well aware of what a small minority of the population can deal at all effectively with spoken English. And, surprisingly, almost every single Japanese begins the study of the English language in the seventh grade, so that even that half of the population which does not go to college ends up with five years spent studying the world's international tongue.

---

* Plural indication is used for a few words; for example, the two syllables for *hito*, "person," are repeated: *hitobito* is used to indicate "people," and the suffix *tachi*, as in *gakusei-tachi*, renders "student" into "students." However, linguists do not consider this authentic pluralization.

Like any social phenomenon, there are several reasons for Japanese difficulty in mastering spoken English. Part of the problem stems from the small sound spectrum mentioned above, which makes it difficult for most Japanese to mimic the sounds of any foreign language. Another reason relates to the size and economic power of the society. One must understand that many places that are so determined to produce a large portion of their population with competent English skills do so out of necessity.

For relatively small countries such as The Netherlands and Norway, for example, it would be impractical to translate into the native language every kind of technical and scientific material. There just aren't enough readers of those languages to make translation of every kind of publication cost effective. Since there is an adequate amount of information of every type available in English, it is understandable for people in those countries that the study and mastery of English is a requirement for most serious professional work.

Japan, on the other hand, is a large and affluent society with a huge reading public in every genre. It is more cost-effective to translate foreign writing there because of the huge reading public. Almost every type of material of interest or value from any language is translated into Japanese. Just as is the case with average people in the United States, in spite of the obvious commitment on the part of the education system, the average Japanese does not usually feel that it is absolutely necessary to know a foreign language. Monolingualism is normal for people of all walks of life in both societies. And this is generally true even for the highly educated portion of the nation. When international science meetings are held in various parts of the world, English is usually the language of communication. The Japanese delegates are easy to spot. They are the ones wearing the earphones.

There is actually a combination of reasons for such a small percentage of fluent English speakers. One of these reasons is the way foreign languages have traditionally been taught in Japan. English in Japan tends to be taught as something to be translated, not necessarily something to be spoken. In Europe it is a simple matter to hire native English speakers from close by Britain as instructors of the language. Japan is a long way from any English-speaking community, and a very high percentage of the teachers of English are native Japanese who have been taught in the same way.

Geographic location, however, is not a completely convincing reason for the paucity of English speakers, since Chinese and Koreans have done much better in recent years in producing competent English speakers. There are internal cultural reasons as well for the relatively poor performance in English. A strong theme in Japan is the compulsion to do well whatever task one takes on. This cultural feature tends to make excellent and effective workers, but it can work to inhibit the learning of a spoken foreign language. Clumsy, incompetent behavior of any type is painful to Japanese, especially the realization of incompetence in oneself.

Of course, learning any foreign language is a progressive experience in which beginning and intermediate stages are fraught with clumsiness and imperfection. We are convinced that many Japanese are unwilling to speak imperfect English because they think it makes them seem foolish. Less like people in other societies, they seem to have little courage to engage in less than highly developed adult-level communication. And because they are reluctant to try to use the language, the only way to improve, most of them remain essentially as non-English speakers.

We leave the basic characteristics of the land and the people here and next begin a somewhat simplified version of the history of Japan, starting about 1,500 years ago.

Chapter 4
The Classical Period

Humans have inhabited the Japanese islands for a very long time. Remnants of pottery and other evidence of settlement date back several thousand years. However, as far as civilization goes, Japan does not have a truly ancient history. Unlike its neighbor China, which was one of the original cradles of civilization and traces its recorded history as far back as four thousand years, the history of Japan is about as old as the history of Britain. On the basis of available evidence, we can divide Japanese history roughly into five periods covering all together about 1,500 years. And because social and cultural change has tended to speed up in recent centuries, the closer we get to the present, the shorter these periods become.

The first of these we call here the Classical Period, extending from around 500 AD to shortly before 1200. Japanese historians usually subdivide this span of time as constituting the Asuka (飛鳥), Nara (奈良), and Heian (平安) eras. It covers the time when Japanese began importing elements from China and eventually changing these elements, molding them around native themes to form a distinctive tradition which can be truly called Japanese civilization.

The second period, lasting from roughly 1200 to just prior to 1600, was characterized by almost non-stop civil war between rival states, small independent territories controlled by warlord families. During this period, the samurai, an elite group of military professionals, came to center stage, and some of the starker forms of Japanese culture—Zen, the tea ceremony, ritual suicide—grew to maturity.

The third period, from 1600 until 1868, covers a time when the entire nation was united under the control of a single ruler called the Shogun. Japan was cut off from the outside world during that period, and in a technological sense became frozen in time.

The fourth period, from 1868 until defeat in World War II in 1945, can be considered a single period of Japanese history; it was during that time that Japan modernized and became an imperialistic military power.

Finally, from 1945 to the present, Japan has followed a path similar to other advanced capitalist nations in nourishing authentically democratic institutions and providing a high standard of living for its citizens. Following is a closer look at each of these periods.

THE EARLY CLASSICAL PERIOD—500–900 AD

Ancient China was the only civilized tradition that the pre-civilized Japanese people had any contact with, and it was from China that the core of what was to form a Japanese version of Asian civilization was borrowed. Many elements of that borrowing can still be seen today.

The first written records giving some insight into human life in Japan come from Chinese seafarers who visited Japan between 200 and 300 AD. They describe what to them was a primitive society made up of many semi-autonomous areas, each with local chiefs, some of whom were women. These units were called *uji* 氏. One *uji* seemed to be dominant, and most other groups considered it a kind of political center. That was probably the Yamato (大和) *uji*, centered west of the present city of Nara. It is thought that leadership of the Yamato *uji* became the source of the Imperial line as Japan copied a version of the Chinese system of political administration centered around an Emperor.

There must have been some contact with Chinese culture as early as before the beginning of the Christian era. By the beginning of the Classical Period, most of Japan had wet-rice agriculture as well as bronze and iron, and we can only conclude that these elements were brought over from China or at least by people who had been influenced by China.

But as late as 500 AD, we still could not consider Japan a civilized part of the world because it did not have literacy, anything we could call cities, any organized form of civil administration, or most of the other requirements of civilization.

It is not surprising that Chinese culture spread to Japan at that precise time. In Chinese history the seventh, eighth and ninth centuries saw two of the most powerful and prosperous dynasties, Sui 隨 and Tang 唐, reach their fullest flowering. It was a time when China surpassed all other civilizations in technology and artistic achievements. It was not simply that Japan discovered China then, as is usually described, but rather that China at that period could not be ignored by any of her neighbors, even the relatively isolated Japan.

If China and Japan had been linked by land, the Japanese would have found out about all that China had to offer a simple tribal people much earlier. But a great deal of water separated the simpler Japanese from the mainland, and unlike the Greeks and other people in the Mediterranean at about the same time, the Chinese, for all their accomplishments, were not a great seafaring people until much later.

When some Japanese began to grasp what civilization really meant, they must have been overwhelmed by Chinese advancement. Or perhaps they were more impressed by their own relative backwardness when compared with all things Chinese. Whichever the case, the leaders in Japan were in a mood to take in everything Chinese possible, regardless of the watery distance between them and in spite of the fact that China continued to more or less ignore them. We have already mentioned what literacy must have seemed like to a pre-literate people.

Japanese who managed to make it to China were, of course, deeply moved by the pageantry surrounding the Chinese Imperial Court. The governmental structure was interpreted by many leading Japanese as a magnificent way to bring order and logic to Japan's rather chaotic tribal system of authority.

It was not easy for Japanese at that time to get to China, and not many Chinese were eager to go to Japan. Many of the parts of Chinese life that the Japanese got came from Koreans who had been far earlier affected by the great Chinese tradition. It was from Korea that Japanese first got Buddhism, and along with its first sophisticated religion came the Chinese writing system and the Chinese way of building large structures. Like simpler people when confronted by the magic of civilization, the conclusion was that a powerful people must have received part of that power from a powerful religion. Although there was some resistance to the idea in some quarters, soon most members of the elite class in Japan wanted to learn about the dominant Chinese religion of the day, Buddhism, which they saw essentially as a magical system superior to native systems of magic and divination.

Massive borrowing from China began for the Japanese in the fifth century AD and continued for three hundred years or so. Following this period of intense importation of Chinese ways, Japan began a process of digesting Chinese artifacts and turning some of them into native patterns, producing a purely Japanese application of the original imports.

The written language is a good example. The non-phonetic Chinese writing system was adapted to the Japanese language, something not easy because the Japanese and Chinese languages are extremely different in both structure and sound, as pointed out in the previous chapter.

The importation of Chinese learning, Chinese building, Chinese dress, Chinese government structure, Chinese Imperial roles and pomp, Chinese religion and all the rest didn't happen by itself. There were several people in positions of power who championed the importation of Chinese culture. One of these people was a regent to a reigning Empress (who was his aunt) by the name of Prince Shotoku (Shotoku Taishi 聖徳太子 in Japanese) who served from 593 to 622. He was able to move aside some parts of the existing elite who saw Buddhism and other aspects of Chinese civilization as a threat to their position of power.

Prince Shotoku set up a formal court, with several formal ranks with official duties surrounding an Emperor, after the Chinese model. He issued a kind of constitution doing away with independent authority of *uji*. This was the beginning of centralized government. Governors were appointed to control the entire area of Japan south of Hokkaido, which only came into the Japanese cultural orbit much later. At least at the top of the society, Japanese were beginning to think of themselves as constituting a nation.

In spite of the efforts of Prince Shotoku, there were still pockets of resistance to so much foreign influence. Finally in 645, a young generation at the Imperial Court decided on an even more rigorous plan of adopting Chinese institutions. It was called the *Taika* 大化 (Great Change), usually called the "Taika Reform" in English. A Chinese style tax system was instituted for the entire country, and the first census of the population was conducted. The government was restructured to resemble even more a scaled down version of the Chinese system of governance.

Some Chinese cultural elements were at odds with basic Japanese ideas, and certain components of the classical civilization of the mainland were not copied, for example the examination system briefly mentioned in the previous chapter. It was used for identifying leadership from among the people of all ranks of society, a process at least a thousand years ahead of its time. By about 400 AD, China had instituted the Imperial examination system as a way of selecting the personnel to occupy many of the positions of power in the government. Although it was never based on practical knowledge, but rather on memorization and interpretation of the classical Confucian literature, it nonetheless broke from heredity and nepotism as a way of choosing leaders. The Emperor and a few of the highest position were peopled through birthright, but much of the rest of those in power came to be selected through a type of scholastic merit. Many historians are convinced that this way of choosing leaders was partly responsible for China's durability as a great civilization.

From the earliest time, Japanese have had a deep faith in blood lines, and that far-sighted program of merit selection was never adopted. Ironically, in today's Japan, selection by examination is as pronounced in that country as in any other society. But traditional Japan did not trust the masses, and authority remained strictly with families that managed over time to manipulate themselves into aristocratic stature.

Strange as it was, for all the copying of things Chinese, especially in governmental structure, the one aspect of China that was undoubtedly the most conspicuous was not reproduced for more than two centuries. It was China's great cities, capped by the great seat of Imperial power at

China's capital. We know that Japanese emissaries visited the great Tang capital at Chang An 長安 as early as 500 AD; Chinese records clearly show that. But it was several generations before even a modest city was ever planned in Japan.

There are two reasons for this: First off, we must understand that then as now, the Chinese population was the world's largest, with around 26 million during the Tang Dynasty, compared with less than one million people in Japan at the time. Another factor was the old Shinto preoccupation with purity and the practice of abandoning the seat of power after the death of each *uji* leader, which carried over to abandoning the place where the last Emperor had died.

Finally, in 707, the leadership decided to discontinue that practice and build a Chinese-style capital city. The first Imperial capital built as permanent home to the Imperial Court was a slavish copy, a kind of scale model version, of the Chinese capital city of the time. It was Nara, completed in 710. Unfortunately for the planners, it turned out not to have a water table sufficient for well technology of the time to support the growing population, and so it was abandoned in 784.

After a short period when the capital was moved to what is now the city of Nagaoka, Emperor Kammu in 794 embarked on a plan to build a larger and more magnificent capital he called Heiankyō 平安京, "Peaceful Capital." Over time, the first two syllables were dropped, and Kyoto 京都, "the capital city," was the official capital of Japan, at least in theory if not always the actual political center, for the next 1,074 years.

THE JAPANESE EMPEROR

Japan borrowed much at this time, but all the while it retained a distinct cultural core, always keeping to a unique Japanese identity, and not becoming merely part of China. Geography was partly responsible for that important sense of distinctness from the rich civilized tradition on the mainland. Not until much later, until the fifteenth century, was China ever much of a seafaring power, with Japan just far enough away to be left alone. What Japan got from China, it got because some people in Japan wanted it. Nothing from the outside was ever forced upon them. Imported ways of doing things brought in from China, and later on things brought in from the West, have always been seen by the Japanese as interesting additions to older native ways, and somehow, the older native ways are more likely than in other places to be honored and preserved along with the imports.

The institution of Emperor is a good example of mixing imported elements of culture with Japanese ways. The Emperor in China was conceived of as the pinnacle of Chinese society. The rule of his family line was rationalized, as was the case in traditional Europe, as divinely sanctioned. On the other hand, there has always been something very different in the way the Chinese and Japanese defined and reacted to their Emperors. Chinese throughout their long history have been aware that the reign of an Imperial lineage comes and goes, and the blood line of Emperors has been replaced by a new lineage many times. Japan may not be as old as China, but the blood line of its Imperial family has been far more durable than any of the Chinese dynasties. In fact, there is no royal family anywhere on earth that comes close to the longevity of the Japanese Imperial lineage.

Actually, the origin of the Japanese Imperial family is not exactly known. As stated above, it is likely that the present Imperial line stems from the leadership of the most powerful *uji* or clan in the pre-Chinese period. There seems to have been only one Imperial line, and it begins well before written records were kept in Japan. We know that until the influence of Chinese Confucianism, with its strong emphasis on the father as center of family authority, there were Empresses in Japan. Both before and after the impact of China, the role has always been deeply intertwined with the Shinto religion.

The Japanese Emperors have always been more like honorary head priests of Japan than actual rulers. In fact, Emperors of Japan have almost never in recorded history been real holders of significant political power. They have been, in a way, something much more important. Right up to the twentieth century, the Emperor of Japan was accepted by a majority of Japanese as a direct connection with divinity itself, a manifestation of the most powerful *kami* 神, the supernatural force which resides in spirits and in nature, and which is the foundation of the Shinto religion. Japanese Emperors have played a role which could be described as high priests of an entire people, situated above the concerns of the secular world and political conflicts.

Although administrative orders emanated from the Imperial household, from sometime in the 7th century, they very rarely came from the person of the Emperor. Another hereditary line, the Fujiwara 藤原 family, who for hundreds of years served the court as regents of the Emperor, held far more actual power.

A good illustration of the role of the Emperor in Japan is to appreciate the nature of the Imperial residence during most of Japanese history. From the middle of the tenth century until 1868, when the Imperial residence was moved to Tokyo, the Emperor resided in a palace in Kyoto. As we shall see in the following chapter, at many times from the twelfth through the middle of the seventeenth centuries, Japan was a bloody place with vicious civil wars fought all over the land. But during all of this mayhem, throughout this period of mass and protracted carnage, no Emperor was ever in any danger. Unlike palaces of the warlords, with their thick walls of heavy stone and systems of motes, some of which are still in place, the walls around the Emperor's palace in Kyoto were never more than about ten feet high, built of adobe and wood for privacy rather than for protection. It did not occur to those struggling for military advantage that anything could be gained by harming the Emperor.

Today, royalty of Europe and elsewhere have given up the power to rule and have become symbols of national unity and a connection to history. In a way, the Japanese were ahead of their time during the past thousand years. Modern politics and governance have not forced the Japanese Emperor to give up anything. That is exactly the way the role of Emperor has always functioned in Japan.

It is a fact that for hundreds of years during the feudal and Edo periods, around 600 years until the big events after 1868 described later, the Emperor was not paid much attention to. At times, life at the Imperial Court became a little threadbare, and as always, the Emperor played no political role whatsoever. But even during those times, the Emperor was never forgotten. The calendar is counted by the number of years in the current Emperor's reign (2010 is the 21st year of the current Emperor's reign, and therefore the current year in Japan is referred to as Heisei 21).

In chapter 6, you will read about the long reign of Tokugawa family, a stretch of over two and half centuries, usually called the Edo Period. During that time, all political power was in the hands of a secular regime three hundred and fifty miles to the east of Kyoto. But the Tokugawa government went to great lengths to preserve the prestige of the Imperial Court back in Kyoto. The Court was more resplendent than it had been for hundreds of years. The Edo regime paid the expenses of the Court, which became a virtual dependent of the regime, but the fiction that it was the Shogun who served at the pleasure of the Emperor was strictly upheld. At the death of the Shogun, his son would make the long journey with a huge entourage all the way to the Imperial Court in Kyoto to be formally consecrated by the Emperor as the next Shogun. It was all for show; the Emperor had no real authority over the Shogun whatsoever. But this was Japan, and things must be done properly.

The ceremonial importance of the Emperor in Japan can be seen in many large and small ways. He ceremoniously plants the first rice transplants, which officially opens the spring planting season. In recent centuries, the Emperor's birthday is a national holiday, and his death initiates an official period of mourning. Before the end of World War II (when the Emperor formally renounced any direct connection with divinity), he was a living god for many people. Even many highly educated Japanese accepted the Imperial institution as a kind of spiritual uniting force, giving the Japanese race a special bond with its own origins.

As the war wound down in 1945, Japan lay in ruins, and any chance of staving off defeat was completely impossible. The Japanese military delayed accepting surrender terms, at considerable cost in lives and material, because America and its allies refused to grant Japan's one and only request, that of not removing the Emperor from his throne.

THE LATER CLASSICAL PERIOD—900–1200

By the middle of the ninth century, two transformations which were to have a great impact on Japanese history began to take place. The first one was that Japan stopped thinking of itself as a cultural client of China. It was around that time that the Japanese began to gain a much greater sense of self-confidence. Things brought in from China were no longer seen as sacrosanct in their original form. The Japanese began to change them to fit their own way of doing things and their own point of view. We have already seen how this happened with the role of Emperor and how the Chinese writing system was slowly modified to apply more to the Japanese language.

For several centuries, Japanese continued to write in Chinese, but by about 800, a long collection of over 4,500 poems, called the *manyōshū* 万葉集, was written in Japanese using Chinese characters as sound elements. It was the first great literature achievement in the Japanese language, but it was only the beginning.

Slowly, impressive literature began to appear, together with graphic and plastic arts, which had only faint connections to Chinese prototypes. A wonderful example of this new, purely Japanese, artistic expression is a book written around the year 1000. It was a long narrative novel based on the life of a fictional male courtesan by the name of Genji. It was written by a female courtesan in the Heian court with the rank of *murasaki*, "purple" 紫. Her name was Shikibu 式部. That book, *Genji Monogatari* 源氏物語 "The Tale of Genji," is over a thousand pages in length in the original unedited version, written entirely in Japanese phonetic script. Its descriptions of people and events are vivid and sophisticated enough to hold the interest of readers through the centuries, and a shortened version is still widely read today.

Kyoto at first was hardly more than a palace surrounded by a series of Buddhist temples. However, by the 10th and 11th centuries, it started to take on the flavor of an authentic urban place, the first large city in Japanese history. As it grew in population, commerce flourished. All kinds of guilds for silk weaving, sake brewing, metal working and other crafts lined the main streets. Since it was the only major city for several centuries, and because it was the home of the Imperial throne, it towered above every other place in prestige. As mentioned in chapter 2, at that time, one of the most severe punishments given to a courtesan who had done something bad was to be banned from the capital.

We know quite a bit about life there because of the literary accounts written by people at the Imperial Court. We know almost nothing about life in the countryside. The illiterate peasants were not interesting to those who described their own lives, and so were ignored in literary accounts.

The growth and maturing of the Buddhist religion during this time was another stimulant to the expansion of written records in Japan. Two of the great sects of Buddhism were formed in the later classical period, the Shingon 真言 and Tendai 天台 sects. Mt. Hiei, just north of the capital, became a kind of religious sanctuary, with several important monasteries constructed there between the 9th and 10th centuries.

The other great transformation in the later classical period was perhaps even more momentous. It turned out to be a development that eventually brought about the formation of feudal states in Japan, something that was to characterize the country for most of the next 700 years.

Prince Shotoku's plan—a nation patterned after Imperial China with a central power ruling over a unified nation—came only briefly to fruition in Japan. Even in China, that structure usually fell apart after the first two hundred years or so of each dynasty. Japan didn't have enough experience with the various levels of local administration, and it had too many natural geographic divisions for the plan to work for any length of time, at least with the technology of that period.

The administrative system set up by the Prince had a fatal flaw. The appointed governors of local regions, usually people related to the Imperial family, did not have military or other resources to actually control their designated areas. They had to hire overseers to actually manage the regions and collect taxes. The overseers, in time, with actual power of taxation in their hands, began to ignore the appointed officials, keeping the taxation for themselves. More and more, these unofficial usurpers gained in power. As the officials appointed by the court in Kyoto became irrelevant, most of them simply gave up any pretense of authority and moved back to the capital. Eventually, the usurpers became virtual warlords, the actual rulers of most of Japan. They built fortifications to protect their holdings from other warlords of nearby lands. These fortifications eventually evolved into castles, and a system of feudal estates similar to medieval Europe came into being. And just as in Europe, these upstart warlords passed their power on to their sons, and so became hereditary rulers with absolute control over everyone living in their domain.

In this way, Kyoto eventually lost control over the countryside, and the Imperial Court had to make do with a tax base hardly larger than the area immediately surrounding the city. But a shrinking tax base for the Imperial Court was by far not the only serious condition caused by Japan's decentralization at this time, as we shall witness in the next chapter.

Chapter 5
The Period of Feudal Warfare, 1200–1600

ollowing the period of intense borrowing from China, Japan in the 11th and 12th centuries became once more quite isolated from the mainland of Asia. In the provinces, the authority of the government, which ruled in the name of the Emperor in what was then the capital city of Kyoto, gave way to local control by warlords with only theoretical connection to the Imperial Court. These warlords ruled virtually as kings of the areas they controlled. Competition, jealousy, and greed, all familiar ingredients of relations between adjacent mini-states, resulted in the inevitable—military struggle between these mini-states—and became a way of life in Japan. The civil wars continued off and on in most parts of the country for several hundred years, creating one of the most warlike cultures ever known. A social system developed that was very similar to European feudalism, with castle towns dominating a surrounding countryside and forming a kind of fief, what really amounted to a miniature kingdom.

The endless civil wars of this period were all about which rival chieftain would dominate over the fiefs in his area. People who did the actual fighting evolved into a kind of Japanese version of feudal knights who practiced their fighting skills all of their formative years, and very often met death in combat in their twenties. As you know, they were called *samurai* 侍, and Japanese literature, (and more recently Japanese television and movies) fell hopelessly in love with them, as Hollywood once embraced the western gunslinger as the epitome of courage and masculine virtue.

An entire warrior class developed with a point of view and a set of ethics completely different from the court nobility in Kyoto. The aristocrats in Kyoto were a cultured lot, spending time writing poetry and enjoying nature. The military men of the feudal period glorified in a life of warfare, in self-discipline, and in mental and physical toughness. Loyalty and personal honor, as in European feudalism, were strongly emphasized. Bravery, valor, and frugality were the highest of virtues. Skill in battle, in horse-mounted archery, and in the use of the lance, were practiced from childhood. Swordsmanship, and even more so, the technology of sword making, reached levels never seen before or since.

A form of ritual suicide came into being as a way of atoning for failure or dishonor. It was called *seppuku* 切腹, "stomach slitting." And it was surely the most painful and gruesome form of suicide ever envisioned.

THE KAMAKURA SHOGUNATE

Two warlord families came to control large areas of central and eastern Japan. They were the Taira 平 and Minamoto 源 clans, both encouraged and to some extent sponsored by rival factions at court. In the middle of the 12th century, it appeared that the Taira clan had won the war between the two. The victorious Taira leader took an important post in the imperial government in Kyoto in 1160 and married his daughter to the crown prince.

He made one big mistake, however. He neglected to physically wipe out the Minamoto clan he had previously defeated in battle. Remnants of the Minamoto clan went into hiding in a mountainous area northeast of present-day Tokyo, nursing a deep desire to avenge their defeat. During the subsequent generation, a new Minamoto leader, the ruthless Minamoto Yoritomo 源頼朝 (remember, in Japan, family names come first), raised an army and swept the Taira forces into oblivion. By 1184, Yoritomo headed the strongest military force in Japan, and by forging alliances with all the other powerful clan leaders, he set himself up as political head of a new regime, which controlled most of the country.

Being Japanese, Yoritomo followed the timeless tradition of pretending that he ruled Japan as an agent of the Emperor. All military rulers of Japan in later periods participated in this same fiction. He avoided Kyoto because he didn't want interference from the Fujiwara family, and so he set up his capital in a remote and sparsely populated area to the east, a place called Kamakura 鎌倉, now a suburb of Tokyo. Yoritomo revived an old title previously given to the general in charge of subduing the aborigines, *shōgun* 将軍, a title used later during the Edo period by the Tokugawa rulers. This period of a loosely held together feudal system with the Kamakura Shogun at the top stayed in place until 1333, when central authority again fell apart and no one military force could any longer control most of the nation. It is called the Kamakura Period.

The early part of the Kamakura Period was relatively peaceful, with only minor outbreaks of military action between clans. However, there was one very large military venture, actually divided into two sets of actions. It was the attempted invasion of Japan by an enormous Mongol/Chinese military armada.

By the mid-1200s, the forces of the great Mongol Khan, Kublai, son of Genghis Khan, controlled all of China and Korea. The only part of East Asia still remaining outside his province was the islands of Japan. It seems Kublai assumed that Japan would see the hopelessness of resisting the military might of Mongol China and agree to become a tribute-paying vassal of his regime in Beijing. When he sent emissaries to Japan demanding capitulation of "your little nation" he completely failed to grasp the mindsetet of the warrior families of that nation.

The Kamakura regime was officially conceived as a military power dedicated to serving and protecting the nation for the Emperor, and surrender was out of the question. Representatives sent to accept Japan's compliance were dismissed without even a formal audience, and when Kublai kept sending them, they eventually were beheaded by Japanese authorities. Outraged, Kublai set up a government department, "The Office For The Punishment of Japan," which began planning for an invasion.

A huge armada of 300 ships was constructed in Korea to be manned by 50,000 Mongol, Korean and Chinese troops, together with 20,000 horses. It set off for Japan in the late summer of 1274 and landed in an area in northern Kyushu near the present city of Fukuoka. For the first few days of the invasion, the Mongol/Chinese army made good headway, burning many coastal towns and driving the samurai warriors several miles inland. The weather started to turn bad with the arrival of a storm, and the invasion leaders became concerned that the rain and wind would cut it off from supplies and a fall back position. The invasion was cut short after one week, and the fleet returned to Korea.

Frustrated, Kublai decided to build another armada twice as big with an invasion force of 100,000 troops. It took seven years for Kublai to prepare for the second invasion, and that gave the Shogun and the clan leaders time to be better prepared. A stone wall was constructed at the place the Japanese guessed the attack would come, virtually the same place where the Mongols had landed before. The Shogun also ordered the construction of small attack boats so the Japanese could harass the armada at night, before it could even reach the shore.

When the Mongol fleet returned in 1281, it confronted a more effective Japanese defense. The small Japanese attack boats burned many Mongol ships, drowning their soldiers and horses before they could even make land. But again, it was the weather that won the day. This time, a much bigger storm, a typhoon, struck at northern Kyushu, the very place where the Mongol forces were attempting to come ashore, wiping out a third of the fleet. Mongols and Chinese were essentially land based people. They had little understanding of the sea, and even less of the storm cycles which commonly threatened Japan precisely during the late summer, when both attacks were planned.

Hundreds of ships did make land and were able to unload soldiers and horses. According to Japanese accounts, many of the horses were apparently so terrified by the storm that they could not be used as mounts. Kublai's warriors charged the beaches on foot. In close range fighting, their bows and arrows were no match for samurai swords. Many Mongol and Chinese fighters tried to surrender, but as samurai did not recognize such a practice, they were slaughtered on the spot. The loss of life is not known, but it must have numbered in the tens of thousands. The remains of corpses continued to wash ashore for years as far north as Niigata.

Kublai never tried to invade Japan again, and the threat from Mongol China was over.

That second invasion turned into a catastrophe for the Mongol Dynasty of China. Kublai lost the bulk of his military and a huge part of his treasury in the vast undertaking. Although Mongol rule was able to hang on for another eighty-some years in China, it was never as strong, and in 1368, Chinese rebels were able to sweep it away and establish the purely native Ming 明 Dynasty.

There were two significant outcomes to the attempted Mongol invasion of Japan: The court at Kyoto, while unable to help in any military way, spent a lot of time praying to the Shinto gods to somehow save Japan from the overwhelming Mongol force. When both invasions were thwarted with the aid of natural forces, many in Japan concluded that the gods had indeed played a role. The storms were called *kamikaze* 神風, "wind from the gods," giving rise to the notion that Japan would forever be protected by the gods from invaders. As you are probably aware, the term was revived during World War II when man-made *kamikaze* tried to destroy the U.S. fleet as it attacked Japanese positions in the Pacific.

The second outcome was that it weakened the Kamakura shogunate; some scholars believe it was indirectly responsible for the end of the Kamakura system of government. The regime was desperate to save the nation from foreign domination and exhausted its treasury in preparing for the attacks. But the Shogun's resources were not enough to defray the cost of the defense. The warlords of Kyushu were asked to use their own resources in the effort, with the shogunate promising to pay them back later. When the Shogun's regime could not do that, the whole idea of warlord loyalty to the regime came into question. Feudal systems work only when loyalty stays intact in both directions.

Even before the Mongol invasion, the Shogun's authority had fallen out of the Minamoto family and into the hands of Yoritomo's wife's family, the Hojo 北条 clan. By the early 1300s, the Kamakura system was wilting, and in 1333 another family, the Ashikaga 足利 family, took over the role of Shogun, moving the shogunate back to Kyoto.

The Ashikaga shogunate never had any real power outside of the Kyoto area, and like the Imperial throne, finally came to have only honorary importance. As the power of a central military regime evaporated, warring clans once again began the struggle for control, only this time, the civil wars were to last much longer and cause much greater destruction across the land.

THE SAMURAI WARRIOR

These warring clans came to be called *han* 藩, and the hereditary warlord head of a *han* was called *daimyō* 大名. They were like small independent nations. They collected taxes, made laws that applied to all who lived within their domain, and pressed peasants into service as a work force for the *han*. They were completely independent of the court at Kyoto, while paying lip service as always to the honorary importance of the emperor.

The center of each *han* was the main castle where the *daimyō* and his family resided, together with all the service personnel of the *han*. All services were important—horse handlers, cooks, record keepers, blacksmiths, and craftsmen of all sorts—but the most crucial of all factors in a *han* was survival. And survival lay in the hands of the most important service personnel of all—the samurai.

The bigger the *han*, the more secure. If one *han* could invade and absorb another *han*, it would increase its power. Each *han* began to view nearby *han* as actual or at least potential enemies. The way to survive and/or expand was to develop an effective fighting force. It is not surprising, then, that samurai evolved into legendary fighting machines. They practiced their fighting skills from childhood. Fencing, archery, horsemanship, and fighting without weapons all had to be practiced over and over throughout life. Bravery was quite literally considered more important than life itself; death in battle was considered a noble deed. Physical conditioning bordered on masochism. Samurai would go for days without food or water, walk into freezing mountain pools in winter, and meditate for hours without moving a muscle.

Himeji Castle, about sixty miles west of Osaka, is one of the best preserved 16th century medieval castles in Japan. 150 years ago, there were almost 300 such castles, which were originally the center of all Japanese urban life. During the first hundred years of modernization, many were torn down or so neglected that they were beyond restoration. Today, the few still standing are preserved as historical treasures.

It should not be imagined that samurai learned nothing but military arts. Unlike the knights of Europe, they were universally literate, learning intricate Japanese poetry styles and striving to write with beautiful calligraphy. Many of them painted in water colors. Most samurai studied the art of tea ceremony to hone their sense of spiritual control. As the people outside the castle developed a popular form of Buddhism, samurai practiced the stern, ascetic *zen* 禅 Buddhism.

Horseback archery and the use of mounted lance warfare were the military tactics used most often in the early feudal warfare period. But as time went on, it was the Japanese sword, the *katana* 刀, which came to personify the warrior class. In some cases, fighting between *han* was carried out between sets of samurai who would pair off, recite their personal pedigrees and accomplishments, and then enter into a sword fight to the death with their paired off opponents. Samurai wore armor made of thick strips of leather, flexible and much lighter than the clumsy iron armor worn in Europe.

Most samurai were the sons of samurai, but during this period, the role was not strictly hereditary. A healthy looking and bright young peasant boy could be recruited to join other young samurai for training. In the following chapter, you will read about Hideyoshi 英吉, who was born to a peasant family, studied to reach samurai status, and eventually become a warlord and, finally, military ruler of Japan.

It happened on occasion that a *han* would be overrun, and its samurai would escape to fend for themselves in the countryside. These samurai without connectedness to a *han* were called *rōnin* 浪人. At any one time, there were several thousand of them. With their carefully honed military skills, they often lived by terrorizing peasant villagers who were helpless to fight against them. The famous motion picture "The Seven Samurai," under the direction of the late renowned director Kurosawa Akira, tells the tale of seven "good guy" *rōnin* hired by a village to stave off the yearly attack of "bad guy" *rōnin*.

Gradually, the samurai way of life was formalized into an articulated philosophy. It was called *bushidō* 武士道, the "way of the warrior." It spelled out the nature and processes of samurai honor. Undying loyalty to one's *daimyō*, disdain for material comforts, and even disdain for material rewards, were central to *bushidō*. Bravery became a religion to the samurai, and refusal to surrender even in the face of certain death was another central, if sometimes only theoretical, part of the philosophy.

The Warring States Period lasted from the mid 14th until the late 16th century. One result of all the fighting was the suppression of the position of women in aristocratic society. The samurai and their superiors never represented more than perhaps a bit over eight percent of the Japanese population. As in any agricultural society, the great bulk of the people were peasant farmers. On the farm, women played a role equal in importance to men. But people inside the castles had a way of creating the dominant values which eventually filtered down to the rest of society.

A fact of life is that in a society which is predicated so much on the success of warriors, women play a less important role. Samurai women were moved to the background and fell to a position of anonymous service.

As Kyoto became less the center of national life, some of the towns which formed for protection around feudal castles began to grow in size and importance. Osaka, Sendai, Fukuoka, and Nagoya were the most important of these. They became centers of commerce, and in the cases of Osaka 大坂 and Fukuoka 福 岡, developed as ports for trade with China and Southeast Asia. The process of decentralization was completed. Prince Shotoku's ideal of a centralized national state had become a patchwork of feuding independent mini-states.

EUROPEANS, RIFLES AND CHRISTIANS

In the middle of the 15th century, when the first Europeans came to Japan, Europeans were not in any broad sense more technologically advanced than the Japanese. They were just as divided as the Japanese, and their standard of living and craftsmanship were not superior to those in Japan. Not superior, with two notable exceptions: First, Europeans had better oceanic navigation techniques and bigger and faster ships than any Asian society. After all, the Europeans came to Asia, not the other way around. Second, and this was to completely change the nature and direction of feudal warfare in Japan, they had firearms.

The first Europeans to reach Japan were Portuguese who landed in southern Kyushu in 1543. Adopting so much from China in an earlier period instilled in the Japanese mind a principle which has served them well all during their subsequent history. They have always been good at seeing the usefulness of foreign technology, studying it carefully, and then producing it in great quantity, often with better quality. Europeans invented the piano late in the 17th century. Japanese had never seen one until late in the 19th century, around 1875. Today, they produce more pianos than any other nation, some of them with the finest quality, used in famous concert halls all over the world.

And so it was with firearms. Leading Samurai of some major *han* in Kyushu noticed the guns of the Portuguese, saw how they could be used to bring down birds, purchased some, and turned them over to their craftsmen; and the process began. Within ten years, musket rifles, in some cases superior to the ones used by Europeans, were being produced in Japan in large numbers. As their use spread throughout Japan, military tactics were revolutionized.

A brand new type of warfare developed with a completely new brand of fighter. Samurai did not go away; in fact, in some ways their role was even more crucial. They came to play the role of military tactician, a kind of officer class, supervising peasant foot soldiers bearing arms. It doesn't take a lifetime of training to learn to use a rifle effectively. Suddenly, fighting between *han* was no longer a few dozen samurai engaging in individual combat. This was modern warfare with movement of troops, massive destruction of property, and huge loss of life. The *han* with the largest population of male subjects had the greatest advantage in this kind of mass military warfare.

The Portuguese were followed by the Dutch. Both groups were motivated to come to Japan for trade purposes, and soon several hundred Europeans had set up small communities, mainly in Kyushu. The traders were accompanied by missionaries. Some Kyushu *daimyō* had good relations with these foreigners, and a few actually converted to Christianity, ordering all subjects in their domains to do likewise. By 1560, there were half a million Christians in Japan, about the same number as today, but representing about a fifteen times greater percentage of the population than they do now.

REUNIFICATION

As the battles got bigger, a few *daimyō* gained ascendancy by swallowing up all the other *han* in their region. The defeated *han* usually didn't disappear, but remained as vassals of their conquerors. Whole groups of *han* under the leadership of a central authority now began vying for control of the entire nation. And it finally happened. A single *daimyō* managed to put together an alliance of subjugated vassals, and he convinced other *daimyō* he had not been able to conquer to recognize him as the new

Shogun, the military ruler of all Japan. All the *daimyō* of Japan were persuaded to grant him allegiance, and once again, Japan was united under a single authority.

His name was Oda Nobunaga 織田信長. He entered Kyoto in 1568 under the pretense of helping the last Ashikaga shogun re-establish his authority. Within five years, he had disposed of the meaningless Ashikaga shogunate and established himself as ruler of the nation.

Nobunaga (like Napoleon, he is almost always referred to by his given name) immediately set out to rebuild a central government. He reinstated a national tax, which all *daimyō* had to pay based on size and productivity of their *han*. One of his most important moves was to destroy the power of the Buddhist monasteries. The larger monasteries around Kyoto had participated in feudal wars with armed monks trained much like samurai. Nobunaga feared that these monasteries would never accept secular authority, and so he had his army attack Mt. Hiei 飛栄, where the most important monasteries were located, burning most of the structures and killing hundreds of monks. Buddhism was never again to have military or political power in Japan.

He was an able and farsighted administrator, bringing about many reforms considering his relatively short rule. When he was assassinated in 1581, he was succeeded by one of his loyal vassals, the man born of peasant stock mentioned earlier, Hideyoshi.

Hideyoshi* continued Nobunaga's work of unifying the country. He abolished the toll booths on roads so that commerce could travel more freely. He standardized the currency and ordered the first physical survey of the nation. He was a colorful character, and there are many amusing stories about his flamboyant personality which we cannot go into here.

One idea Hideyoshi had was to lesson the danger of *han* uprisings by siphoning off excess samurai from the larger *han* for an ambitious invasion of China. In 1592, he dispatched about 150,000 soldiers and samurai to strike at China through Korea. The force devastated Korean

---

* Hideyoshi was his given name. Most peasants during that period did not have family names. Later, Hideyoshi adopted the aristocratic sounding Toyotomi 豊臣 as his pseudo family name.

cities and countryside. To this day, the name of Hideyoshi is an anathema to the Koreans. His army never made it to China proper, and it finally withdrew after Hideyoshi's death in 1598.

Unlike Nobunaga, Hideyoshi died a natural death, but just as his predecessor, he was not able to create a dynasty by passing his power on to a son. His much younger wife produced a son when Hideyoshi was quite old (paternity of the child has always been much in doubt), but when he died, his son was still an infant. His wife tried hard to get the major *daimyō* to accept the young son as the future ruler of Japan. What actually happened was a new outbreak of military struggle as the major *daimyō* saw a chance to take over Hideyoshi's role as supreme ruler.

So while neither Nobunaga nor Hideyoshi were able to establish a ruling dynasty that would see power peacefully transfer from one generation to another, the rule of those two men did, by establishing a unified state for a time, set the stage for the next ruler, who was able to keep power in his own family for two and a half centuries. That ruler was undoubtedly the most prominent person in Japanese history. His name was Tokugawa Ieyasu 徳川家康, and we will get to know him better in the next chapter.

Before we leave the era of Feudal Warfare, we should say something about some important cultural developments during the period. The field of religion is one of these developments. Although Nobunaga routed the Buddhist establishment around Kyoto, Buddhism certainly did not die out in Japan. Quite the contrary. It was during this period that Buddhism became a truly popular religion.

During most of the classical period, Buddhism was concentrated mainly among the elite in Kyoto and other larger towns. Perhaps with so much human misery in the land at the time, the people needed a religion that helped them to accept hardship. The monk Nichiren 日蓮 founded the Amida sect around 1250, still one of the most popular Buddhist sects in the nation. By around 1300, almost every village of any size had a Buddhist temple. Ordinary peasants and townspeople embraced Buddhism into their personal lives as an equal to their older native Shinto. In fact, the two religions became intertwined. Both continued to have separate places for religious activity, but to most people, they were simply two sides to a religious panoply.

The way towns tended to form around *han* castles greatly increased the urban population in Japan. This always gives impetus to the advancement of art and technology. Some great literature was created during the period, and the famous *noh* 能 drama appeared at this juncture in Japanese history. When Hideyoshi moved the seat of his government from Kyoto to the site of his original castle at Osaka, it became a port for trade with China, eventually growing into a city almost as large as the capital. It is interesting to note that by the beginning of the 16th century, the historic movement of goods from China to Japan had been reversed. Japan now shipped more merchandise to China that it received from its old teacher—things like swords, fans, minted coins and art work.

Although the period that followed the feudal warfare, the Edo Period, was actually far more instrumental in forming what we now envision as the characteristics of Japanese culture, no period in Japanese history ever captured the imagination of the Japanese people the way feudal warfare did. Movies, novels, and television dramas are all saturated with stories of samurai life of the feudal warfare period. It was the wild, wild East. Courage, bravery, self-sacrifice, and honor; these are features easily dramatized, and they have entertained and inspired Japanese for many generations.

Chapter 6
The Edo Period

D uring the final three decades of the sixteenth century, the civil wars were brought to a halt by an alliance of military strongmen under the leadership of a single ruler. As we have seen, there were actually three of these men in succession. We have also seen that while managing to gain dominance over all other groups and rule over a nation united as a single entity, the first two were not able to create a system of stable transfer of power when they died. The third in line, Tokugawa Ieyasu, turned his considerable ability toward just that problem, and in the early 1600s, he built a dynasty of secular authority that lasted for two and a half centuries. This era of Japanese history is called the Edo Period, or *edo jidai* 江戸時代 in Japanese. It was a time when Japan became a truly national state, with the entire society effectively ruled from a single center of national government.

The Japanese historical period from the early 1600s until 1868, the span of the Edo Period, has been interesting to many historians. There never has been anything that we know of before or after quite like it. The Japanese authorities at that time created a very intricate and successful system—quite impressive when we consider the technology limitations of the time.

When we look carefully at Japanese society up to the beginning of the Edo Period, it follows a rather familiar course of the evolution of civilizations in other places. It is remarkable, for example, how Japanese feudalism during the Feudal Warfare period and European feudalism, although at different points in history, were so much alike. This is especially interesting since the two systems never were in any contact.

On the other hand, as the Edo Period began to be formulated under the Tokugawa regime, Japan deviated from more familiar patterns and became a society virtually unique in the annals of world history. It remained technically a feudal system, in that *han* continued to exist and were responsible for running the affairs of their domain. But it was a strange kind of feudalism, with tight control over all the feudal estates from a single center of power. In fact, Edo Japan was more tightly controlled from a central power source than any place ever, until the development of Soviet Russia in the 20th century. And this was in a society with almost no printing, telephones, or rapid transit, and with very slow and cumbersome travel across a large nation.

ESTABLISHMENT OF THE TOKUGAWA REGIME

Tokugawa Ieyasu had been a loyal vassal of Hideyoshi; in fact, Hideyoshi had been the godfather of his oldest son. But Ieyasu had great ambitions for himself and his family, and when Hideyoshi died in 1598 without an adult heir, Ieyasu decided to use the confusion and power vacuum to further his own fortunes. He was not the only *daimyō* who felt this way, and a power struggle ensued that was reminiscent of the feudal wars prior to Nobunaga's unification of the country.

Within a year of Hideyoshi's death, two great alliances were formed, both locked in desperate struggle to replace the fallen leader as the ultimate ruler of Japan. One of these was centered in Hideyoshi's castle at Osaka; its goal was to continue the line with Hideyoshi's son, who was now a teenager. Their rival on the other side of this power struggle was the group of *han* lead by Ieyasu.

It all boiled down to an enormous battle in the spring of 1600, involving thousands of foot soldiers and samurai, at a place east of Kyoto called Sekigahara. Ieyasu was not just a great military leader; he was extremely clever in dealing with people and situations. His side would probably have lost the battle except through promises and wile; he persuaded one of the leading rival generals to come over to his side. He was victorious, and later he laid siege to the castle at Osaka. When his forces couldn't breach the walls, he simply had his soldiers disassemble them, finally entering the castle and killing Hideyoshi's widow and her son.

Tokugawa Ieyasu was now the undisputed ruler over the entire feudal system, and in 1603, he revived the title of Shogun. He was a child of the feudal wars, and he well knew how difficult it would be to keep control of so many of the proud *daimyō*, especially the ones who had fought against him. Apparently, he thought a great deal about this problem. We know this because Ieyasu, his son Hidetada, and his grandson Iemitsu wove together a system that proved to be virtually rebellion-proof.

Ieyasu's dream of establishing a family dynasty that would rule over the land for a very long period was realized. The Tokugawa family produced 16 Shoguns in all, not all the sons of the former Shogun. Occasionally, a Shogun would die before an heir could be produced, and the next Shogun would be selected from one of the cadet families of the Tokugawa clan. The first three Tokugawa Shoguns were men of immense personal power, often making far reaching decisions completely on their own. But after that, in more typical Japanese style, the office became more ceremonial than an actual seat of personal power. Some Shoguns reached the position before the age of twenty and knew virtually nothing of how to run a nation. It was the two councils, the *toshiyori* 年寄 "Elders," and the other council called somewhat strangely the *wakadoshiyori* 若年寄, "Junior Elders," that actually made and carried out government policy.

Each new Shogun made the long trek overland to Kyoto for a meaningless coronation ceremony with the Emperor presiding. The Kyoto court nobility had not had it so good for centuries. The Tokugawa regime decided that it was their responsibility to maintain the dignity of the Emperor and the court, transferring lavish amounts of money to Kyoto to support the nobles in style. It was the peasantry that ended up paying for the operation of the central government, for all expenses of keeping the samurai, and to support the Court. All *daimyō* taxed their peasants forty to fifty percent of the grain they produced. Local *daimyō* kept a part of it for their own support, with the rest going straight to Edo.

The first thing Ieyasu did when he took power was to begin building a physical center of government in the spirit of Minamoto Yoritomo, far from Kyoto and away from all the intrigue and political entanglements of the Imperial Court. He chose the location of a small castle belonging to a distant relative in eastern Japan, near the Edo River and a village with the same name, Edo 江戸. It was that small village that gave its name to the castle, to the city which grew up around it, and eventually to the entire period of history.

Ieyasu's ambition was to be the greatest ruler Japan had ever had, and for that he needed the greatest castle Japan had ever had. There was very little there besides the small castle when work started; in fact, most of the site was swamp land and had to be drained before construction could even begin. When it was finally completed after 1670, it was easily the largest fortress/castle in the world. It covered several square miles of area. More than 7,000 people eventually lived inside the castle, serving the regime in various capacities. Part of it still remains in Tokyo, taking up a huge area in the center of the city. However, the old Edo castle was partly torn down to make room for modern Tokyo, and what remains as the Imperial Palace is less than one third the size of the original Shogun's palace.

Exactly as in the case of the castle built by Yoritomo in Kamakura, the offices of government were established and manned before the castle, even in its earliest form, could be occupied. As before, officials had to work and live temporarily in tents, and as in Kamakura, the regime until its demise in 1868 was known as *bakufu* 幕府, literally "tent government." The name stuck and came to mean "the real government" as opposed to the honorary government in Kyoto.

The Tokugawa regime did not anchor itself in tradition. It set out on an audacious program that was self-consciously revolutionary in its nature and scope. An example of this is when, for one of the few times in history, an important technological trend was reversed. Japan at that time probably had more firearms per capita than any other nation. Gun powder weapons, of course, represented a major step in military effectiveness. Ieyasu decided that they were simply too effective and too dangerous in the hands of non-governmental sources. He ordered all firearms to be turned over to the *bakufu* for destruction, and in fact the *bakufu* itself destroyed its own firearms. No *han* could henceforth press peasant men into service as foot soldiers. Only samurai were allowed to have or carry weapons. Ieyasu, in essence, turned back the clock to an earlier time in history, when fighting could only be done by hand with traditional weapons.

Because the program of reinventing Japan by the first three Tokugawa Shoguns had such massive scope, it had to have a massive bureaucracy to carry it out. The *bakufu* divided all some 260-odd *han* into different categories, some of which were considered loyal enough to participate in the government. The two councils mentioned above were set up to establish the basic rules and regulations for the entire nation. Below them were a series of sub-councils charged with more specialized regional policy and record keeping. To enforce the rules, Ieyasu developed a huge samurai army of police who had absolute power over commoners. They, in fact, were authorized to kill anyone on the spot who disobeyed their orders.

It is impressive to contemplate just how many rules and regulations there came to be, all written by hand, reproduced and delivered to locations the length and breadth of a large country. Movement around the country was strictly controlled, with checkpoints on every main road to determine if people could show permission from the *bakufu* to travel.

Eventually something called *buke shohatto* 武家諸法度, "comprehensive rules for all warrior families," a set of laws governing the activities and behavior of all member of the *daimyō* and samurai class, was gathered into one large document. Everything was spelled out in this set of regulations: Stipulations for requesting travel or permission to marry, for castle maintenance, for a strict dress code, for limiting communications between *han*, and for the number of samurai allowed according to han size. There was very little that people in any *han* could do on their own without reference to regulations laid down by the *bakufu*.

Just as later in Stalinist Russia, the regime suffered a great paranoid fear of insurrection and was determined to keep as tight a control on the population as possible.

SANKIN KŌTAI

One supposes it natural for someone like Ieyasu, who came to power through military means, to be fearful of men with potential military power. Ieyasu died in 1616, but the programs he designed were faithfully carried out by his heirs. Around 1630, his grandson, Iemitsu家光, instituted another of Ieyasu's ideas. This one certainly sprung from the paranoia mentioned above, and it turned out to be extremely effective in squashing any chance of military uprising against the regime. It also produced an amazing byproduct, as we shall see.

It was called in Japanese *sankin kōtai* 参勤交替, usually rendered in English as "alternate residence." It actually was an elaborate and complicated hostage system. It worked like this: All 260-some *daimyō** were required to build a mansion around the grounds outside the new castle as it was being built. The size and location of the mansion depended on the amount of rice produced each year by the respective *han*. It had to be big enough to house all of the retainers who accompanied the *daimyō* to and from his home place, which in some cases amounted to more than 200 samurai and other service personnel.

All *daimyō* were required to be resident with their entire families for about half of each year in the Edo mansion. For the remaining part of the year, they could return to their *han* to take care of affairs there, but family members had to stay put in Edo. Every *daimyō* was completely aware that even a hint of insurrection while back in his home domain would mean the immediate assassination of all family members in Edo. While in Edo, they all were, of course, under the eyes of the powerful *bakufu* samurai police.

After receiving permission to travel, each *daimyō* was given exact dates his entourage had to be at each road check point along the way to and from Edo. A list of every member of the entourage was given to every check point to make sure that family members could not sneak back to the *han*. It seems to have worked. Not a single uprising of any type was reported in Japan all during the Edo Period, until finally, after 1853, when the system became no longer enforceable.

---

* We can't be any more specific about the number. Several *han* were taken over and dissolved by the regime for tax shortages or failure to follow some rule, so that the number of *han* kept changing.

Sankinkōtai was without a doubt one of the most effective methods of controlling powerful military rivals ever devised. But at least as important was something that came about more or less by accident. It turned out to be one of the greatest urban development schemes ever put into place. Think about what it meant to suddenly have over 260 wealthy aristocratic families, together with all their retainers, ordered to build large mansions in what was, in the beginning, the middle of nowhere. Almost overnight, there was a desperate need for everything—carpenters, masons, mat makers, and gardeners. All these were needed by the hundreds. But it wasn't just people who built the mansions that were needed. These were lords, accustomed to luxuries of every kind, with funds to pay for them. They wanted the best food and sake, the best garments, the best decorations; they wanted entertainment—all the things inherent in the good life.

Craftsmen of every kind, together with all the other service people needed to sustain aristocratic living, were all of a sudden drained from Kyoto, from Osaka and from anywhere else they could be found. The village of Edo, the only place for miles around with even a store of any kind, quickly became a town, and then as it began to surround the castle, as the population shot upward, it became a small city. By 1700, it was a large city, and finally, by 1750, it held a population of around one million inhabitants, making it the largest city in the world at that time.

Edo Castle, as it came to be called, was closed to residents of the city except by command. Like the city surrounding the castle, it also kept growing in size and number of people who resided and worked there. Something like the Kremlin in Moscow, it was the citadel of administration for a large and complex society.

SHI-NŌ-KŌ-SHO

The people of the merchant class were not favorites of the *bakufu*. As a theory of how a society should be organized, leaders of the regime were attracted to a new kind of Confucian philosophy developed in Sung Dynasty (993–1287) China. Sung theorists had it that in order to better organize and control a society, four ranks should be established according to the importance of the contributions they make to running the society.

The ranks were scholar/administrator, food producer, craftsman, and merchant. The *bakufu* liked the idea partly because it put the merchant class last. These were people who were perceived by the Edo leaders as mere parasites, offering nothing of any real value to a just society.

The Japanese leaders had to modify the meaning of the ranks a bit. After all, they were not ruled by scholars, but by warriors. The Japanese reading of the four Chinese ranks was *shi-nō-kō-shō* 士農工商. The Chinese characters for *shi-nō-kō-shō* continued to be used to describe the system, but in the Japanese mind, the top ranking, *shi* really came to stand for *bushi* 武士, the Japanese word for warrior or the warrior class. The entire population was designated as being in one of these categories, which was supposed to be a permanent caste-like system. All castes were ordered to dress according to strict caste-related guidelines and were forbidden to marry outside their category. Actually, as a practical system, it was never perfectly applied. Peasant farmers in reality certainly were not in a position next to the top of society. They were actually at the bottom, viciously exploited and treated hardly better than food producing slaves.

Shi-nō-kō-shō was more than anything a way of setting apart the ruling class from everyone else. All *daimyō*, together with all samurai, and even somewhat illogically, all members of the court nobility in Kyoto, were given *bushi* status. Only that group could wear silk as an outer garment, only they could carry weapons, and everyone else had to use special honorific phrases when addressing them. All other classes had to behave with exaggerated courtesy toward any member of the warrior class. Members of the *bushi* class looked down on the merchants as parasites, but it was they, the samurai, that in truth where the parasitical class. They produced nothing and had to be supported with a huge tax burden on the peasants.

Hypocrisy occasionally crept into the ranking. The ranks were supposed to be hereditary, but as some merchants became very wealthy and members of the ruling class wanted to share in their fortunes, they sometimes declared the merchant family as *bushi* to permit a member of the warrior caste to marry the daughter of such a family. Peasant farmers who were supposed to stay at home and remain farmers had a way of drifting into urban areas to become apprenticed to craftsmen and merchants. As the economy in places like Edo grew, many farm boys were hired by merchants as their businesses expanded. The officials tried to stop this by putting a limit on the number of unrelated persons who could work at any private enterprise. Merchants got around this by simply adopting the young men as family members. Apparently, the *bakufu* had no policy to interrupt this subterfuge, because we know it became quite widespread.

FORMAL ISOLATION

Japanese Christians, as well as other forms of foreign influences, worried Ieyasu. He was aware that the Philippines had been taken over by the Spanish, after being initially, as in Japan, approached by traders, followed by missionaries. Some of the *daimyō* who fought against him at Sekigahara were Christians from Kyushu. Hideyoshi had banned Christianity earlier, but never completely carried out the policy. Ieyasu and his grandson Iemitsu were more thorough. They were determined to wipe out Christianity from Japan and expel the remaining foreigners from the southern part of the country.

A group of Christians rebelled against the policies of the *bakufu* in 1637, and *bakufu* samurai attacked them at a castle at Shimabara 島原, in Kyushu. There were over 2,000 of them holed up there. They held out for several months, but were finally overrun, and every single one was killed. Suspected Christians were forced to step on a wood-block print, supposedly of the face of Christ, to symbolically deny allegiance to the faith. If they refused, they were killed on the spot. Some remained as secret Christians, but as a religious force, Christianity disappeared from Japan for 250 years.

It was decided that foreign influence would best be avoided by simply closing Japan to all overseas contact. Japanese were prohibited from leaving Japan by the regulation called *sakoku rei* 鎖国令 in Japanese, something like "locked country rule." Japanese living abroad were given a set number of years to return, and if they did not return by that time, they, along with everyone else, would be prohibited from entering Japan. For the remainder of the Tokugawa regime, even ships in distress could not land in Japan in emergencies. Anyone who did was arrested, usually kept for years in horrible circumstances, often dying without ever being repatriated.

Japan kept one tiny window open to the outside world. It was a small island in Nagasaki harbor called Dejima 出島. A few Chinese junks were allowed to call there each year, and the Dutch were allowed to bring a single ship there each year for trade. Neither Chinese nor Dutch were allowed to traverse the few yards of water over to the actual city of Nagasaki. They all had to remain all of the time they were there in quarters provided for them on Dejima, as if they carried some horrible communicable disease.

The overall effect of closing Japan at this time had several results. · It succeeded in protecting the country from the colonization that was happening to almost every other Asian society. By 1750, all of Southeast Asia save Thailand had fallen under the control of European powers. Even China, proud and powerful as it had been, was not able to resist the power of European military technology and slowly lost control of many coastal areas. But Japan was more organized and more warlike than any part of Southeast Asia; Europeans concluded that Japan was not worth fighting for.

The other result was that Japan gradually fell woefully behind in technological progress. In many ways, Japan had an advantage. It was better run, had a more robust economy, and had a literacy rate higher than any European nation in the early days of the Edo Period. But isolated as it was, it completely missed out on the Industrial Revolution. At the time of the closing, Japan's technological level was about the same level as that of most of Europe. Later, however, steam power, new designs in military hardware and ship building, the factory system, and eventually electricity and new printing techniques, all made a new world. Japan missed out on all of this until they were forced to face it in the middle of the 19th century.

SOCIAL EVOLUTION IN EDO JAPAN

One of the great ironies of history is the system of ranking and social order in Edo Japan. What we had there was an hereditary warrior elite, descendent of actual warriors, probably about eight percent of the population, with no possibility of engaging in any kind of military activity—fighters with no one to fight.

Not all samurai commanded great power. *Daimyō* in charge of very large *han* were in the *bushi* caste, together with ordinary samurai, but many lower ranked samurai were nothing more than professional guards with no real power at all. They received no pay for their services, and in fact, it was undignified for a samurai, until near the end of the Edo Period, to even handle money. But even the lowest ranked samurai were completely set apart from all other Japanese by costume and by manner, and of course by formal ranking. As we have seen, only samurai could wear silk and carry weapons, and all others had to speak to them with special honorific language. They lived in castles, removed from ordinary people, and of course counted themselves as far superior to all those ranked beneath the samurai class.

So what was the role of the samurai within the peace that the regime had so successfully created and maintained? It actually took several forms. Some still honed their military skills with constant training. They never used that training, but they kept training nonetheless. Other samurai gravitated to more intellectual pursuits, studying the Chinese classics and their own Japanese history. Remember that their development had always included the arts and literacy. It was some of these types of samurai that in the 19th century began to ask dangerous questions, questions such as, "Why do we have Shogun rule rather than Imperial rule?" It was questions like that which eventually brought down the regime.

As we know, real life has a way of following its own course, ignoring, in many cases, the path laid down by rule-makers. This carefully planned system of a small elite ruling over an unchanging agricultural society was, in time, countermanded by the growth of power of the lowest ranked group of all, the merchants. The samurai as a class continued to hold all political power, but the peace the Tokugawa regime so successfully enforced created an excellent environment for commerce. It was the merchants who actually benefited most from the Tokugawa organization of society.

The regime tried all sorts of ways to limit the growing power of merchants and their money, but try as they may, the role played by merchants in a slowly developing capitalist system continued to eat away at the central position the samurai were supposed to represent. Many *daimyō*, and even the regime itself, came to be in debt to people with this new kind of power in Japan—the power of great wealth.

As the merchant class grew in size and wealth, it could serve itself, and not just the samurai; merchants became the super consumers of Japan. Everything money can buy flourished in urban Japan during the Edo Period, while back at the castles, things went on pretty much as before. Life inside the castles and life on the outside grew to be so different that they seemed to be on separate planets.

Outside the castles, down in the cities, all kinds of entertainment, with its new rich audience, became professionalized and reached very high standards. Artisans, who in theory were to produce products for the samurai, themselves became capitalists, and in spite of the rather simple technology of Japan then, made wares as fine in quality as anywhere in the world. In the cities, publishing of various kinds probably surpassed any society in Europe of the time. Woodblock printing was introduced,

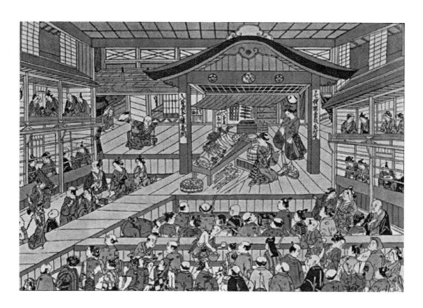

and soon periodical magazines were very popular. Even some interesting popular pornography was widely circulated. This was the time when haiku poetry reached the highest levels of artistry under such great poets as Basho 芭蕉, and the wonderful woodblock art often called *ukiō-e* 浮き世絵, widely prized by art collectors since that time, reached its zenith.

The lively commercial life on the outside of the castles was driven by what the Japanese call *chōnin* 町人, "townspeople," a population that had grown up in the urban environment. They had a totally different outlook on life from samurai. These were the kind of people who could take quickly to the changes brought about after 1868, a population that made the transition to modernization much easier for Japan than for many other people.

The stark difference between what passed for entertainment inside the castles and the rambunctious theater and literature of the *chōnin* is especially informative. The *bushi* caste continued to watch *nō* 能 theater, an extremely quiet and sober tradition that concentrates on the spiritual qualities of historical events. There are hardly any props, and actors wear masks, move very slowly, and have many moments of complete silence. It is all supposed to be very contemplative. We often wonder how many times anyone ever smiled inside the castles of Edo Japan.

In urban areas, theater took place in an altogether different atmosphere. Their theater was *kabuki* 歌舞伎; literally, "song and dance styles." It seems old-fashioned now, but in the Edo period, it was the newest epitome of fun. It is loud, colorful, and dramatic—a truly popular form of entertainment. People would bring box lunches and spend half the day watching several performances. *Kabuki* performers, all male, became as famous and adored as movie stars are today.

The tension between these two worlds with different mentalities and ways of life, one a center of political power that used agricultural produce as its currency, the other strictly a money economy, was finally dissolved in the Meiji period. At that time, the two worlds came crashing together, as we will see in the next chapter.

Chapter 7
Meiji Japan

The early part of the Edo Period was a time of revolutionary change in Japan. The political system, the organization of society, the role of samurai, and the enforced peace all represented a new Japan, altered significantly from its predecessor. However, after the first hundred years or so, change slowed down, and for the remainder of that period, Japan experienced a retrenchment, and in fact became a society with an almost static lack of change.

The continuity and stability of the Edo Period was all blown away, however, with the cataclysmic events of the middle of the 19th century. Japan was once again the scene of great transformations, and in fact, the monumental developments that took place as the Edo Period finally ended were far more rapid, much more continuous, and even more revolutionary than anything the country had experienced up to that point. This was a time in which the country not only modernized more rapidly than any society before or since, but saw Japan actually join the imperial powers of Europe and America as equals in a community of the most powerful nations.

To more appreciate this stunning set of changes, consider the following: As late as 1853, Japan was in a society that had never seen a steam engine, did not posses machinery of any kind, had no cannon or other modern military weapons, had no sea-going vessels, and in which virtually all the documents of government were written by hand. There were no paved roads, all weaving was done by hand, no glass was used in constructing buildings, time keeping was done by the sun*, the only artificial light was candle light, and there were virtually no wheeled vehicles.

By 1890, a mere 37 years later, Japan had fifty miles of railroad with steam powered engines, steam driven sea going vessels, modern artillery, Western-style buildings, horse pulled trolleys in five cities, and brick pavement in the built up areas in two of the largest cities. All that remarkable achievement in just over three decades! Fifteen years later, Japan had a military force large enough and sophisticated enough to defeat a major European power on land and at sea.

The period is called the Meiji Period because that was the "reign name" given to the current emperor's reign. All members of the immediate Imperial family have one name only. There is no family name for the Imperial line. The name of the young boy who became the Meiji Emperor was Mutsuhito. When a man or boy becomes emperor of Japan, his name is never used again officially. A committee of important people—historians, government officials, experts in Shinto lore, even including famous fortune tellers—meet to choose a reign name for the new emperor. No reign name can ever be repeated, and it must be easy to pronounce and not overly difficult to write in Chinese characters. Once the reign name is chosen, that Emperor is forevermore known by the name of his reign. The reign name chosen for Mutsuhito was Meiji 明治. In that way, Mutsuhito became Emperor Meiji, or *Meiji Tenno* 明治天皇 in Japanese.

Meiji Tenno's reign was from 1868 to 1913. There have been three reign periods associated with three emperors since the death of Emperor Meiji. Together with their reign periods, they are: Taishō 大正 1913–1926; Shōwa 昭和 1926–1989; and the present emperor, Heisei 平成 1989 until the present.

---

* There was at least one spring-driven clock in the castle at Edo, purchased from the Dutch, but in general, the statement is accurate.

THE END OF BAKUFU

It is interesting to speculate how long the Edo Period, with its isolation and relatively simple technology, would have gone on. Many observers think it would not have been long because discontent with the social order was beginning to rise above the surface in the group that mattered most in issues of politics—among the samurai class itself.

In 1853, an event occurred which brought discontent to a fever pitch, and although it took fifteen years to finally come about, it was the ultimate spark that caused the collapse of the Tokugawa regime. During the first half of the nineteenth century, several nations had made contact with *daimyō* located on Japan's coasts in an effort to open Japan's ports. These attempts were rebuffed. It was an American fleet that finally forced an audience with the leaders of the *bakufu* by sailing in unannounced to the very walls of the Shogun's palace in Edo.

In July of 1853, four steam powered American ships sailed into Edo Bay. It was an intimidation that made a profound impression on all Japanese who were witness to the event. The Japanese had never seen vessels of that size, and they were amazed that they could operate against the wind. The Americans came ashore in small boats, and the *bakufu* officials, in a state of shock, did nothing to stop them. The confrontation was not particularly hostile. Commodore Perry, commander of the ships, ordered a scale model steam train to be set up nearby, and the teenage Shogun was given a courtesy ride.

The ships left after two days, but returned the following year with a series of demands. They wanted to open ports in Japan and be allowed to set up delegations to manage trade between the two countries. Soon France, Britain and Russia followed with the same demands. The Tokugawa regime had taken over rule of Japan by military force, and continued to rule by threat of force. When it was shown to be powerless in keeping out the intruders, the image held so long of an all-powerful regime evaporated.

For the leaders of Japan, it was like breaking open a beehive. Everyone began trying to figure out what to do. The next fourteen years was a time of endless debate about the future of the country. That period is called *bakumatsu* 幕末 in Japanese, something like "swansong of the *bakufu*."

Daimyō far from the Edo capital, together with factions of the Imperial Court in Kyoto, came up with the idea of resisting any further encroachment by foreigners. The *bakufu*, on the other hand, were more realistic and could see clearly that Japan was helpless in the face of the military technology of the intruders. Thus divided into two separate points of view, some groups actually squared off for battle, engaging in the first organized fighting in Japan for over two hundred years.

At first, the *bakufu* was successful in putting down these outbreaks of rebellion, but when it began to lose engagements, the weakness of the regime became increasingly obvious. Finally, young samurai from *han* in the extreme southwest of the country took events into their own hands. They raised an army including peasant soldiers, marched on Kyoto, and took over the imperial palace, declaring that the Emperor, not the Tokugawa Shogun, was the legitimate ruler of the nation. The forces of other *han* joined them, and after some half-hearted fighting by samurai loyal to the *bakufu,* the regime that had reigned supreme for over 250 years, longer than the United States has existed as a nation, simply gave up. We almost wrote here that the young Shogun abdicated, but that verb is normally reserved for royalty, and of course, the Shoganate never laid claim to royal status; it was always only the hereditary leadership of a military government.

The last Tokugawa Shogun, Yoshinobu, simply resigned and became a citizen of the new Japan. He was just a lad of 15 when Perry let him ride on the model steam train in front of the Edo castle, and he was still a fairly young man of 30 when the end of the regime finally came. Neither he nor any part of the Tokugawa family was ever harassed in any way following the change of government, and Yoshinobu lived a fairly luxurious life until he died at the age of seventy-six in 1913. There are still people with the family name Tokugawa in Japan today. Some are descendants of the last Shogun, many of whom continue to live and thrive in the country.

THE NEW REGIME

The young samurai, self-declared as the leaders of a new Japan, brought the Emperor, who was only sixteen years old at the time, to Edo and set him up in the Edo castle, which they renamed as the new Imperial Palace. They also changed the name of the city of Edo to Tōkyō 東京, "eastern capital." These young men—there were only about a dozen who actually functioned as the movement's top leaders—then had to face the colossal job of quite literally building from scratch an entire new society.

One of the most impressive things that these samurai did, something quite rare in the annals of history, was to give up their own hereditary privileged status. The new leaders announced that the shi-nō-kō-sho ranking system was officially abolished. This meant that the *bushi* caste, long the hereditary ruling class of Japan, was to officially cease to exist. All *daimyō* and samurai were to be equal with those of formerly lower ranking. Now, of course, this did not go over well with many samurai. One group of samurai in Kyushu resisted to the point of rebellion against the new government and had to be put down with a large military force, using newly imported European and American technology.

What made the surrender of status more palatable was the fact that all former *bushi* were to be given a generous grant of money, mostly issued as government bonds which were to mature in several years time. This clever ploy insured that these men, capable of causing a great deal of trouble for the new government, were committed to the success and continuation of the regime. This development turned out to be of considerable importance later in the Meiji Period. Eventually, the government was unable to finance the development of a modern industrial system by itself. It became necessary for private investors to begin and maintain industries under the guidance of the government. The former *bushi* class had available funds to finance these undertakings.

How serious the young ex-samurai in charge of the new regime were about eliminating their class was demonstrated by the fact that many young unmarried samurai leaders made a point of marrying women not from former samurai families. This is something many people of former aristocratic lineage in Europe have not been able to bring themselves to do even today.

Everyone in Japan, save the imperial family, was now to be a citizen, technically equal in status and official ranking with everyone else. There was one exception to this equality, however. The new leaders saw the West as Japan's new teacher, much as China had been seen as its teacher at an earlier time. They particularly admired Britain, which at the time was the most powerful nation in the world. They also were puzzled with what to do with the Court nobility in Kyoto in a new modern society. The British peerage system seemed the perfect answer. Nobles in Kyoto were given new European-style titles—count, baron, etc. (although Japanese language equivalents were always used). When a two-house legislature was formed to show the world how modern the new nation would be run, an upper house similar to England's House of Lords was created. This Japanese peerage system continued to exist until dismantled by the U.S. occupation authority after World War II.

Han were renamed *ken* 県, usually translated as "prefecture" in English, with governors appointed by the new central government. In most cases, the governors at first were simply the same men who had served as *daimyō*, but the status was no longer hereditary. Later, the *ken* were redrawn to make them more equal in size and population, and the old hereditary leaders eventually died out. With the old former *daimyō* gone, new governors were at first appointed by the central government; later, a system of prefectural election was installed.

The young men who usurped the leadership of the Meiji regime (most were under thirty years of age) found a way to guarantee that their program would not be opposed. They cleverly used the historic image of the Emperor as a figure of divinity, or at least semi-divinity. The Emperor had always been interpreted as connected to the Shinto creation stories of the first Emperor's decent from heaven. Using the figure of the emperor as the center piece of religious nationalism, they established the Emperor as the official head of state. That meant that any rule or policy issued by these men through the Emperor was beyond criticism.

The young Emperor had no idea of the events happening around him, and in reality was not in a position to personally issue anything. He had no more personal authority than he'd had back in Kyoto. But all of the policies of the new regime were issued under his seal. He likely was not even aware of all the various proclamations, but they "came from" the Emperor nonetheless.

The leaders of the new regime faced a daunting task. If they were to avoid being swallowed up by the great powers of the West as their neighbors had been, they had to create a society strong enough and modern enough to face the West on equal footing. And they had to do so in a hurry.

In many ways, it seemed like an impossible undertaking. When we look back at how they pulled this off, we can see that they did have some important advantages. Tokugawa Japan was not as socially or politically backward as one might assume. It was in much better shape in terms of adopting modern life than many third world countries are in the contemporary world as they try to modernize today.

Most importantly, they inherited a society that was tightly unified, with clockwork administrative efficiency from top to bottom. For two centuries, the Japanese knew nothing but following rules with discipline and respect for authority. There were no rival religions, no competing ethnic groups, no language disparities—all things which plague many modern third world nations. In addition to this, they were provided a symbol of unity in the newly elevated status of the Emperor. Although in practical terms it was a new role for the Emperor, the people had always honored the institution, and no Japanese had any trouble accepting his new position as a symbolic unifying force.

Although the social system of the Edo Period was based on an antiquated feudal structure, the market system that grew up in spite of it—city-bred capitalism—was as robust as that of most Western nations. Japanese cities had a banking system, stable value of currency and a fairly high standard of living. The literacy rate of Japanese urban areas in the late Tokugawa period was equal to the rates of Europe and America of that time. So the new leaders of Japan had a head start as they began their work, but to build a modern nation out of a technologically backward one would require enormous effort, including considerable sacrifice.

As in the founding of the new nation of the United States of America, one great blessing of the new Meiji regime was the intellectual quality, the dedication, and the energy and sense of purpose of its leaders. Unlike leaders of many contemporary third world nations, the young samurai who took over as leaders of the Meiji regime were not looking for wealth or for power for its own sake. These men were afraid of the threat from abroad; they were dedicated to the idea of saving Japan by making it strong, and that meant, above all, making it modern.

BUILDING A MODERN SOCIETY

The military might of the monstrously powerful Western foreigners was easy to see. The Japanese knew that the power of the West came from the type of society they had at home, but this society was something the Japanese could not easily comprehend and interpret from the great distance that separated them. There was no choice but to go to where the foreigners lived and learn first hand the way they did things. Russians had gone westward to learn about modernization in the 18th century. But it had been much easier for them. They were fellow Europeans and Christians who didn't look or dress much different from the more advanced western Europeans they were attempting to learn from.

One can imagine how difficult it was for young, mostly ex-samurai, accustomed to a position of honor at home, to be sent to distant foreign lands to study how to build a modern nation. They arrived not knowing the local language, dressed in what to the foreigners must have seen as an absurd style, had to eat strange food, and were looked down on as some weird men from heathen or even barbaric places. It took most of them more than a year just to learn enough German or English or French to function at all in these strange environments. But they persevered; they studied ship building and modern manufacturing techniques in England, how to construct and manage the organs of a modern government in Germany, railroad construction and locomotive design in America, and modern military methods in France.

But it wasn't enough. They needed demonstration of how these things would work back home in Japan. The new Japanese government set off on a campaign of trying to get foreign technicians to come all the way to Japan and to live there as teachers. But it was difficult. Japan was far away, unknown to Westerners, and not a place many wanted to travel to, let alone live in. Initially, there were no residences foreigners would accept and no food they would eat. Even when these things were provided, the new Japanese government had to pay Americans and Europeans three or more times their normal salaries to get them to come, at least twenty times more than Japanese of similar status earned at the time. It was an expensive undertaking, but it worked. Engineers of all kinds, advisors, and teachers, all of whom knew how to help the Japanese modernize, eventually did come to Japan in considerable numbers.

In a breathtaking program of massive innovation, Japan created for itself much of the infrastructure of the modernity of its time: A telegraph system linking the entire nation was set up, a mechanized system of silk production was initiated, mining and manufacturing was completely altered with the latest Western technology, a modern port system was built, the monetary system was modernized with the yen as the unit of exchange, and roads and railway construction reached a fever pitch. There were electric lights in the *ginza* 銀座, the main shopping area of Tokyo, by 1888, only six years later than their appearance in lower Manhattan. In a remarkably short time, Japan began to look more like the nations of the West than any other Asian society of that time.

The new Japanese leaders were aware that in order to be accepted as a modern society, they needed to adjust to international standards of law and propriety. For the first time in two centuries, Christianity was allowed to be practiced openly. Foreign missionaries, mostly from the U.S., were active in setting up schools and hospitals in major cities. They weren't notably successful in converting many Japanese to Christianity, but for a time they were the chief source of learning the English language.

Unlike China, which pretty much stuck to its original culture when confronted by the West at a slightly earlier time, the Japanese were eager to imitate Western ways. Suddenly, city life took on a completely new look. Western clothing styles for both men and women quickly became standard dress. Western musical instruments were studied enthusiastically, and soon native orchestras were proficient in playing classical Western music. Beer and other Western alcoholic drinks, which had never been tasted a few years earlier, were suddenly the rage, and within a short time, Japanese were not only drinking them, but producing them in large quantities.

Through all this copying from the West, the new leaders of Japan were wise enough to see one thing as more important than all the rest. In fact, they copied the idea and implemented it more effectively than it operated in any Western society at the time. It was education. Many important people saw education as Japan's ticket to joining the modern club of powerful nations. An ambitious plan for compulsory education for the youth of Japan was not easy to implement, and it was not really applied to all the population for some time. But that was the goal, and before long, Japan had a population as educated at all levels as any Western nation.

Part of the plan was to open a network of national universities, beginning with Tokyo Imperial University, set up in the 1880s, to train the brightest of Japan's youth for service as government administrators. There were also private universities established at this time, although very small at first—probably what we would call colleges. One of these was Keio University 慶応大学, founded by a former samurai who was an enthusiastic Westernizer. His name was Fukuzawa Yūkichi 福沢諭吉; he published a manual in his younger days attempting to teach Japanese people the basics of Western living. Another private university, Waseda University 早稲田大学, was begun by Ōkuma Shigenobu 大隈重信, who also founded one of the first political parties in Japan in 1881.

In the governmental arena, another ex-samurai, Ito Hirobumi 伊藤博文, wrote Japan's first constitution. He admired the governmental structure of Germany of that time and actually traveled to Germany to study its government. Under Chancellor Bismarck, the German government had a legislature, but most power was centered in the appointed ministries, such as the ministry of finance, the foreign ministry, etc. The new Japanese government was set up along those lines. There was a prime minister and two houses of what is called in English the Diet,† but neither

---

† The term "Diet" is of Latin derivation and is used in Japan only when writing in foreign languages. The Japanese word for legislature is *Koku Gikai* 国議会.

had as much power as the major government ministries, and this is true to a great extent even today.

The outline of the new government structure, called the Meiji Constitution, was presented as a gift to the Japanese people from Emperor Meiji in 1889. It allowed for elected members of the lower house of the Diet, but for the first fifteen years of the Meiji period, the franchise was limited to men with large property holdings; it only expanded to include most male adults after the turn of the century.

After two decades or so with so many secondary school and university graduates in the population, a middle class began to arrive on the scene; this was not the *chōnin* middle class of earlier times, but a modern middle class that read the newspapers which had sprung up in the major cities—a new middle class, interested in politics and curious about the world. For the first time in Japanese history, people who were not part of a hereditary class began to be interested in the affairs of state. It was this part of the population which demanded more of a voice in the new society and began to support the new popular political parties. Japan, in a shorter time than anyone could have imagined, started to take on the character of a truly modern nation.

JAPAN BECOMES AN IMPERIAL POWER

There were many young nationalists in other parts of Asia who viewed what was happening in Japan with great interest. They admired the way Japan had been able to achieve virtual parity with the technology of the West in such a short time. However, in the next chapter of the story of Japan, in the minds of many of those same Asians, Japan was transformed from hero to villain.

Many Japanese leaders of that time were not oblivious to the fact that some European countries, notably Britain and France, had taken over vast areas of the world as colonial holdings.

They also knew that those imperial powers brought cheap raw materials back to the home country for processing—a system which fortified the economy of the nations considerably. It was perhaps natural for the Japanese to conclude that exploitation of weaker societies was one of

Emperor Meiji at about age 40.

the rewards of being a modern industrial power. Japan, as an emerging power, wanted to get into the act. Of course, the regions of Africa and South Asia were already taken by England, France and Holland. Much of northeast Asia, on the other hand, was still "available."

Along with all the other great feats of rapid modernization, Japan began to build up a sizeable modern military machine. The military leaders of Japan were itching to test the strength of the new armed forces, and they picked a fight with China over the control of Korea in 1894. To the surprise of the world, the Japanese army utterly humiliated a much larger Chinese force, sweeping it from the Korean Peninsula within a few months. Japan took over as the controlling influence in Korea and took over Taiwan and portions of coastal China as part of the peace settlement.

At that point, the Japanese were taught a stinging lesson. Three major European powers banded together to force the Japanese to give back China's coastal Shantung Province. Germany then cynically took over

Shantung for itself the next year. Although Japan had easily defeated the Chinese military, Europeans were not ready to accept an Asian nation as an equal in the club of military/industrial powers.

That kind of rebuke may have goaded Japan's leaders to an even greater motivation to show its military capability. The greatest fear the Japanese had from foreign nations at the time was that presented by Russia. Imperial Russia was rapidly consolidating its control over Siberia, and it had designs on Manchuria and Korea. Japanese military leaders began thinking about an inevitable clash with Russia as early as the 1890s.

It may seem quaint now, but at the turn of the nineteenth century, there was the popular idea in Europe and America that modern industrialism was part of the legacy of the white race. Yes, Japanese were able to imitate Western ways up to a point, but they could never actually create and run a truly modern society in the Western sense. After all, they did not inherit a great civilized tradition from the Romans and Greeks as had the Westerners, they were not Christian, and most importantly, they were not of the Caucasian race. Only the British were impressed enough by the Japanese to actually take them seriously. They signed the first co-equal treaty with the Japanese in 1902, and that guaranteed that other Western powers would not interfere with Japan if it went ahead and challenged Russian power over areas of East Asia.

In February of 1904, the Japanese decided to initiate a surprise attack on the Russian fleet, initiating a full-scale war between the two nations. Many people in the West found the idea of an Asian nation fighting against a European military force amusing, if not outright laughable. But the war did not turn out to be very amusing for mother Russia. The extent of Japan's progress in building a huge industrial complex capable of building modern battle ships, state of the art artillery, and the most efficient weaponry of all types, was simply not appreciated by most people in the West. Japan also had much greater motivation than did Russia. It knew the world was watching, and unless they could defeat the Russians, they felt the Japanese would remain as a backward people in the eyes of foreign observers.

Many Europeans and Americans expected Russia to crush little Japan within weeks. The war actually lasted over a year and a half, but it was the Russians, not the Japanese, whose army and navy were badly beaten in the fighting. Japan's loss of life was great, but Russia's was even greater. Finally, in September of 1905, Russia had had enough and sued for peace. The U.S. President, Theodore Roosevelt, presided over peace talks, for which he was awarded the Nobel Prize. Japan got southern Manchuria and half of the Island of Sakhalin, together with some smaller islands off the northeast coast of Hokkaido. What the world got was the great shock that an Asian society could be strong enough to play the international power game with the big boys. From that point on, very few people thought of Japan in the old way. It was the beginning of the end for theories of white supremacy.

Victory over Russia increased Japan's control over the Korean Peninsula. Even though Russia had been defeated, Japan remained wary of Russia's long-term intentions in Asia. Japan decided to administer Korea as a military region for security purposes. The military mindset usually makes for horrible civil administration; this was shown later by the Ottoman Turk administration in the Balkans and by the U.S. Federal military's administration of southern states at the close of the U.S. Civil War. What happened over the following fifty years in Korea has been very difficult for Koreans to forgive and forget. The Japanese are a reasonable and practical people under most circumstances, but the brutality and short-sightedness of Japanese military rule in Korea ensured a long lasting bitterness in the minds of the people of that nation.

With hegemony over Taiwan, Korea and large sections of southern Manchuria, all of which had populations that were not Japanese, Japan was now a full-fledged colonial power. A nation which only 40 years earlier had been officially sealed off from the rest of the world—a backward agriculture-based economy, completely without modern institutions of any kind—now faced the world as a military and economic entity on equal, or nearly equal terms with any nation on earth.

Emperor Meiji reigned for 44 years, and although his grandson was to have an even longer time on the throne, it was a very long period in the minds of his subjects. By the time he died in 1912, there were not many adults who could remember a time when he did not serve as the living symbol of their nation. When something very important lasts that long, it is always shocking to find it gone. We shall see in the next chapter how Japan coped with a world without Meiji.

Chapter 8
Japan After Meiji

Emperor Meiji died on July 30, 1912, at the age of 62. The entire nation fell into a fit of mourning. He was the only Emperor who had ever reigned outside of Kyoto and the only Japanese head of state who had ever presided over a modern nation. In his name, Japan had transformed itself and headed into a completely different future. Several military and political leaders could not fathom a life in Japan without the great symbolic leader and simply committed suicide.

His son was given the reign name Taishō 大正, but while his father had been a handsome figure—tall and masculine-looking with a fine Western style beard—Taishō Tennō was short and spindly, with a strange personality that hinted at mental deficiency. He embarrassed the Japanese several times with weird behavior as he officially opened international forums. After five years, those around the Emperor had had enough, and for all official functions, he was replaced with his twenty year-old son, Prince Hirohito, the future Shōwa 昭和 Tennō, who served as Imperial Regent until his father's death in 1926.

In spite of the disappointment with the new Emperor, the period began with the highest of hopes. Japan was not only now a great military power, but its economy as well was coming to maturity. The dream of creating a rich and powerful new country had been realized. What could go wrong? Well, as it turned out, a great deal could. The period of the two reigns, Taishō and Shōwa, covering the years 1912 until the death of Emperor Shōwa in January of 1989, were in many ways the most eventful in the history of the nation.

That period turned into a virtual historical roller coaster ride. It began with peace and relative prosperity, but then there was the great depression. At that time, military men became the real force behind the government. With a war in China, followed by Japan's participation in World War II, what they call the Pacific War, Japan suffered as complete a military defeat as any country in the annals of warfare. Its industrial infrastructure was nearly destroyed, over eighty percent of its rail system was obliterated, and with no way to get food into urban areas, many people came close to starvation.

Then, Phoenix-like, Japan rose up from the ashes of defeat and rebuilt its economy, eventually becoming far more prosperous than before. Prosperity, depression, militarism, war, disastrous defeat, reconstruction, economic success, and a return to prominence in the world—all in the span of a half century!

SOME SIGNS OF DIFFICULTY

Superficially, the governmental structure of Japan under the Meiji Constitution seemed to reflect the norms of the Western democracies. But there were some important differences. The samurai, now of course ex-samurai, who had set the whole structure in place, had not disappeared. Actually, in a sense they did disappear, but they certainly had not lost their power. What they did was to function behind the scenes, controlling imperial mandates. They were called *genrō* 元老, "the founding elders." They were well known figures; some of them served as government officials, while others never took any official titles. Until they all died off in the 1920s, they continued to have enormous power. An example of this power is seen in the way the prime minister, together with all cabinet ministers, were appointed rather than elected until late in the 1920s. Unlike other parliamentary systems, in which the prime minister and his administration are chosen by the legislative body, under the Meiji Constitution, those offices were determined directly by the *genrō*.

Another weakness to the system was how the *genrō* had stipulated that branches of the military were to be under the direct control of the Emperor, which, of course, meant under the control of the men who interpreted what was called "Imperial will." That condition worked to a degree, as long as the *genrō* were around. When they all died off, it meant that the Japanese military establishment was not effectively under the control of any organ of civilian government. The army and navy were free to formulate their own foreign policy—a situation that eventually got Japan into a whole lot of trouble.

In the early part of this period, political parties and politics in general entered Japanese life in a big way. Important in this development was the way it created such a strong backlash. The designers of the new Japan had in mind a paternal governmental structure, with the Diet not much more than a harmless debating society. As the voting franchise was extended during the early 1920s, the public and media began to clamor for a more "normal" type of administration, in which the Diet would play an increasingly important role. Eventually, a compromise was reached in which the prime minister continued to be appointed, but cabinet ministers, who slowly began to have some real authority, were selected from the leading political parties.

As you can imagine, the result of these changes was the kind of political haranguing typical of political bodies all over the world. It was the beginning of real democracy with all its warts. In fact, the political situation in the Taishō and early Shōwa periods is often called "Taishō democracy."

But many Japanese were not accustomed to the messiness of democratic government. In several ways, Japan began to turn into two separate societies. Rapid industrialization had created the *zaibatsu*, huge conglomerates with great economic, and even indirect political presence. Small business activity did not share in all the expansion of the economy. Especially, the countryside lagged behind the rest of the country. Forty-five percent of the people who worked the soil were tenant farmers who lived simple lives in comparative poverty. The way the economy and political system was being run was intensely disliked by a growing number of people. Many became dissatisfied, yearning for a time like the early Meiji period when, as they saw it, dedicated and selfless men worked for the good of the country without seeking reward.

The onset of the Great Depression greatly added to a sense of malaise in some quarters of the population. As a society that had slowly come to depend a great deal on international trade, Japan was hit especially hard by the world-wide economic slowdown. Perhaps it was inevitable that some of the discontent was directed outward toward the other industrial societies. It was interpreted by some Japanese that, as their economy began to perform less well, the cards were stacked against them. And in a way, they were. Americans and Europeans were free to move to the vast continental areas of Australia, the American continent, Africa and other areas where they held colonies. Japanese could not emigrate to Australia or to any European society, and with the passing of the U.S. Exclusion Act in 1924, which excluded Japanese from emigrating to the U.S., it was obvious that the nation had no real friends among the other industrial societies. In this atmosphere, the Japanese military felt it was justified in taking things into its own hands.

JAPANESE MILITARISM

In 1931, a group of military officers staged an incident in which some Japanese rail equipment in southern Manchuria was damaged, allegedly by local rebels. This was used as an excuse to take over all of the remaining area of Manchuria by force. When other countries objected, the Japanese military set up a puppet government in a new state called Manchukuo, claiming that it was a completely independent nation. When the League of Nations, the precursor of the United Nations, demanded Japan's withdrawal from Manchuria, Japan left the League, causing it to eventually collapse.

Some in the army saw themselves as a cleansing force bringing order to the disorder of parliamentary rule. They saw the poverty in the countryside in bitter contrast to the life of luxury of business leaders and politicians. Their goal was quite frankly the military seizure of power in Japan. In 1926, an attempted military coup by young officers almost succeeded in taking over the government. Cooler heads prevailed, and the highest military authorities arrested and put to death the perpetrators. But that certainly did not end the military as a slowly emerging political power in Japan. Elements of the military had an ally in an emerging right wing in Japan. Ironically, some of these right-wingers were the very industrialists radical military officers were set against.

At any rate, the military struck again soon, this time in China proper. China, which had been torn apart by regional fighting as the Ching 清 Dynasty deteriorated, was now at least partly in the hands of a new national government. A new generation of Chinese was flexing a revived sense of nationalism. When the leader of the new Chinese government, Chiang Kai-shek 将介石, objected to Japan's encroachment in the north of the country, the Japanese army decided to tame the upstart regime with a full-scale military invasion of China in the summer of 1937.

At first, the Japanese military was as successful against Chinese forces as they had been in 1894. A series of easy victories fanned the flames of patriotism at home as the army pushed deep into north China and took the southern coastal area. They expected the Chinese to quickly sue for peace as they had done before, but the Chinese nationalist army kept fighting as they retreated southward, and a new group of Chinese communists began harassing Japanese forces in the north. Nanking became capital of a Japanese-occupied government, and many Chinese collaborated with the Japanese, but the Chinese outside the Japanese controlled areas would not surrender and kept up the fight.

The military adventure on the mainland had the effect of strengthening the hand of the army and navy, and the Japanese government came to be increasingly dominated by an alliance of the military and right wing zealots. Finally, in 1940, the government ordered all political parties to join something called the Imperial Rule Association, effectively temporarily ending the democratic system.

This was a momentous development for Japan: From the beginning of the Meiji Period, Japan had slowly adopted many of the features of a modern liberal democracy, certainly according to the somewhat paternalistic standards of the time. There had been a free press with open debate and a way of criticizing authority (except for the Emperor). People could travel and communicate freely. Current ideas, such as Marxism, were openly publicized. Then, suddenly, much of that changed. A version of secret police, actually a part of the army, called *kenpei* 憲兵, was developed and given enormous power. The *kenpei* could arrest people and hold them for as long as they wanted for reasons they did not have to explain to anyone. Liberalism of any kind was their enemy, *kenpei* spies infiltrated university classrooms, and newspaper editors were bullied into avoiding any criticism of the military and its adventures. They were plain-clothed, operated in secret, and were always on the lookout for "unpatriotic" behavior.

For a short time, until the end of the war, Japan was transformed into a virtual police state, in which people were afraid to discuss politics or the affairs of the nation outside of their most intimate associates. It is true that not many people were assassinated or executed by the *kenpei*, but thousands of labor leaders, members of left-wing political parties, professors, writers and others were arrested after 1940 and remained imprisoned until the Occupation began in Autumn 1945. Japan never became as tightly controlled as, say, Stalinist Russia, but each year, the country drew closer to that reality.

The right wing and military controllers of the Japanese government at the time decided on a fateful decision—to join the fascist states of Nazi Germany and Italy, forming what was called the Tripartite Pact, becoming part of the Axis alliance. From that point, war with one member of the Axis was war with all.

Growing tension developed between Japan and the United States over Japan's continued military presence in China. Important Japanese military and business leaders began formulating a plan for Japan to control all of East and Southeast Asia, to act as the center of a new economic and political empire. The name they gave to it was *dai tōa kyōei ken* 大東亜共栄圏 "The Greater East Asia Co-prosperity Sphere." The plan was to subdue China and then strike south and take over all of Southeast Asia, with its rich supply of petroleum and other natural resources. The U.S., with its large naval presence at Hawaii, stood in the way. Japan decided to cripple the U.S. navy and then take over control of the Pacific area before the U.S. Pacific fleet could be built back up.

Japanese military planners were not stupid; they knew that the sheer size of the U.S., to say nothing of its productive capacity, would make it impossible to defeat the entire American armed forces in a head on war between the two nations. But they thought they had a way around this situation. They made two calculations which ultimately led them to calamity. First, they knew that the Tripartite Pact would obligate Germany to declare war on the U.S. if war were to break out between the U.S. and Japan. They guessed that the salvation of England and the rest of Europe would take precedence over fighting against the Japanese. They were certain that not even the U.S. could fight a war in Europe and at the same time take the offense in the Pacific. The idea was to solidify an expanded area of control that the U.S., when it finally turned its attention to the Pacific, would be too weary and too unwilling to expend lives and resources to dislodge.

The second miscalculation was based on the estimate of how much military material the U.S. could produce in a given year. Military engineers in Japan seriously underestimated the industrial capacity of U.S. factories. Apparently, they failed to fully comprehend how far below capacity the U.S. was running at due to depression era low demand.

THE PACIFIC WAR

The outbreak of war in Europe in 1939 seemed like a godsend to the Japanese. It distracted attention away from their occupation of China, and with the defeat of France in 1940, it permitted Japan to take over France's large colonial holdings in Asia as ally of the victorious Germans. With Britain fighting for its life against a possible German invasion, there were not sufficient British resources available to defend its colonies of Hong Kong and Singapore. Japan easily took over both early in 1941.

Although many at the top of Japanese military leadership were anxious to take over such a vast area even if it meant a war with the United States, not all Japanese in leadership roles agreed with them. The admiralty of the Imperial Navy, for example, thought it was a bad idea. Some Japanese officials made a last ditch desperate attempt to negotiate with the Americans, promising a gradual withdrawal from China if the U.S. would end its embargo of steel and oil to Japan. But a hard-line nationalist, the army general Tōjō Hideki 東条英機, had become prime minister, and soon it became obvious that there was no way to stop the march toward war. Even the Navy reluctantly agreed, and it was from that source that the war actually began.

Japan struck by surprise in the morning of December 7, 1941 (December 8 in Japan), causing great damage and great loss of life at the naval base in Pearl Harbor, Hawaii. Things went very well for Japan at the beginning of the war. Within a few weeks, Japanese forces overran all of European colonial holdings in Southeast Asia. The Philippine Islands, an American protectorate at the time, held out for five months, but eventually ran low on food and supplies, surrendering to the Japanese army in May of 1942. By March of that year, the huge Dutch East India colony, later to become Indonesia, was under the control of the Japanese military. Within a year, Japan controlled a vast region stretching from the borders of India to the middle of the Pacific Ocean.

Suddenly, Japan was managing a huge area from Sakhalin in the north all the way to New Guinea in the south, a distance of some 5,000 miles, plus nearly forty percent of the entire Pacific basin. If the coastal area of China is included, the population under Japanese control by mid-1943 represented about one fifth of the human population of the earth.

Alas for the Japanese, that expanded empire was not to last very long. By late in that same year, 1943, the U.S. began a relentless push across the western Pacific, invading island after island within the area controlled by Japan. The Japanese were dismayed at how soon the Americans had been able to rebuild their navy. To the surprise of the Japanese, the U.S. had both the ability and the will to fight a two front war, and to fight very effectively. With great loss of life on both sides, U.S. forces finally took over islands close enough to send bombers to the Japanese homeland.

The bombing of Japan began. It was on a small scale at first, but eventually every major city of Japan, with the single exception of Kyoto, was seriously damaged. Initially, the U.S. lost many planes, but with the supply of petroleum from the south cut off by the steady loss of its merchant ships, the Japanese air force slowly began to run out of fuel, and American bombers were free to fly over Japan unmolested.

By 1944, the military position of Japan was, by any objective measure, hopeless. The Philippines were retaken that year, and Okinawa, historically part of the Japanese homeland, was overrun by U.S. forces, with over 200,000 Japanese casualties. But in true samurai tradition, the army and navy fought on. Finally, in August of the next year, with large parts of its urban areas flattened, and after the dropping of two nuclear bombs on the cities of Hiroshima and Nagasaki, Emperor Showa called together the military high command and urged them to accept surrender terms submitted to the Japanese by the U.S. and its allies. No Emperor of Japan had exerted that kind of influence since ancient times.

U.S. OCCUPATION

On August 14, 1945, the military and civilian population of Japan heard the Emperor's voice for the first time. He had never spoken over the radio before. He told his people that further military resistance would bring complete destruction to the nation. Although he didn't exactly say so directly, everyone listening understood that the Emperor was explaining that Japan had lost the war and would surrender to the enemy. He went on to tell them that they would have to "endure the unendurable," referring obliquely to foreign occupation. Through their tears, the bulk of the population emotionally collapsed in relief and exhaustion. They had struggled as hard as they could to preserve the honor of their Emperor, but their military had let them down. They had fought off the Mongols and later pulled off the miracle of modernization, but now Japan lay prostrate in defeat.

They expected the worst from the victors. Many of them knew how brutal the Japanese had been when they were victorious in China and in the Philippines. Many Japanese braced for a series of bitter reprisals against the now defeated and helpless nation. They steeled themselves against what they thought would be revenge against Japan for all the loss of life and treasure by the victorious forces. What a pleasant surprise it must have been when the U.S. military set up shop early in September 1945. Those tall, smiling soldiers who arrived in Japan seemed completely uninterested in revenge. They were usually friendly, often helpful, more like visiting students than a conquering army. As the war often seemed to bring out the worst in the Japanese character, the occupation of Japan by the Americans seemed to bring out the best in theirs.

The Americans, for their part, were pleasantly surprised as well. The only Japan they had ever encountered was the Japanese military—fanatical fighters who died in suicide charges rather than surrender; the kamikaze pilots flying full speed into U.S. ships. Many Americans probably expected a sullen population in Japan, hostile and resentful, maybe even willing to engage in violence against the occupiers. What they found was something quite different, a Japan they had not seen in the war. When the Emperor mentioned "endure," that meant acceptance and cooperation to the Japanese. What the Americans found was a disciplined, surprisingly peaceful people, polite to the point of caricature. Not a single "Go Home Yankee" sign was ever seen in the early days of the occupation. Even the military cooperated completely with its own dismantlement. After all, they saw themselves as the Emperor's warriors, and he had told them to give up.

The administration of President Franklin Roosevelt had been impressed by one important fact of history. The heavy handed treatment of Germany at the close of World War I was a bitter and humiliating experience for the German people. Germans were dealt with like a race of criminals. When Adolf Hitler came along, most Germans were willing to follow his radical policy if it would restore Germany's dignity. To avoid the kind of smoldering resentfulness that had eventually led to World War II, it was decided that the defeated nations of Germany and Japan would be handled differently this time.

Both nations would be helped to renounce militarism and embrace true democracy, to become allies of the very nations that had defeated them.

Months before the end of the war, as victory loomed as a certainty, the Roosevelt administration began planning for the reconstruction of Japan. It was decided that Japan would be reformed institution by institution, with specific people, experts in various areas of society, running special groups or missions. There was the government mission, which was to bring some alterations to the Japanese way of ruling their society; a human rights mission to guarantee new rules of civil rights; an education mission, which would be charged with completely redesigning Japan's education system; an agricultural mission dedicated to ending the negative effect of absentee land holding in Japan; and a labor relations mission guaranteeing labor's right to organize.

It took some time for the various missions to be up and running at the beginning of the Occupation, but some things happened immediately. All Japanese armed forces were disbanded. The Imperial Japanese Army and Navy, proud traditional institutions of enormous size and importance, simply ceased to exist. The U.S. military took responsibility for bringing war criminals to justice, and several dozen former military officers were convicted and hung. A long list of politicians and business leaders considered to have aided the war effort were put on a list of people barred from any positions of power indefinitely. All army officers were added to the list.

It seems strange to contemplate now, but for almost six and a half years, from early September 1945 until mid-May 1952, the U.S. effectively ruled Japan. It was supposed to be a unified system of administration by all of the allies that had been enemies of Japan during the war. Something called the *Supreme Command of the Allied Powers* was created. It was set up in theory as sort of a committee to make decisions concerning the establishment and operation of a new Japan under occupation. The committee had representatives from China, Russia, France, Britain, the Netherlands, and, of course, the United States. This group was to meet as equals in making all important decisions regarding the reconstruction of Japan. However, that idea was completely derailed by one important development.

That development was the man chosen by President Roosevelt to head the Command. He was General of the Army, Douglas MacArthur. General MacArthur had led U.S. forces in their bloody island hopping across the Pacific. It was Americans who had paid the price for victory in blood. And committee or no committee, he was not about to let any non-Americans interfere with the running of post-war Japan. The Command committee continued to meet and make proposals for the entire six plus years of the Occupation. MacArthur continued to ignore them. The Occupation of Japan was to be an all-American undertaking.

In a way, Douglas MacArthur was a fortuitous choice to play the role of supreme authority of the nation of Japan—in essence, to take on the job of running the country. And run it he did. He was a complete egomaniac. He acted more like a king than an administrator. He could not abide taking orders from anyone, and he was eventually fired, toward the end of the Occupation, for refusing to obey a direct command from President Truman. MacArthur looked and acted the part of a virtual demigod. All decisions by him were final.

Far from resenting MacArthur's arrogance and overbearing nature, the Japanese quickly warmed to their new ruler. The population there was used to authoritarian leadership, and the unquestioned military superiority demonstrated by the U.S. gave MacArthur more prestige than any native source could match. SCAP, which was supposed to stand for the international committee, gradually came to stand for Supreme "Commander" of the Allied Forces. From early in the Occupation, whenever the letters SCAP were used, it referred to MacArthur, not the meaningless committee.

Fortunately for the future of Japan, MacArthur, although in his past considered a conservative Republican, had the good sense to let the young "New Dealers"* do their work without much interference. He could have stopped these people at any time, but he listened to their arguments:

---

* For those of you not familiar with American political history, that term "new deal" refers to the left-wing, in some cases almost socialistic, policies of the Roosevelt administration.

For example, that Japan's leftist labor organizers should be encouraged to form left-leaning unions to check the power of corporations.

His good sense was observed in other ways. Many in the U.S. government wanted the Emperor to be deposed and tried as a war criminal. MacArthur saw the Emperor as a stabilizing force. It had been the Emperor who announced Japan's surrender, and MacArthur was impressed at how utterly silent the Japanese military instantly became after the announcement. That kind of power could be used to the advantage of the Occupation, and he refused to listen to any arguments favoring the Emperor's removal. MacArthur met with the Emperor at the General's residence. They were photographed together, standing as equals. In the eyes of most Japanese, SCAP could no longer be the enemy.

The missions began their work, and, in some cases, they brought about permanent and revolutionary changes; in other cases, their work was undone later. Mission members did not act openly as dictators of a new Japan. They worked with their Japanese counterparts, and the results of their work were always presented as coming from Japanese sources. Not many people were fooled; Japanese citizens with any degree of sophistication knew who was calling the shots. The missions' greatest successes were in the areas of education and human rights and with the agricultural population. They were less successful with reorganizing business life and the government. There was some lasting influence in those areas, but much of their effort was muted later, and in some ways reversed.

In education, it wasn't so much that the U.S. education mission to Japan brought in new attitudes and new commitments, but that by restructuring the system, it enabled prevailing Japanese values and attitudes to be more fully realized. The Japanese public school system before the end of the war was based roughly on the French system of the early 20th century. It was complicated and highly exclusive, with many vocational paths producing a tiny proportion of students who could qualify for higher education.

Japan had always used entrance examinations for entrance into colleges and universities, and they were not forced to give them up. The system was otherwise tremendously simplified and given a decidedly American accent. Every Japanese child was to attend six years of elementary, three years of middle, and three years of senior high school. High schools were divided into academic and vocational versions; most Japanese chose to attend academic ones. The number of colleges and universities was increased fivefold. And the percentage of college-age Japanese attending higher education increased tenfold, from three percent in 1940 to thirty percent in 1950! It was a well educated generation of engineers and administrators that led Japan to economic revival in the 60s and 70s.

The human rights mission was given the task of writing a brand new constitution for Japan. Japanese officials were aware that MacArthur did not like the Meiji Constitution, with its ambiguity and references to Imperial Will. Some Japanese officials tried their hand at writing a new one, but when MacArthur looked them over, they seemed to him to be just more of the same old ideas. He assembled a group of young Americans and gave them just five days to come up with the draft of a completely new outline for Japanese governmental structure. The draft they presented to MacArthur was later proclaimed to be issued by the Japanese government as the official constitution of Japan, but in fact, no Japanese had any hand in it at all.

It was a progressive document, in many ways more so than the U.S. constitution. The new constitution declared the Emperor to be a mere symbol of the state, with no power whatsoever—not a big change, actually. One clause stood out as very significant. The new constitution renounced militarism for all time. Japan was forbidden to have normal military forces, and although a self-defense corps was later allowed, it is not permitted to carry arms outside the confines of Japan. There are those in Japan today who would like to strike that clause from the constitution. However, it is still supported by a majority of the Japanese population.

In the long term, probably the most important change brought about by the U.S. Occupation was the transformation of rural Japan. Before the Occupation, almost half of all farm land in Japan had fallen into the hands of owners who lived in towns and cities and were not farmers at all. Prices for farm products were very low, so that even those who owned their own land could barely make a living. The agricultural mission changed all that. The land that tenant farmers worked was sold to them at token prices. Owners were not given a choice. Generous farm subsidies were set up to guarantee that farmers could have a respectable income. This caused a great fall in wealth for a few landowners, but the farm population, a third of Japan in those days, was suddenly transformed from virtual share-croppers into middle class capitalists. The incentive to produce more for their own income had the effect of tripling agricultural production within five years.

UP FROM THE ASHES

For anyone visiting Japan at the end of the war, it must have seemed that the days of that country as a leading industrial nation were finished. Just clearing away the rubble caused by American bombers would take the Japanese more than a year. Housing was in such short supply that many people slept in large drainage pipes. Few people starved, but hardly anyone had an adequate diet. But the Japanese had done it before, and they were determined to build a new and prosperous economy once again.

In 1950, war broke out between North Korea and South Korea, in which the U.S. became heavily involved. It was a great gift to Japan. American forces needed to assemble and repair a great deal of equipment to fight the war, and U.S. factories were too far away to do this efficiently. Within the next two years, over 120,000 Japanese were working either directly or indirectly in the Korean War effort—a tremendous economic shot in the arm at precisely the right moment.

Slowly, the economic sector began a painful comeback. With wages and salaries very low, Japanese began making merchandise and selling it on world markets at very low cost to consumers. At first, these were cheaply designed and shoddily made items, such as toys and crude electrical devices. The Japanese had lost the war, but they had not lost their sense of diligence. Gradually, as manufacturers gained more confidence, the products made in Japan got better. A long evolution of products entered international markets with gradually increasing complexity and quality—radios, watches, small motorcycles, larger motorcycles, and cameras.

In fact, cameras provide a good example of Japan's post World War II breakthrough in world markets. Up until the late 1950s, almost all professional photographers used a camera made near Frankfurt Germany by the Leika Co. Engineers at a small lens manufacturer in Japan, *Nihon kōgaku kōgyo* 日本光学工業, examined the Leika hand-held, through-the-lens camera for a year, experimenting with their own design. They finally produced a camera that was the equal of the Leika in every dimension, with at least the equivalent performance. With one exception: The cost was about one half that of the Leika. They marketed it as *Nikon*, and photographers, being practical people, flocked to it. Within a few years, it was difficult to find a professional photographer anywhere in the world, including Germany, who did not use the Nikon as his or her primary camera.

Finally, the Japanese entered the automobile market, and if you have any doubt about what happened after that, you should get in touch with an American automobile executive. He or she will tell you all about it. By the 1970s, Japan was producing more cars and trucks for sale world-wide than the U.S.

Up from the ashes, Japan became an industrial giant, with greater shares of markets in many products than it could have dreamed of in the era prior to World War II. The standard of living in Japan, except for living space, is equal to any of the other industrial societies.

As the Occupation finally came to a close, the Japan that entered the Occupation and the Japan that existed when it ended in 1952 were barely recognizable as the same country. Twenty years on from that point, the change again was stunning. The U.S., as it set out to rebuild Japan after the war, no doubt hoped that it would rebound and become a self-sufficient economy once again. Indeed, the U.S. was instrumental in helping Japan regain its industrial vigor. It is likely that very few, if any, Americans of that time could have predicted what Japan would become. On a per capita basis, Japan's industrial capacity and output is almost equal to the nation that defeated it in World War II. Japan is no longer our client, it is our competitor. The two nations don't always agree on important issues, but they have a great deal in common and have learned to deal with each other as equals.

This concludes our brief description of the place, the people and the past of our subject. In the following chapter, we begin an exploration of how Japanese think and act in the world today. We begin by taking a look at some general aspects of the contemporary cultural environment of the society, followed by a more specific investigation of important institutions such as family life, the education system, and the religious part of Japanese life. Unless you already know Japan well, you will probably be surprised at some of the things you read in the next three chapters. Japan was largely isolated from cultural intrusion for a long time; this gave the Japanese a chance to formulate their own way of doing things. Some Japanese exaggerate just how unique their cultural features are, but no one could deny that life in Japan is, in important ways, not like life anywhere else.

Chapter 9
Cultural Themes

W e humans share many traits with the other creatures that inhabit the earth with us. There is, however, a dividing line that separates us fundamentally from all other animals. It is a difference generated by the evolution of the human brain. Only humans have fully blown language and the ability to codify language into writing. Only humans have systems of behavior which can change rapidly in changing circumstances. Only humans have creative adaptation, resulting in technology. Only humans have religion, philosophy and other fruits of abstract thought. All this is due to what we have come to refer to as *culture.*

Culture, then, is really what makes us truly human. It pervades everything we are and everything we do. Strangely, it has been studied scientifically for only a little over a hundred years. We still don't understand all the ways it is created and evolves, but some things have become clear. We know, for example, that there are two important features of human culture that, while they may seem to be opposite, are nonetheless both true. Stated simply, they are: First, cultural themes can be extremely durable; and second, human cultural systems are very adaptable and can mold quickly around new circumstances. An example of the first principle can be seen in the writings of the French aristocrat Alexis de Tocqueville, who traveled through the U.S. in the early 1820s. Upon his return to France, he wrote a book translated as *Democracy in America,* in which he described with keen insight the kind of society he encountered here.

Sociologists and historians are always fascinated at how much of what he described sounds so familiar in the American society of today, almost two centuries later. This, after the nation was transformed to an industrial society, its people moved from farms to towns and cities, and it absorbed millions of newcomers from every part of the world.

De Tocqueville noticed that Americans were more egalitarian, more independent, more distrustful of authority, gave more status to women, and were more generous to strangers than any people he had ever been around. He commented on the strength of religious beliefs of the people he met and noticed that Americans were obsessed with machinery and other gadgets. If one had to list ten basic features of American culture today, in spite of all the growth and transformation, those seven surely would have to be included.

In Japan as well, we can see some basic themes that have held sway even as the society was completely transformed from a backward agricultural economy to an industrial giant, with all the changes in lifestyle that such a transformation entailed. Several of the themes introduced in this chapter, which are exclusively concerned with contemporary Japan, have antecedents which go back hundreds of years.

The second characteristic of culture, its adaptable nature, can be seen clearly through the story of Japan's real life Rip van Winkle. His name was Onoda Hirō, a soldier in the Pacific War who served in the Philippines. During the fighting there in 1944, his squad got separated from the rest of his unit, and he and two other comrades hid out in the jungle. They lived off the land and from what they could steal from local farmers, avoiding capture by staying in a trench with camouflage cover during daylight hours. After several years, the other two Japanese soldiers with Onoda died, and he just stayed there hiding out, not knowing that the war had ended. He survived there in the jungle for nearly *thirty years*! Finally, a Japanese journalist convinced him that the war was over and brought him home in 1974.

The Japan Onoda found when he returned was a place he did not know or feel comfortable with. Although Japan had already been an industrial society when he'd left, most of the population up to the 1940s was what we would call "working class." Spartan values predominated, people worked hard and saved what they could for older age, and there were virtually no public social services. There was, of course, no television and no jet travel. Loyalty and obedience to social superiors, especially to the Emperor, were fundamental and closely adhered to values.

On his return, Onoda confronted a middle class society that he saw as well fed and self-indulgent—a society in which the Emperor was casually accepted as a mere symbol of the past. The idea of giving up one's life willingly for the Emperor would seem rather silly to most people of this new land Onoda suddenly fell into. All this sounds like improvement to us, but to Onoda-san, it was very confusing. He could not adjust to so much emphasis on material possessions, to so much political and social freedom, or to all the cars and the fast pace of life. After a couple of years, he emmigrated to Brazil to live in a more traditional Japanese-based community.*

Of course, all the other Japanese of Onoda's age had experienced the same changes that were so obvious to him. But the changes to them happened on a day by day progression. As the technological and social environment changed, the people changed along with them. To someone who had not witnessed all the things that had happened over those thirty years, Japan had become a place with a profoundly different culture.

Trying to understand the culture of any society, even the society one grew up in, is not an easy task. When we try to look into the fabric of any cultural system, we have to avoid ascribing too much importance to root or basic themes. These underlying motifs can last for centuries and be at the bottom of many aspects of the cultural personality of a society. But, as the experiences of Onoda-san reveal, fundamental changes in secondary themes can be just as important to consider in understanding contemporary life. In some ways, it might be easier for young adults in Japan to grasp the approach to life of young American adults than the approach to life of their own grandparents.

Another thing to keep in mind when trying to understand cultural reality is that culture is often inconsistent and varied within large societies. Even basic themes cannot always be generalized to extend to every

---

*   Later, in 1997, Onoda Hirō returned to Japan to run a camp teaching survival techniques for hikers and campers. He married a Japanese woman and lived in rural Japan the remainder of his days.

circumstance. The very opposite tendency can often be seen existing right alongside the cultural feature being explained. For example, Americans are usually described as placing great emphasis on the individual, and conversely, Japan is usually described as a place where personal identity is found more as part of a group. In many important ways, these descriptions are valid, but as you will read in the following chapter, within marriage, Japanese spouses are actually much more independent than Americans, who far more than Japanese tend to merge their identities together as a married couple.

It is also interesting to observe that the traditionally "group oriented" Japanese originally never had any team sports. All athletic and sporting events—archery, Sumo wrestling, judo—were events where individuals performed or competed without being members of teams. It wasn't until late in the nineteenth century that they finally got their first team sport—baseball—from those die-hard individualists, the Americans.

With these cautions in hand, let us now briefly explore what most observers would agree are some of the most characteristic Japanese cultural themes.

GROUP ORIENTATION

Strong attachment and loyalty to some sort of identity group is certainly not unique to Japan. Deep and emotional ties to family and clan characterize much of the traditional world. Japan, on the other hand is a modern nation, and when we compare that country with various other modern societies of Europe and America, it would be hard not to notice a particularly strong attachment to doing things as members of groups. We have known a few Japanese loners, but the great majority of people there are comfortable submerging their identity in a group setting. They work in groups, they travel in groups, and more than Americans or Europeans, they tend to identify themselves with the groups they belong to. Where we identify as individuals, Japanese often relate to the groups they are members of. This is reflected in the language they use in referring to themselves and to others. To a Japanese, one's grandfather is often referred to not as *my* grandfather, but as *uchi no sofu* 内の祖父 "the grandfather of our family." Or, instead of using the word for "you" in conversation, it will often be replaced by *otaku* お宅, "(a person of) your house."

Americans like to call each other by their given or first names. Japanese, and East Asians in general, normally use family names—Kato-san, Nishimura-san, etc.—except for the most intimate of relationships. First names, of course, identify an individual, while family names identify a family line to which one belongs.

When we look at Japanese history, and especially at the workings of the Japanese village in historical perspective, we can see some important specifics that have an especially broad influence over the people there. Working together in rice planting, creating and maintaining irrigation ditches, harvesting crops, and many other ventures, was not based strictly on kinship ties as was and still is in many other traditional societies. It was the village as a work organization, cutting across family lines, that molded the spirit of group cooperation in Japan. Other wet rice cultures have developed this sense of cooperation as well, but outside of Japan, kinship organization tended to trump non-kin groupings.

The feeling of group togetherness is comparatively strong in Japan and can be demonstrated in many ways. For example, Japanese workers often will take much less individual paid vacation time than offered by the company, perhaps ten days out of twenty or thirty that they could take. The reason Japanese workers do this is because of a kind of obligation they feel toward fellow group members. After all, so much time away from the work the group does will put extra stress on the other members.

This idea of working in a group extends to the entire organization one works for. The organization is accepted as a body of which every member is a part. That kind of talk is made in many places as a way to encourage worker morale. In Japan, it has none of the ring of corniness it usually does to Americans. Commitment to an organization does not have to be encouraged in Japan; it just sort of happens naturally. All personnel at large companies wear small company badges on the lapels of their jackets. Sometimes, neighbors will refer to a family by the name of the company associated with the head of household—"the Sanno Bank family," "the Aiwa family," etc. It is common for men to take a week-long vacation trip in the summer, not with family, but with his work group, with family left at home. The first author once asked a retired neighbor in Japan what kind of work he did before retiring. His answer was interesting; he didn't say I worked at this job or that job as an American might do. He said "*I was a Seibu*† *man for 37 years.*" The particular work was less significant in his eyes than the organization he belonged to.

Westerners often complain about working in giant organizations, of being just a cog in a big, impersonal machine. There usually is less of this feeling in Japan. Typically, Japanese yearn to work for these kinds of organizations. They seem to derive a personal satisfaction in belonging to something large and powerful. And they really do feel like they belong.

Japanese businesses, from top to bottom, are formed into all kinds of groupings that start with local organizations and then pyramid into larger groupings, ending as huge national institutions. Farmers' cooperatives are a good example. Every farmer belongs to the local cooperative. It may loan the farm money for materials, offer technical advice, and also serve a social function. The cooperative elects members to represent it at the next higher level, the regional cooperative, which elects members to the prefectural cooperative organization, which is topped by the national organization. At the national level, the All Japan Agricultural Association, as it is called in English, is a powerful lobbying agency, keeping prices high for many agricultural products, and it is partly responsible for Japan's rather astonishingly high food prices.

Professional people such as physicians and dentists likewise all belong to grouping like this. Americans belong to these kinds of organizations as well, but in Japan they are more widespread and are taken more seriously by individual members.

Hobbies, activities and interests people engage in for fun or relaxation or stimulation have wide expression in societies all over the world. Sometimes Americans have hobbies which require other people forming teams and such, but for Americans, hobbies can be something that can be followed all by oneself, in complete isolation, with no organizational involvement whatsoever.

---

† A large nation-wide retail and rail line corporation.

In raising this subject, it should be pointed out that the English term "hobby" is not a very good translation for what the Japanese call *shumi* 趣味. There is no English word that conveys the seriousness and important role *shumi* plays in Japanese life. Almost every Japanese adult has a *shumi*. Some *shumi* involve action and athletics such as hiking, judo, or ballroom dancing. Others relate to classical pursuits such as playing the koto, classical Japanese dance, or reciting traditional historical narratives. Very common ones are flower arranging, calligraphy, learning to speak colloquial English or French, and photography.

But in Japan, one doesn't normally pick up a hobby and practice it all by oneself. Time may be spent doing one's *shumi* alone, but he or she will almost always get started by joining a *shumi* group around a particular pursuit. Groups like that have formal levels of proficiency, which a leader or teacher will grade and advance members through over time. If the group is not very large, say not more than a dozen people, it is not uncommon for the group to stay together for the remainder of the lives of members. A *shumi* group may even take trips together, attend weddings and other important events of group members, and of course, be present at funerals when *shumi* members finally die.

Political parties are always divided into smaller groups called *habatsu* 派閥, which are like smaller versions of the larger parties. Members of these groups remain fiercely loyal. The political fortunes of an individual politician on the national level depends more on the size and power of his or her *habatsu* than on anything he or she actually does.

University life, as well, is built around group orientation. Although the situation is beginning to change, professors are traditionally arranged around a senior individual with perhaps five or six faculty of lesser rank. These *koza* 講座, as they are called, have their own budgets and promotion policies, and they interact with other academic groups usually even less than do academic departments in the U.S.

On the student side, as you will learn in chapter 11, they really don't have to study very hard once they gain entrance to a university. Most of their energy is expended in clubs. Having said that, it might not sound so different from American student life. But clubs in Japanese universities play a much deeper role in the lives students than is normally the case in the U.S. In a large university, there may be as many as 100 official clubs on campus, covering just about any interest one can imagine. Some clubs have an academic flavor—the French literature club or the Steinbeck club. Others involve activities such as wind surfing or skiing. There are clubs for Japanese *manga* 漫画, or comics. Team sports are club activities in Japan—baseball, tennis, wrestling, American football, etc. The institution provides facilities, but (except for baseball) coaches and all equipment are paid for by the participants.

The important point here is that club membership is the focus of social life in a Japanese university. Members will have parties, socialize together, and for those of the same year-grade, commonly remain as friends for their entire lives.

INSIDE-OUTSIDE

As a side effect of the strong emphasis on belonging to groups in Japan, in many interesting ways there is an unusually strong sense of *inside* and *outside* in Japanese life. This tendency runs through the entire scale of social dimensions, from the way people interpret their residence unit to the way they see themselves as a people. There is a keen awareness in Japan of just who is and who is not Japanese. Some observers have called this the *gaijin* 外人 complex. Gaijin is usually translated as "foreigner," but it does not mean the same as the English word foreigner, especially as used by Americans. To Americans, "foreigner" is a status that can easily be outlived if one stays in the U.S. and comes to think of him or herself as part of American society. In Japan, gaijin means non-Japanese. It is a definition that can never be outlived; one can be "in" Japan, perfectly accepted and functioning normally with no disadvantages. But in the truest sense, one who has not been born of Japanese parents can never be "of" Japan.

This is part of a strong inside/outside consciousness, but it goes farther than national identity, extending into every facet of life, even, as mentioned above, to such things as personal residences. Japanese do most of their socializing outside the home. Normally, with a few exceptions, only relatives and the most intimate of friends see the inside of a person's residence unit. Traditional Japanese houses have an alcove called *genkan* 玄関, which is at ground level below the rest of the house, located at the entrance. This is as far as most salesmen, neighbors and other non-intimate outsiders get when visiting a Japanese home. Inside the home is for people on the "inside." All others are outsiders, and are usually kept outside. In personal relationships, that same strong sense of inside and outside prevails.

The organizations a person is associated with—hobby groups, informal groups of close friends, people who have gone to the same schools, and of course work groups—form networks of belongingness which to the Japanese is their social *inside*.

As discussed at several junctures in this book, students at a Japanese university are not under pressure to study very hard in order to remain as students at their universities. In fact, some students hardly study at all, and still they are virtually guaranteed of graduation after four years of university attendance. If you understand the way concepts of inside and outside work in Japan, the principle of passing students through makes more sense. Students at a university have passed the entrance examination and thereby have become associated with the university. Students there *belong* to the university; they are part of the inside world of the institution.

Some day, you may refer to a university as your *alma mater*, but frankly when you use that term, it will simply refer to a place where you went to college, and many of you will have more than one. When Japanese use a similar term *bokō* 母校, it has a far deeper meaning, a meaning perhaps only Princeton, Yale and Harvard graduates could begin to appreciate in the United States. It is, with few exceptions, the only college or university they have ever attended. It is a place they will identify with in the deepest personal manner all the days of their lives.

Conversely, as part of its own special inside, for everyone associated with that university, the institution could never treat its students in a cavalier way. The students are theirs; it is truly their mother school and will always be theirs, and like a mother. The university is there to help them, not to give them a hard time. It will guarantee their graduation (regardless of study habits or lack thereof), and it will use all the resources at its command to help the students secure employment after graduation. We can tell you from experience that a flunking grade given by an uncaring foreign professor is definitely not part of mother's plan, and such a grade will almost surely be changed by the administration.

HIERARCHY

A famous Japanese sociologist[‡] refers to Japan as a "vertical society." What she means by this is that although the society can be said to be "group oriented," as we have seen, the social structure puts more emphasis on ranking than in most other places. Members of groups are usually arranged in ranked categories, commonly with specific rank titles. As some of you are aware, in a Judo group, all members are ranked according to their level of proficiency—white belt, brown belt, black belt—determined by the teacher, the *sensei* 先生, who is formally ranked above all members.

Age itself, seniority as we say, is taken far more seriously as a form of ranking in Japan than in Western societies. Sometimes, in recent years, the rule is broken, but there is a rule nonetheless in Japanese groups that the highest status accrues to the oldest member. In business circles, for example, Americans and other Westerners are comfortable with using merit alone as the criterion of promotion and leadership. In a group of traveling Japanese businessmen, no matter how sharp the younger members of the group, no matter how much they contribute, they find it natural to defer to the oldest member as the titular head of the group. Even though younger members may be smarter and actually more valuable to the company, it is they who open doors for the senior members and bow slightly as senior members pass through them.

Japanese learn the lessons of formal ranking early in life in their own families. Japanese don't have so many children nowadays, but when there are multiple children, an iron-clad rule is always in force: Older siblings call younger siblings by their given names, but younger siblings always call their older siblings by their title. If son Hiroshi is nine years old, and

---

[‡]   Chie Nakane, who taught for many years at both the U. of Calif. at Berkeley and Tokyo University.

daughter Keiko is seven years old, Hiroshi will call his sister Keiko, but Keiko will never call Hiroshi by or refer to him as Hiroshi, but always use the title "older brother," *o-niisan* お兄さん. If the older sibling is a female, then the title "older sister" *o-neesan* お姉さん is used. When the two are all alone, even when Keiko is fighting with or complaining about Hiroshi, it will always be *o-niisan*; there are no exceptions.

As Japanese go through life, the lesson stays with them. In any organization, people senior to oneself are referred to as *sempai* 先輩, and those junior to oneself are referred to as *kōhai* 後輩.§

Another way in which hierarchy comes into play in Japanese interpersonal relations is the importance given to personal titles. Anytime people have titles in Japan, they usually become substitutes for personal names. Americans value egalitarianism, and they like to pretend that people are on the same level (even when that is clearly not the case). The dean of a college in a university may be a person by the name of Helen Smith. But being an American she will probably insist on being addressed as "Helen," rather than Dean Smith, or Dr. Smith, or even "Dean."

In Japan, this is not the case. A dean may be every bit as friendly and approachable as Dean Smith above, but if the dean's name is Hiroshi Kato, no faculty member would ever think of addressing him as "Hiroshi," and even his peers, the other deans, would never address him using his given name.¶ Most Japanese wouldn't even say "Dean Kato." He will almost always be addressed and referred to by his title, *gakubu-chō* 学部長, simply, "Dean."

The man the first author usually works for when in Japan, and has known for more than thirty years, started out with a small English language school but eventually built a kind of empire of private schools and colleges. He is a close friend. Our wives are close, as are our children. But as close as we are, we always call each other by our respective titles; *hakasei* 博士, the title referring to an academic Ph.D., and *sōchō* 総長,

---

§   These are never used in addressing people, but only as second person pronouns, such as, "He is my sempai."

¶   The only people to do so would be perhaps his wife, older siblings, or lifelong boyhood friends.

something like, "general director." The only time these titles are dropped is when speaking English around other Americans.

You are likely to find the above strange. "Why would intimate friends call each other by their titles?" It sounds absurdly formal and unfriendly to Americans. Using titles instead of names does not detract from any degree of warmth and intimacy among friends in Japan. It is just the Japanese way of identifying each other. One's rank in society doesn't disappear just because two people become close friends.

There is one way in which the Japanese definition of rank identity does indeed interfere with social relationships. It has already been described above that age seniority tends to be formally recognized in Japan. People are either in a category older than oneself, about the same age as oneself, or younger than oneself. There are some exceptions, but in the main, close friends can be chosen only from that category of people close to one's own age. The older people get, the broader these categories become, but for young people in Japan, it is unusual to see close friendships form from people even a year or two in either direction. The reason for this is that for the categories above and below in age, more formal and polite language must be used from down to up. One can share strong interests, and in some ways behave like good friends with someone in a higher age category, but in public, the ethics of formal ranking between the two tends to get in the way of intimacy.

Friendship in Japan is an interesting subject in itself that perhaps we should consider a bit here. Perhaps because the population of people with whom a person can form close friendships is somewhat restricted, due to the limitations of ranking, friendships in Japan seem to have a longevity that is on average greater than for Westerners. Americans, for example, can be as supportive as friends as people anywhere. But, perhaps because we move around so much in such a big country, friendships have a way of cycling to rather dim memory over a long period of separation. Some Americans continue to have close relations with their friends from high school, but this is certainly not always the case. In Japan, although a person's circle of friends may be somewhat smaller, friendships more often last an entire lifetime. When people who have been raised in Japan return after a long absence, it is common to get together with old friends from schools dating back to early childhood. Again, this trait is not unique to Japan, but it is considerably more prevalent there than in the U.S.

THE INDIVIDUAL

The way Japanese tend to live their lives as members of groups and put so much emphasis on group orientation is very easy to see. What is not so easy to see are the ways in which Japanese partly balance out this cultural feature with a kind of Japanese-style individualism. Yes, Japanese people interpret the group context a person exists in as in some ways more important than the individual. For example, the term *uchi* 内 "inside," as suggested above, is commonly used as a pronoun for "I" or "me." Japanese refer to the company where they work as *uchi no kaisha* 内 の会社, which is to say, in effect, "the company of which I am a member." Think about that.

But in spite of all that, there are areas of personal life where Japanese do indeed express a very personal side of their lives. In fact, we insist that in some ways Japanese are more individualistic than average Americans.

Almost as soon as a way to write their own language was available fifteen hundred years ago, the Japanese have been avid diary writers. We don't know what percentage of Japanese keep diaries these days, but it is almost certainly greater than in the U.S. Some have become famous when published as diary-novels. Diary writing in Japan is never just a chronicle of everyday events, as it often is in other places. Japanese ruminate about life in their diaries in a deeply introspective manner. When you read them, they sound more like prose poetry than a list of happenings in an individual's life.

Poetry itself plays a much, much greater role in Japanese life than in any other country we know. There are well-publicized poetry contests. Haiku poetry competitions are very common things in Japan. Major newspapers sponsor such contests, and the finalists' work is prominently reproduced in full pages of the most important newspapers in Japan. The winning poem for one national contest is read in the presence of the

Emperor, who also always reads one of his poems to the attending dignitaries. For a Japanese student, businessman, or housewife to occasionally compose some form of poetry is considered a normal thing to do.

There are, of course, poetry magazines in the U.S. as well, but in Japan, there are more of them, and the leading ones sell far more copies per capita than similar ones in the U.S. Poetry, like diary writing, is a very personal act. Naturally, being Japan, there are poetry circles which function like other interest groups, but the actual writing of poetry, by its very nature, is a completely individual undertaking.

In spite of the ubiquity of television, the internet, and all of the other electronic and other distractions in modern life, the Japanese have never given up on reading. Among nations of the world, only the people of tiny Iceland read more than the Japanese. Newspaper reading has fallen off precipitously in the U.S. over the past twenty years, but Japanese newspapers have experienced only a very slight decline in readership. They read more magazines than any other people, even more than Icelanders. And fiction reading of both native and foreign books is about double the U.S. per capita average.

In discussing any kind of individualism in Japan, perhaps more important than how much the Japanese read is the nature of the material of what they read. A typical Japanese novel of course tells a story, but usually, more importantly, it reads more like an essay on how the protagonist feels about the situations or relationships or life experiences. With some notable exceptions, Americans tend to have a rather practical approach to figuring out how to live, and by and large have limited patience with a great deal of pondering about the "meaning of life."

In public life, Japanese people seem reasonably cheerful and purposeful. However, from what they read and what they write, we can definitely discern a considerable philosophical bent to the Japanese psyche. Some of this manifests itself as a kind of pessimism. There are many differences in religion between America and Japan; only a very small portion of people in Japan believe in a hereafter, in heaven, or in any type of life after death. Japanese seem to be more conscious than Westerners of just how short life is, of the temporariness of existence. It is this kind of sober reflection that pervades some of what they think and write about. The point here is that people in that society ponder these things in a decidedly individualistic way, and this tendency can certainly be considered a very authentic expression of individualism.

SOCIAL CONTROL

Differences in the way societies control the behavior of their members are rather subtle, things anthropologists and sociologists notice after long and careful observation. The way people actually behave on a day-to-day basis doesn't actually vary much in practical terms from to society to society: Most people follow the rules of proper behavior most of the time, but under the right circumstances, some will lie and cheat and do other devious things when it benefits their interests. In this regard, the Japanese are not so different from any other people. What we describe below is not so much a difference in behavior as a difference in the route taken to achieve that behavior.

There is a tendency in Western societies to conceive of morality in terms of broad abstractions of *good* and *evil*. Western societies have had a long experience with monotheism, and traditionally in these societies, ethics and morality have been interpreted as coming from religion, or perhaps more specifically, from the commandments of an all powerful God. Except for the tiny minority of Christian and Moslem Japanese, people in that society have never worshiped a monotheistic God. In fact, there is not even a very good word for God in the Japanese language.

Originally, when referring to foreign ideas of God, Japanese used the word *ten* 天, a Chinese term denoting a vague supernatural holy place beyond the reach of humans. Beginning around 1920, Japanese writers coined the term *kamisama* 神様 to render the concept of a single God into Japanese, taken from *kami* 神, which traditionally referred both to the many demigods in Japanese polytheism and to a kind of supernatural force inherent in various elements of nature. The *sama* 様 part indicates an honorable role or personage.

Throughout history, morality and ethics have not in Japan ever emanated from God or in any other way from religion. Ethics and morality in

Japan are not as universalistic, but are based more on specific obligations to people and institutions.

Western religions are full of universal concepts. The Ten Commandments, for example, are presumably meant to apply to all situations in life. People in Western societies, whether religious or not, have been taught to see standards of behavior in that kind universalistic perspective. The Japanese do not have a strongly developed sense of universal good or evil. They do have an extremely well developed sense of personal obligation. This is not obligation to a set of principles, but obligation to specific people and organizations.

In understanding the historical context of morality in the West, one must be familiar with the concept of *sin*. There is no exact translation for the word sin in Japanese, at least not in a religious context, but two words are equally important in understanding the historical context of morality there. They are *giri* 義理 and *on* 恩. They mean roughly the same thing, and in contemporary usage, they are often treated as synonyms. Both terms are commonly translated into English as "obligation." In a strict etymological sense, however, there is a difference. *Giri* is more associated with "achieved obligation," and *on* tends, at least historically, to relate to "ascribed obligation."

Giri traditionally has carried with it the meaning of obligation acquired through some act of help (or kindness or mercy) received from someone who was not obligated to give it. In other words, *giri* is the feeling of debt owed to someone who did you a significant favor when they didn't have to. *Giri,* of course, must be repaid, and the favor must be returned with at least as significant a benefit as received. The longer one waits to repay *giri,* the deeper *giri* gets, and so the obligation should be increased accordingly. It is felt by Japanese people that really very deep *giri* can never be paid off, but that one must sort of pay on the interest throughout life, meaning that you will be in someone's debt forever and owe them certain kinds of smaller favors from time to time.

On tends to refer to obligation owed to someone or something just because it is there—a factor of support or protection or nurture built into one's life and for which one should feel gratitude. For example, people owe *on* to their parents. The Chinese character meaning teacher is pronounced *shi* in Japanese, and people there often refer to a favorite or particularly helpful teacher or professor as their *onshi* 恩師. Before the end of World War II, all Japanese were taught that they owed *on* to the Emperor, a way of emphasizing commitment to the nation in a particularly effective way.

Actually, the word *giri* is not heard very often in Japan nowadays, except in its specialized use to denote in-laws and step relatives, such as *giri no chichi* 義理の父, father in-law or step father. Many young Japanese will tell you that *giri* is not a part of modern Japan at all, motivated by the desire not to be seen as somehow old-fashioned or different from the people of Europe and America. The word *on,* as well, is more often a part of period literature than everyday speech.

Don't believe them, however. While not often articulated these days, and certainly not as powerful a determinant of behavior as in the past, the spirit of *giri* and *on* still influence how Japanese respond to social reality.

Due to space limitations, this hardware store places merchandise where no store personnel can monitor it during hours of operation. At closing time, when they bring it inside, none of it will be missing.

The words themselves may not be used much nowadays, but just beneath the surface, the idea of obligation to people and institutions is still a strong determinant of how people judge themselves and others.

There is less of a tendency in Japan than in the West to think of something as inherently good or bad, and conversely, more of a tendency to evaluate how behavior affects others within one's social network. Some writers call this tendency "situational ethics," and the label often has a negative interpretation in the U.S. and other Western societies, where it is thought of as a kind of creeping moral sloppiness that deviates from timeless standards of right and wrong. But in Japan, it definitely does not represent any type of "creeping." The Japanese have, throughout history, interpreted moral behavior more in terms of obligations, and of course, obligations depend on one's social relationships at the time—in other words, on the situation.

While Japanese mechanisms of behavior control might not always make sense to outsiders, no one could deny that they work. Japan has remarkably high standards of ethical behavior in the context of a large, complex society full of anonymity. Every foreigner who has ever lived in Japan for any length of time can relate stories of valuable items left out in public places that were still there when the owner returned hours later to look for them. As shown above, Japanese retailers have a hard time with space, and retailers often stock items for sale during hours of operation around corners on the outside of the store, completely out of sight of store personnel. Virtually no merchandise ever turns up missing. Can you imagine what would happen if a store tried that in a large city in the United States?

CONFORMITY

After reading the above, it should come as no surprise to learn that the parameters of self expression in Japan are narrower than for people who live in the United States. A great deal of Japanese conformity is a direct result of Japan's homogeneity. They have never had to adjust to significant numbers people with different traditions and different ways of speaking and thinking.

When spending any time in Japan ,Westerners will normally be struck by the uniformity of personal presentation. Japanese, perhaps influenced by all of the minute regulations of the Edo *bakufu,* including how everyone had to dress, have a habit of rather strictly combining costume with situation. Japanese know how things are in Western countries, and there is a bit more individualism in dress than in the past, but there is still a strong tendency to dress according to defined format.

We remember one time accompanying a group of students on a summer retreat to a kind of mountain tennis resort. The idea was to play tennis for a few days, or to learn to play the game if one had never done so. Some of the students had never held a tennis racket in their lives. But even those complete neophytes showed up on the courts the first day all wearing name brand tennis gear, including top of the line shoes, rather expensive shorts and tops, and rackets far better than needed by beginners. For Japanese, when you play tennis, damn it, you show up looking like a tennis players!

Fads in clothing and dress style, especially for young people prior to taking full-time employment, is a fact of every modern society. But when it comes to fashion, the speed and completeness of how it spreads across the land is more pronounced in Japan than in any society we know of. A few years ago, boots worn by young women with exaggeratedly high platform soles made their appearance around early April. By summer, it was rare to see a young lady not wearing them.

Weddings in Japan, besides being unbelievably expensive, as discussed in the following chapter, are also highly standardized. There are all kinds of settings, types of services, degree of formality and other choices possible for Americans when they decide to get married. For Japanese, the choice range is all the way, as the old joke goes, from A to B.

About seventy percent of young Japanese who get married,** get married in a Shinto ceremony. The ceremony is attended by relatives and a few others, but the banquet that follows actually is kind of a party, where

---

** They are almost always below the age of forty. Women over that age getting married are interpreted by most Japanese as somewhat ridiculous.

people give speeches and everyone (except the principles, who never seem to smile) has a good time.

Another twenty percent get married in a Christian ceremony with a larger group in attendance. Sometimes this takes place in a Church, but more often, it takes place in a hotel facility presided over by a young foreigner with absolutely no clerical status—merely a young man with a side job posing as a priest or pastor. In many cases, at least some members of the precession are completely aware of this. It is simply not an important issue. Few people who get married in a Christian ceremony are actually Christians. People of that persuasion constitute only a little over one percent of the Japanese population. It's just that the Japanese think that Christian weddings are "cool," or *kakkō ii* 恰好いい, as the Japanese would say. The Christian ceremony is followed by the same kind of banquet, which is really the formal introduction of the married couple to their social world.

There is one alternative, which several thousand young people take each year. It is to get married in a foreign country by the local custom of whatever place they choose. However, even for those kind of extra-brave newlyweds, upon their return, they almost always have a banquet that turns out to be remarkably like the traditional wedding party.

WOMEN IN JAPAN

There will be more to say about the role of women in Japan when we get to the next chapter, dealing with family. However, it is such an interesting and misunderstood subject outside of the country that we thought a separate section on it would be useful here, as we discuss cultural themes.

There is one thing you can count on: Glib and simple statements about the role of women in Japan are always at least partly wrong. Women in Japan play completely different roles in different social contexts, so that no one-sided depiction can come close to the truth. In fact, we can make two statements, both of which are backed up with solid evidence: First, women of Japan are the most put upon and exploited, and have the least power of women in any other industrialized nation. Second, women of Japan have more personal freedom and more power and influence in their society than women in any other industrialized nation. Both statements are equally valid, depending upon on which aspect of the lives of Japanese women one focuses.

Before the period of Chinese influence in Japan, women there had an unusually high status for women in an agricultural society. Until the end of the eighth century, women occasionally served as Empresses. Chinese Confucianism, together with the importance of the male role during the long period of inter-clan warfare, reduced women in Japan to a service status, but some of that early matriarchal spirit never went away. It is true that in many ways, Japan is almost as male dominant as Islamic societies.

The double standard of sexual behavior, for example, is as alive and well in Japan as in any Latin country. Men, both married and unmarried, have a good deal of sexual license. They drink at bars after work, where girls are hired to flirt with them, engaging in mildly off-color banter that they would never have with their wives or other "nice girls." That sort of thing doesn't usually involve actual sex, but some amount of sex is available in other kinds of establishments if a man really wants it, with far less social risk than in the U.S. Wives (especially after a few years of marriage) and other women in a man's life are generally expected to look the other way and not get too concerned about these kinds of things, if the behavior doesn't become excessive or cost too much money.

Unmarried women in Japan have come to include sex in their lives to about the same extent as women in other modern countries. However, once married, the social and personal tolerance for anything that even hints at sex outside of marriage for women comes to a screeching halt. Men can often get away with flirtatious relations and even sex with other women under certain circumstances, but any evidence of extramarital relations for married women would be strong grounds for divorce, and worse, devastating to her image as a respectable person.

It isn't so much that men dominate women in Japan, but rather that men and women are more separated into *outside* and *inside* arenas of adult control. At work and in the formal world of governance and business, the tradition is for men to play the role of the adults in authority, but inside the home, men, along with children, become dependents of women, who turn out in most cases to wear the mantel of real adult responsibility.

There is an irony surrounding the role of women in Japan that lies in the fact that men expect women to be extremely feminine and completely non-threatening in public, while at home, women take what might be considered a commanding posture. It isn't that they are necessarily bossy, but rather that all family members expect wife/mother to be in complete charge of running the household.

There is nothing "subservient" in the role of Japanese women in the domestic arena. After marriage, and especially after children, they expect to follow the role of their mother and grandmother and play the part of CEO of family life. Japanese men are so busy with their jobs and careers that there is little resistance to that arrangement.

It is always interesting to us to observe how powerful women are at home and yet how relatively powerless they appear at work. Female office workers take on almost infantile personalities in the work place. Some women artificially raise their voice to a higher pitch when talking to men at work; they understand that men prefer women to project a childlike image, interpreted in Japan as cute and pleasant. In any group where men and women have to interact together in public, most women make a conspicuous point of deferring to men when opinions are stated and decisions made.

Official Japan is almost all male. Forty percent of the workforce is female, but that statement alone is entirely misleading. Most women work at dead-end jobs. Even though the gender differential in colleges and universities has been greatly reduced in recent years, women college graduates rarely end up climbing the corporate ladder. They have done better in professions than in private industry. Women represent about half of elementary school faculties, and even in secondary schools, there are usually between 15 and 20 percent female teachers. There are women lawyers and doctors, and as translators, they dominate. Women also have made some headway in government service, especially in middle and lower level positions.

But in industry and business, they are pretty much locked out of the top. In medium-sized companies, some wives take over as head of enterprises their deceased husbands leave them. But in the executive offices of large corporations, they are rarely to be found.

In every corporation and government ministry, there are always women who are employed, including those who have graduated from highly ranked universities. But they most often serve as what are called OL in Japan. It stands for the English term "office lady," what really turns out to be office servants. They make tea, do filing, run copies, and now serve the important function of running computers for offices, something which surprisingly few male staff seem able to master.

Manufacturing in Japan is run pretty much along gender-specific lines. Work with large machinery, such as automobile assembly lines, are male jobs. But when it comes to the hugely profitable electronics business in Japan, while men are the engineers, the administrators, and handle all the shipping, almost all assembly is done by young women. Women who work in those kinds of jobs are not college graduates, and though their work is very important, they almost always plan to work only a few years, quitting by their mid-to-late twenties at marriage, or if not then, at the advent of their first pregnancy.

A growing feeling in Japan is that the best life of all is as a young, unmarried woman. Many postpone marriage as long as they can, even into their thirties. Some are not getting married at all, a factor which worries some social commentators in Japan. It is typical for a young lady with a full-time job to live with her parents, pay no rent whatsoever, not contribute in any way to household expenses, and to spend all of the money she earns on herself—on clothes, travel, eating out with other female friends of her age, and living a carefree and luxurious life that she knows will end the moment she marries.

As mothers and wives, on the other hand, women are expected to be paragons of strength and good judgment, and in those roles, men more readily defer to women than in the United States and other Western societies. Women bear the burden of running all the really important affairs of the family, almost as if their husbands had stored all responsibilities in their lockers at work. If a Japanese man puts on too much weight, for instance, rather than placing any blame on him, some will end up criticizing his wife for overfeeding him. After all, it is her job to "take care of things" at home, and this includes the personal welfare and appearance of her husband.

Except for the very wealthy, family finances are run almost exclusively by the wife in the Japanese family. When a Japanese family goes out on Sunday to a restaurant, a rather common practice these days, the waiter or waitress normally gives the bill to the wife, expecting her to be the one who pays bills for the family. In the unusual event that a husband accompanies his wife to a supermarket, he normally stands idly by while she pays for the groceries.

Wives are referred to as *okusan* 奥さん "the inside person," a term which has come to have a connotation of "ruler of the house." It is she who takes care of and guides virtually all domestic life. She normally decides what people of the house wear when venturing outside, she manages school work for children, and she, as mentioned above, is completely in charge of the household budget.

In informal discussions among women, occasionally quite realistically reproduced in television dramas, there is an undercurrent of feeling that, along with the other duties of being a wife, women must bear the additional burden of "raising" their husbands. While this idea is prevalent to some extent in the United States as well, in Japan it goes much further and seems to be more pervasive. Young men, after being pampered by their mothers as children, are not expected to be ready to take care of social responsibilities. Young males, considered to be inherently immature in their personal lives, are expected to be compelled toward maturity over time by the triple forces of school, employer, and wife.

During the daytime, men are completely in charge of running the important affairs of Japan. These caretakers of the businesses and services of one of the most dynamic economies of our time, once they leave their jobs, tend to be seen by adult women as grown up boys in need of careful supervision.

Women, of course, are only part of the most basic institution in any society, that of the family. We now turn to a brief exploration of some more specifics of family life in Japan in the following chapter.

Chapter 10
Family Life

S pecies other than humans commonly have a form of family life as well, but only human beings, among all the creatures we know about, live by cultural traits and not primarily by following instinctive patterns. The great advantage of culture as a foundation of behavior is that it is flexible, and family life for people everywhere, while meeting similar needs and providing basic required functions, is to a great extent customized to meet the demands of particular situations in a wide variety of ways.

Because the possibilities of social organization are limited, similar situations, for example similar economic circumstances, result in similar types of family and kinship models. The people of Japan, like those in rich Western societies, live in a mature industrial society, and a description of family life in Japan is similar in many ways to how we might define the contemporary American family.

That similarity is because, to a great extent, the structure and function of family life is dictated by the organization of work. In peasant societies, people work the land with their families, while in industrial societies, people work at jobs away from their families. The major cities of all modern societies look very much alike, and the life routines that people in them follow are also quite similar. Japan is a modern society, and at least at a superficial level, it shares a great deal with people who live in other industrial societies all over the world. This is true regardless of differences in things such as history, language and religion.

From the outside, a typical Japanese family and a typical American family share many things in common. For the members of each to live for a time in a household of the other would not be all that difficult, and in fact, university students from both countries experience just such exchanges all the time. It is also true that over time, family themes in Japan have become more like those of the West, as they share more of the aspects of modern life together.

However, when we explore beneath the surface, we begin to understand that, while the broad patterns may be quite familiar, Japan has its own version of modern family life. No society today, regardless of its level of economic development, is either all modern or all traditional. Even the most advanced industrial societies mix the baggage of cultural history together with pressures to adjust to the present, and in this way blend tradition and modernity.

Japan has conformed to some basic trends of life in the post-industrial world, but we can also notice more traditional aspects than in contemporary Europe or the United States. Japan did not experience industrialization until a little over a hundred years ago, a full century and a half after parts of Europe had begun to be subject to those particular kinds of changes. And unlike the United States, Japan is not a transplanted culture; its cultural roots go deeply into the soil, right where the Japanese live today. It is easier to break away from traditions of the past when the past is not with you in a geographic sense.

THE JAPANESE EXTENDED FAMILY

If we look at the broad sweep of history over the past several thousand years, it is easy to witness the close connection between family systems and the basic economic organization of societies. When some parts of the world developed horticulture, or gardening, as their basic support system, clan structures were formed because of the need for more formalized, large-scale decision-making in those societies.

As modern plow agriculture enveloped large sections of the human population, once again, societies evolved the kind of family system that best met their economic needs, and the extended family was born. As plow agriculture slowly replaced other forms of subsistence agriculture, starting around six thousand years ago, the extended family came to be the most common family system throughout the world. With industrialization, however, things like a money economy, social and geographic mobility, urban life in general, and the growth of government influence over everyday life tend to diminish the vitality of the extended family system.

Two or three hundred years before the industrial revolution, which was the final death knell for the extended family in the West, patrilineal kinship groups had already began to slowly be replaced by the smaller nuclear or conjugal family system. In that system, the one which modern societies gravitate to, there is more emphasis on a married couple and their dependent children, with less emphasis on the connection to vertical blood ties though the male line.

An aspect of Japan in the modern world which makes it a little different from other modern nations is that the extended family system, only a dim historical memory for most Europeans and Americans, is something which many Japanese sixty or seventy years old grew up with. The movement toward a nuclear family system, with all the changes it eventually brings to a society, only started for most Japanese one or two generations ago.

For more than a thousand years, until well into the 20th century, central to Japanese family and kinship ties was the Japanese version of the patrilineal extended family. From the area a little south of modern Tokyo on to the north, this family system was called *ie* 家, pronounced something like the American slang word, "yeah." In southern and western Japan, most frequently, this family system was called *dozoku* 土俗. The *ie* is a patrilineal extended family system in which the oldest son, and perhaps the next son in line, stay as adults at home and run the farm or other enterprise. Later born sons either move off to form branches of the main family or move to urban environments to become laborers or apprentices. Women leave their own family of birth and become official members of their husband's *ie*.

We call this kind of patrilineal family unit "extended" because it is a larger family grouping than the nuclear family, which became the norm in northern and western Europe a couple of hundred years ago. It includes the oldest living members of a single family—at least one grown son, his wife, all young children, and the oldest male children even after marriage.

Extended families, except for a small ruling elite and perhaps a few other privileged aristocrats, were units of production. Most people in societies with that type of family arrangement are peasant farmers, and, although they may not all live in the same household, the extended family is the basic social unit for organizing work, for teaching children, for carrying out religious rituals, and for most of the rhythms of everyday life.

The Japanese *ie* is similar to a description of extended families all over the world, from contemporary Iran, to rural Mexico, to the Italy of two or three generations ago. An overriding characteristic of the extended family system is an exaggerated gap in gender roles. Men and women are treated almost like separate species, with women relegated to almost complete concentration on raising children and the domestic details of running the household. Men are officially supreme in this kind of family arrangement; only men inherit permanent family membership at birth. Women join a family from the outside through marriage and are only accepted as real members by having children, especially male children. As they grow older, the women come to actually run the extended family household, although they must defer to the men of the family in matters outside the home. New brides play a role similar to recruits in the military; they take orders, do most of the work around the house, and are at the beck and call of their husband's mother.

In most versions of the extended family, emotional ties between husband and wife are not usually very strong, being far outweighed by ties between a husband and his own parents. As people get older, their power and prestige in the family tend to increase, and when they retire from active work, they stay in the household, playing a role akin to elderly counselors. Marriages bind one extended family to another and so are a matter for the family heads to consider carefully, with the young principles having, in most cases, little to say in the matter.

Human beings are not robots, and even though all extended family systems contain certain basic similarities, they, of course, show differences from society to society. In some interesting ways, Japan, by coincidence, was more similar to Europe than to the rest of Asia in matters of kinship. For example, as virtually all European societies have traditionally been monogamous, Japan has also been characterized by monogamy. Wealthy and powerful Japanese men have had concubines, and in modern times, mistresses, but never multiple wives with full legal status of married spouses, as was the case in traditional China and many parts of southern Asia.

Japan was not as influenced by Confucianism as were China and Korea, and the intense consciousness of family lines in traditional China—"ancestor worship," as people outside China often call it—did not take root in Japan, except at the very top of the social order. Until a little over a hundred years ago, most Japanese didn't even use a family name. One reason modernization occurred with such ease in Japan, compared with the rest of Asia, was that the traditional family system there did not get so much in the way. Bureaucratic administration practices, necessary for new ways of organizing the economy and government, did not have to fight as hard in Japan against strong family ties as they had to do in other Asian societies. Cousins, for example, have always been regarded with about the same degree of importance to Japanese as for the British or other Europeans—recognized as part of a family entity, but not people one must accommodate in almost every situation ahead of non-relatives, as was the case in most of the rest of traditional Asia.

THE CHANGING JAPANESE FAMILY

The culture of any society has to be taught to each new generation anew. It is always a complicated business because there is so much volume to human culture, and passing it on is made even more complicated in the modern world because cultural items keep changing during the lifetime of a single person. Ideas of how family life is supposed to be structured and how families are supposed to work is, of course, a fundamental part of any cultural system.

When changes in the way people work and the way they spend their non-working time are brought about by changing technology, these changing circumstances bring pressure for change in the images of family life. When they change very rapidly, there is bound to be some amount of ambiguity and confusion. While most Japanese households are as harmonious and mutually supportive of individuals as in other places, if we look carefully, we can see evidence of friction as one family system replaces another, right before our eyes, so to speak.

Today in Japan, the word *ie* is hardly ever used as the word for family. Nowadays Japanese use the word *kazoku* 家族, a term that for most people has come to have a meaning very similar to the word "family" in English. *Kazoku,* for the most part, is seen as a residence unit: Children, parents, perhaps one or two grandparents. The "breadwinner," the person in the unit who provides the most income (it is almost always a man in his middle years), and his or her spouse, tend to be the main decision makers.

Even farm families, considered to be more resistant to change than city dwellers, and with a very high percentage of live-in grandparents, have, for the most part, also adopted the modern *kazoku*: Older members of farm families no longer have the power over the rest of the family that they once enjoyed, young people are about as free to pick their own marriage partners as are Japanese living in cities, and few brides of farmers would put up with being considered servants of their mothers-in-law the way they used to be.

We should remember, however, that the shift from *ie* to *kazoku* (notice both terms employ the same kanji) has in a sociological sense been rather sudden and recent. Cultural change is rarely well coordinated, especially since some are liberated by the change, while others are disadvantaged. One way of looking at it would be to observe that when basic institutions begin to significantly change, some get the message and some don't. Within the Japanese family system, some people, especially old people, still harbor within the definition of *kazoku* elements left over from *ie*. Old people resented for meddling in the lives of their grown children can be a much more severe problem in Japan, precisely because the issue of who is in charge is not completely resolved. When aged men and women live with their children in the U.S. and Europe, unless they are personally wealthy, it is usually quite clear that it is they, the old people, who live in their children's home, and it is the children's decision to share their resources with their parents. Under the rules of the old *ie*, of course, no matter who provided the actual income, the oldest male was the official head of the family. Old people were the major decision makers, and taking care of the older generation was an immutable obligation that their adult children had to bear.

Remnants of the *ie* are easiest to maintain in three generational residence units. While three generations living together under one roof is still the ideal in Japan, fewer and fewer Japanese families are able to actually do so. As we have already seen, with a population almost half that of the United States, the total land mass of Japan is less than that of California, and more than eighty percent of the total area is so mountainous that use for agriculture or dwellings is very limited.

The bulk of the Japanese population today is crowded together in towns and cities in the few coastal plains available. That kind of crowding together of people makes space an extremely limited commodity. While some houses in rural and suburban Japan are quite roomy, the average Japanese family lives in houses and apartments that are very small by the standards of the rest of the developed world. There simply is not enough space for the older generation to live with adult children in small urban residences of six or seven hundred square feet.

In fact, taking care of the oldest generation looms as a huge problem in Japan's future, a problem that the government is trying its best to deal with, as we shall see in more detail in Chapter 15. Japanese live longer than people in any other large society. The nation also has a quite low birth rate, averaging now less than 1.3 children per family. Early in this century, over 35 percent of Japanese will be over the age of sixty-five. Not a very large percentage of elderly Japanese are provided for in nursing homes, at present, but the number of Japanese who are taken care of that way will have to greatly expand.

COURTSHIP

Love and marriage,
Love and marriage,
Go together like a horse and carriage.
You can't have one without the other.

The famous Italian-American crooner Frank Sinatra made a lot of money singing those words from the Rogers and Hammerstein musical, "Oklahoma." The recording, made more than forty years ago, is occasionally still heard today, and the sentiment underling it is as unchallenged in the American psyche as the law of gravity. As complex and full of turmoil as relations between men and women are in the United States, the central idea of marriage is based on an incredibly simple theory: People meet, fall in love, and get married.

Americans tend to perceive this sequence of events as the normal, even inevitable, course of life, but the welding together of marriage with the emotions of romance, especially as the one and only justifiable reason for getting together and staying together as a couple, is for most of the world a rather recent invention. Even in the United States, romantic love as an absolute requirement for marriage has prevailed for the mass of the population for no more than about a hundred and fifty years.

A large number Japanese are attracted to this concept of a romantic prelude to marriage, and many young Japanese go through a meeting and courtship scenario which does not differ very much from those of Europe and America. However, as appealing as the idea of what Americans would interpret as love being something which by all means is a required preliminary to marriage, for the average Japanese, this ideal still does not have much to do with reality. True, there is an undeniable atmosphere of fantasy promoted by the popular media, but most Japanese actually end up getting married because that's what one is suppose to do. Japanese certainly recognize it as a big step, and in some ways, it is a more profound change of life than in the West, but it is usually not really a culmination of a period of very powerful emotions.

Courtship, which sociology defines as the ways people come together for purposes of marriage, also is still in many ways influenced by ideas rooted in *ie*. Many young Japanese would dislike what is written in the next few lines because there is a rather strong sense of denial by many young people in Japan concerning the effect of tradition over matters of courtship. Japanese young people prefer to think that they are as modern as their counterparts in Europe or North America.

But while many Japanese do indeed follow courtship practices which deviate little from those of other industrialized societies, one does not have to look very hard to see the unmistakable weight of the past in what goes on between young unmarried people. It could be pointed out, for example, that while the amount of dating and premarital sex probably does not differ so much from common practices elsewhere, when it comes to the actual act of marriage, a certain seriousness sets in that is not as common in Europe or the United States. By seriousness, we mean simply that the implications of what is happening in a prospective marriage are more soberly considered, and not just by the two young people themselves. The emotions of romance as a factor of courtship play a far greater role than in the past, but they have never in Japan come to be as paramount in paring off for marriage as in, say, the United States.

Even today, almost a third of marriages are the result of what the Japanese call *omiai* あ見合い, a formal meeting between people of marriage age arranged by someone else. Somebody, perhaps a relative of one of them, an older friend or work mate, or sometimes even a professor who knew both of them as students, schedules a meeting between the two people. Formerly, an *omiai* took place in the go-between's residence, but far more common today is one that takes place in a private room in a rather exclusive restaurant. Parents either are in attendance, or if not, and the meeting goes well (meaning the two people agree to begin seeing each other in earnest consideration of marriage), both sets of parents are introduced rather early on.

Japanese distinguish a marriage that begins with an *omiai* from virtually the only other pattern available by labeling the latter *renai kekkon* 恋愛結婚, literally "love marriage." But that label should not mislead anyone into thinking that people who find each other on their own enjoy the autonomy of people typical in Western societies. Families, and in particular, parents, still usually have far more veto power in Japan over a prospective marriage than all but parents of the very rich in the West. When their children seem to be having romantic connections to someone whose family background they are unfamiliar with, parents still often turn to the services of people involved in a thriving industry in Japan—private investigators who specialize in checking out family circumstances.

Parents have more power over whom their children marry in Japan for several reasons beyond the lingering ideas of marriage as a link between families, held over from *ie*. Although the average age at marriage is about three years older than in the United States, people in the United States marry at a wide range of ages. In contrast, almost everyone in Japan marries while still young, before the onset of financial independence.

Weddings in Japan are very standardized; almost everyone has the same kind of ceremony, and they have come to be huge productions requiring staggering amounts of money. Weddings now average a total expense of around $80,000 to $100,000. Without the help of both sets of parents, of course, it would be impossible to carry off such an expensive affair. Also, far more than in the United States, young women, and even a surprisingly high percentage of young men, have never had a personal address outside their parents' home until after marriage. Setting up an apartment for a newly married couple is not nearly as simple in Japan as in most other countries. A large deposit is required, and the apartment will be totally bare; usually, help from parents will be needed to make it livable.

Many young Americans and Europeans in their twenties are already living far from home for most of the year, and the ties that bind them and their parents are therefore weaker than those of Japanese even several years their senior.

Another way in which the shift to the modern *kazoku* has brought about adjustments in Japan, along with some confusion and friction, can be seen in relations between husbands and wives. The role of wife and mother in Japan has a more traditional feel than in most other developed societies. The ideal of women forgoing any kind of career in favor of a life of devotion to husband and family is still strongly supported in the Japanese popular imagination. The legal system is slowly beginning to support some amount of flexibility in the ideal of feminine domesticity, but even today, a woman is removed from the family registry she was born into and transferred to the registry of her husband's family upon marriage, reflecting the old *ie* premise that a wife "belonged" to her husband's lineage. For this reason, until as late as 1982, a foreign woman married to a Japanese man could rather easily obtain Japanese citizenship, while it was next to impossible for a foreign husband of a Japanese woman to become a Japanese citizen.

THE JAPANESE NUCLEAR FAMILY TODAY

Family life would appear to be more stable in Japan than in the United States; divorce, for example is only about one-fourth as likely between Japanese couples as for Americans. It should not be assumed that there is necessarily less conflict within family circles, however. As in previous times in the West, wives are supposed to bear with circumstances between husband and wife that would routinely cause divorce in the United States, including repeated sexual affairs with other women, perpetual drunkenness, and even physical beating. Not all wives do bear with these things, of course, but divorce is less an option for most women because it is difficult for divorced women to support themselves and their children.

DIVORCE RATES PER 1000 POPULATION

United States	4.8%
Russia	3.4%
United Kingdom	2.9%
Germany	2.1%
France	1.9%
Japan	1.3%
Italy	.04%

Source: United Nations Demographic Yearbook, 2004.

Companionship between spouses is not nearly as emphasized in Japan as in many Western societies. Even in a harmonious Japanese family, husbands and wives tend to have separate friends and to a great extent, separate social lives, and so living together without being very intimate seems to be a bit easier for both spouses to tolerate. It is not that there is any more tension necessarily between married people. The average Japanese couple is quite comfortable spending time together, and the present generation of newlyweds seems to be putting more emphasis on life between spouses. But it is true that most Japanese, including probably even most young people, consider that Americans and Europeans spend an excessive amount of time doing so many things together as married partners. This is especially true for men, who would no doubt find it painful to give up the many hours during evenings and weekends cavorting with male friends, if they were to try to live the life of a typical middle class American man.

Married women, as well, have a social life that in many cases omit their husbands. When children leave home and mothers are free from daily motherly duties, women often take trips to hot springs resorts, temples, or historical sites. Sometimes they accompany their husbands, but far more than in the West, these trips are taken with same-sex friends retained from earlier times.

COUPLES REPORTING SEX IS IMPORTANT IN MARRIAGE

United States	75.6%
United Kingdom	73.8%
France	71.9%
Germany	55.5%
Japan	35.3%

Source: World Values Survey. Shapiro, 2004.

Married Americans (while they are still married) tend to face the outside world as a couple. Japanese married people are not thought of in that way nearly as much. A few years ago, when the first author was teaching in Fukuoka, he decided to run a little experiment with his students. A man by the name of Nakasone was prime minister at the time, quite a popular person for a Japanese head of government. A photograph of his wife appeared in a weekly magazine, and the first author cut it out and put it together with seventeen other photographs of other women of about the same age. In showing the photographs to one of the classes, only four (all female) students out of about 35 identified the correct photograph as that of the prime minister's wife, and probably even one or two of those were fortuitous. Can you imagine only ten percent of American university students being able to recognize the First Lady of the U.S.?

Needless to say, most Americans would not approve of the ideals surrounding married life in Japan. Just as with courtship practices, the roles of husbands and wives in the minds of most Japanese are influenced by the past, and the traditional ideal for wives in Japan still exerts considerable influence over actual behavior. According to that ideal, a woman should dedicate her life to husband and children. If she works outside the home, it should be solely to boost family income, and at the birth of her first child, typically within a year or so of marriage, she should give up most outside involvement to become a super-domestic homemaker. The ideal holds that a woman not in any way threaten the primacy of her husband's role as head of family; she should be demure, gentle, patient, and the support pillar for other family members.

A three-generation household at dinner: Grandfather, grandmother, daughter and granddaughter. The father has yet to return from work. The clutter is unavoidable with space so severely limited.

All this makes Japanese women sound like servants, but the traditional ideal is under considerable pressure for change. Women have made important advancements in many professions, and while still well behind their female counterparts in the United States, they are beginning to be represented more and more in the world outside the home.

No doubt, most young women in the United States probably would not see the position of being a wife in Japan as all that attractive. In fact, a growing percentage of young Japanese women would agree with American women. After living the life of a young single women in her parents' home (for as long as she wants), spending most of her money strictly on herself, being able to travel and date as she pleases, it is hardly surprising that all the demands and sacrifices of being a wife constitute a stark contrast.

In 1950, 15 percent of women ages 25–29 were unmarried. In 2005, the percentage stood at 59 percent.* Eventually most of these women will marry, but fewer than in the past. The freedom of singlehood is so alluring that many will postpone marriage to the point that it will be quite difficult to find a suitable spouse or, even more importantly, to bear children.

Even for those women who follow the more familiar practice of homemaker, however, as briefly described in the previous chapter, there is a considerable degree of misunderstanding concerning the role of Japanese wife and mother outside of Japan. It is true that Japanese women are something like second class citizens in the world of work. They are less likely to achieve important positions in the corporate world than in any other industrial nation. At work in large organizations, women wear uniforms and have an image only a little above that of office servants. Even at home, symbols of male privilege are still much in evidence. Most men in Japan, even the youngest generation of workers, perform almost no domestic chores whatsoever, expecting to be virtually waited on by their wives. However, the position women play within the family is in some ways more powerful than that played by their counterparts in the West.

---

* 人口問題研究所 *jinkōmondaikenkyūjo*. (Population Problems Research Center). 2006.

Men are the official head of most families in Japan, but women there are in charge of family matters more firmly than in the U.S. or Europe.

A tradition developed in the 20th century in the modern Japanese family that placed financial matters—planning, most purchases, saving—almost exclusively with wives. Older children jokingly refer to their mother as *Ōkura Daijin* 御倉大臣, "the minister of finance," because they understand that the family budget is completely in her hands, and when they need money it would be pointless to raise the issue with anyone else. It is the woman of the house who is in control of family money matters, and it is she who typically decides how much money is given over for spending by family members. Children normally receive a monthly spending allowance, and so do their fathers, both referred to by the same word, *okozukai* お小遣い.

While a very large purchase, such as an automobile, will be mulled over between a married couple for some time, everyday budgetary matters are her business alone. Many Japanese men we know personally have only the vaguest notions of their savings and investment profiles, being content, as is the normal pattern, to let their wives handle money matters. As mentioned in a previous chapter, when husbands and wives go together to Japan's new burgeoning supermarkets, as they both stand in line at the checkout counter, it is almost always the woman who hands over the payment.

Another example of the dominant role women play in household finances is the way stocks are purchased in Japan. Traditionally, and somewhat uniquely, many stocks and bonds owned by ordinary people are purchases through door-to-door salesman who visit homes on a regular basis. Online stock purchases have somewhat replaced this practice, but a surprisingly large percentage of stocks are still sold that way. In either event, it is the woman of the house who buys and keeps track of the stock portfolio of a typical family, consistent with her role as manager of family finances. Interestingly, following the stock market crash in Japan in the early 1990s, many wives faced the unpleasant duty of informing their husbands that a large part of their family savings had been lost.

So, in conclusion, we should remind anyone who contemplates staying for a time with a typical Japanese family that the differences from what an American is used to at home are subtle and stay mostly in the background. As pointed out earlier in the chapter, *The People*, the economic level of a society has a lot to do with how people live their everyday lives. As long as we keep comparisons on a general level, Japanese and Americans are not all that different in domestic and personal life.

However, as in many other areas of cultural reality, when one gets beneath the surface and comes to know how family life is played out in intimate detail, there are definitely differences in the how people define situations and how they relate in family-related circumstances. Another aspect of Japanese life which is superficially similar, yet quite distinct from American life, is education. It is wound up closely with family values and follows naturally as the subject of the following chapter.

Chapter 11
Education

Historians generally agree that education was important in enabling the United States to improve its industrial capacity, so that by the middle of the 19ᵗʰ century, it had surpassed the leading European nations. A compulsory school system of four to six years had spread across the U. S. landscape by the time of the Civil War. This country had advanced further in producing a literate workforce, with basic skills in computation and experience with the discipline of school routine, than had its European cousins. The U.S. was one of the first nations to fully realize the advantages of mass education. It developed a primary school system, then followed with secondary education, and finally set in place a system of higher education that was available to large segments of the population. There were other reasons for American economic success, but it was not a coincidence that as schooling progressed, rapid and impressive economic development quickly followed.

At about the same time, as you have seen, young Japanese men were scouring Western nations, peeping into every corner of these societies, looking for the best recipe for becoming a modern nation. The U.S. emphasis on basic learning did not go unnoticed. In an interesting turn of events, it was education that was at the core of Japan's impressive economic surge of the 1970s and 80s. Now it is Americans who look at the Japanese system of schooling with interest.

The fact that post World War II Japan burst onto the scene as first an industrial success story, and then far more than that—as a true economic super power—has focused much attention on the nature of Japanese society and institutions. People everywhere are naturally curious as to just how Japan was able to recover from the rubble of war and grow in industrial power so rapidly. As it became widely known that Japan routinely leads the world in many subjects on achievement tests given to school children, a great deal of interest has been drawn to education as one of Japan's great strengths. Certainly, it is true that in terms of factual information and basic technical learning, it is difficult to find a system available to the mass of people on the primary and secondary school level which matches Japan in quality; this is reminiscent of the way the United States led the world in quality basic education a century before.

There are many facets to the educational environment in Japan which are worthy of note, and in spite of the impressive results mentioned above, not all of them are particularly flattering. An almost fanatical devotion to study by a large portion of school-age children was long ago noticed by many foreign observers. One could also point to the way parents, or at least mothers, often get so avidly involved in the academic progress of their children—something universally touted by American experts as the most important single ingredient in continued success for children at school. There is the overriding importance of entrance examinations at various levels of progress through the system, from initial entrance into high school through examinations that qualify high school graduates to enter universities. As we shall see, these examinations produce an enormous amount of stress in the lives of young people in Japan.

EDUCATION STRUCTURE

Americans will find some aspects of education in Japan more familiar than systems in most other parts of the world. A diagram of the school system reveals a structure similar in most ways to the traditional structure common in the United States since the late 1930s. That structure, kindergarten followed by six years of elementary schooling, then three years of junior high school and three years of senior high school, was set in place by the education mission of the U.S. occupation authority, immediately following World War II. When the formal U.S. Occupation ended in 1952, Japan was free to return to its earlier and quite different

		Grad. S.
Semmon	University Four	
Semmon	University Three	
	University Two	
	University One	
Vocational 3	Academic High Three	
Vocational 2	Academic High Two	
Vocational 1	Academic High One	
Junior High Three		
Junior High Two		
Junior High One		
Grade Six		
Grade Five		
Grade Four		
Grade Three		
Grade Two		
Grade One		
2nd Year of Kindergarten		
1st Year of Kindergarten		
Nursery School		

structure, but it chose to keep the American pattern, and in fact, it has followed that pattern almost without exception for over fifty years.

The U.S. has experimented with varying patterns over the past few decades, with some middle schools for seventh and eighth graders and four full years of high school, or other deviations. In Japan, however, the format of 2-6-3-3-4 has reached an almost sacred position of changelessness. Japan has followed that one pattern far more consistently than have school districts across the United States.

One reason for this is the enormous power of the national Ministry of Education and Science, *monbukagaku-sho* 文部科学省 in Japanese. Like many aspects of Japanese life, education is highly centralized and controlled by the central government. States and individual school districts are pretty much free to improvise any kind of school structure and curriculum they want in the U.S., while in Japan, the structure, the curriculum, and just about everything else, is spelled out in detail by the Ministry. This is even the case for private schools. Just to build a new school, permission from the Ministry must be obtained. All accreditation for colleges and universities is done by the Ministry, and the addition of any new courses of study must be reviewed by that agency.

The two heavy lines drawn above the third year of junior high school, and again above the third year of academic high school, represent points in a student's life when he or she must confront very important written examinations. All ninth graders are tested to determine if their academic attainment is high enough to qualify them for entrance into an academic high school. If the score is high enough, then a student may enroll in a high school which begins preparation for university study. Any high school may be chosen, public or private. The two are more equally balanced in Japan, with private schools in a slight majority.

As described in more detail below, all universities in Japan use entrance examinations to select students. Depending on the ranking of the university, these examinations can be unbelievably difficult, requiring literally years of study and preparation. An additional difference from the American pattern you will notice from the chart is that the second year of kindergarten is attended by virtually all Japanese children. So then, the common expression "K through 12" in Japan actually refers to fourteen instead of the American thirteen years of schooling. Vocational schools (called "industrial schools" *kōgyōkōgakkō* 工業高学校 in Japan) are where students who do not achieve high enough scores on the ninth grade exams are routed. More will be explained about these schools later; it perhaps should be mentioned here that the Japanese take vocational education seriously, and these schools are not holding cages for dummies as they sometimes are in the U.S.

The letters "Semmon" in the upper left of the chart is short for *semmon gakkō* 専門学校, post-high school vocational schools. These are places where young people, almost all graduates from the vocational track who feel they need more job training, are given a chance to become more proficient in a job skill. They study things such as cosmetology, lathe operation, construction-related skills, and even computer programming.

In the chart, the cell indicating graduate study is somewhat exaggerated in size. Only about fifteen percent of university graduates go on for some kind of graduate education, quite less than the thirty or so percent in the U.S.

THE INTELLECTUAL TRADITION

As suggested above, the U. S. may have contributed as a model to the importance Japan placed on education as it modernized late in the 1900s. But by no means was that the only reason the Japanese were inclined to consider education as a paramount institution.

Scholarship and book learning was a pillar of the Chinese civilization that Japan so admired in its early period of development. Scholarship in classical China was always closely connected to morality itself. A young man in classical China demonstrated moral superiority through memorizing classical literature, the basic subject material of the all-important Imperial Examinations. The Chinese used a system of academic meritocracy to choose their leadership. Passing the Imperial Examinations was the path to government positions and eventual power. The Japanese never adopted the Imperial Examination system; nevertheless, due to their respect for China, a deeply ingrained respect for learning was lodged in the Japanese psyche.

Most of the warriors in the feudal period were literate; many were accomplished in various types of poetry and diary writing. All through Japanese history, there has been formal schooling. Buddhist monasteries were more than simple religious institutions; they were centers for learning. Even peasant farmers got some schooling at what were called *terakoya* 寺子屋—priest-run schools that taught basic literacy to local children. It was no coincidence that as the Meiji government was being set up, the Ministry of Education was the second ministry established after the Ministry of Finance.

As much as people in any society, the Japanese truly value book learning. True, that trait is not always a pure advantage, as when Japanese students learn large vocabularies in studying foreign languages, but can't seem to master even the most basic speaking ability. There has always been a type of suspicion in the American popular mind of people who have book learning but little practical experience. Terms like "pointy headed intellectual" have been used to describe such people. In high school and junior high, the term "nerd," certainly not used in any flattering way, describes a person with intellectual but insufficient social development.

People like that should move to Japan. In a Japanese junior high school, the most accomplished students in purely academic terms are normally the most admired. Social skills, on the other hand, are not nearly so important. Unlike in the U.S., to be called an intellectual in Japan, even for teenagers, is a measure of peer respect.

SOME U.S. – JAPAN COMPARISONS

One similarity between the two systems is the very high percentage of high school graduates who attend college—just slightly under half of all college age people are students in higher education in both societies—compared with Europe and other Asian societies, which normally have a much lower percentage. A typical percentage of college attendance in other industrial societies is ten to twenty percent.

However, as with family life and many other aspects of life in the two societies, although the education systems may look similar on the surface, when we begin to look more closely beyond structure, at how the two systems actually work, differences arise and quickly become more impressive than similarities.

In Japan, formal required schooling only extends to the end of junior high school by law, and in theory, high school attendance is strictly optional. But, because schooling in Japan has come since the 1950s to be so closely linked to the type of job a person can get, in spite of the fact that it is not compulsory, almost all Japanese of both sexes—ninety-seven percent—complete high school.

As mentioned above, one enters high school in Japan by passing an entrance examination. About twenty percent of high schools are industrial high schools, or what Americans would call vocational schools, emphasizing practical training for jobs. The examinations for entrance to those kinds of high schools are rather easy, but going to a vocational high school does not prepare a young man or woman to pass the examination for a university or college.

One of the important functions of counselors in junior high school is to guide students toward which high school they have the most realistic chance of getting into. We should repeat here that vocational high schools in Japan are not mere warehouses for dumb students, as is regrettably the case in many American school districts. Vocational schools in Japan offer high quality training with up-to-date equipment donated by industry. Most of these schools are for males only, and their graduates are well qualified for work in many industries. They are literate, know basic science, and have mathematics skills characteristic of only a small portion of American high school graduates. Strong ties between these vocational schools and particular corporations provide a strong incentive for the students to work hard in order to land the best jobs.

Certainly, the fact of separate academic and vocational high schools is not the most dramatic difference between education in Japan and the United States. The biggest single difference is the scale of intensity; in other words, in the way that the pressure of schooling impacts young people in Japanese society. It impacts especially that sixty percent of Japanese who enter or aspire to entire the kinds of academic high schools which have the kind of curriculum that will prepare them for the entrance examinations for colleges and universities. For them, an ordeal begins that is so intense, most of you might have a hard time imagining. If the act of studying from books could be converted into electrical power, surely Japan would be the best lit place on earth. Every society has its share of bookworms; students with good study habits are not confined to any one country or to any one part of the world. It is quite likely, on the other hand, that young Japanese who aim to attend a reputable university, probably seventy or eighty percent of the student body of academic high schools, spend more hours of serious academic study on average than high school-age people of any other society.

The reason they study so hard is rooted in the role higher education plays in Japan. In Japan, higher education is used in a very direct way to identify—at a very early age—leadership for the most powerful organizations in the nation. For those who can attend the most reputable institutions of higher education, status and opportunities will be available to them which are not possible for anyone else. That may sound like a strange thing to say. After all, there are limited opportunities for success in most societies without credentials earned in higher education. So what is different about Japan? It's a little difficult to adequately explain in such a short space, but what makes the Japanese system different is that so much is funneled into a narrow selection process with hardly any alternatives or exceptions. Even the sons and daughters of wealthy and successful Japanese will have a difficult time retaining upper middle class status and standards without traveling that one narrow path.

THE EDUCATION PYRAMID

If we take a wide look at the United States by comparison, the difference becomes clearer and clearer. Of course it helps to go to a reputable university for a chance at almost any successful career. But life in the U.S. has lots of little by-paths and second chance opportunities, so that one cannot always predict how successful a particular teenager will be. Success in an American organization is most often determined during one's working career, dependent on how well an individual works with situations and people. Americans often go back to college for advanced degrees, something which can bring great rewards under the right conditions. In Japan, much of all these determinants of success—certainly at the top of the social system—are wrapped up in one afternoon when a person is seventeen years old. It is the afternoon one sits for the examination for entrance into the university.

What actually drives the system of selection for success in Japan is something the Japanese often call *gakureki* 学歴, which translates literally to "education record," but means something much more than that. *Gakureki* refers to a system of selection and reward in the most strategic areas of society, those things we think of as the highest level of individual success, based almost solely on the rank of the university one has attended—not on grades while at college, not on distinctions of any kind earned while there, just the fact that one attended that particular institution. As explained in more detail below, Japanese universities are easy to get through; in fact, graduation is virtually guaranteed in four years whether one studies hard or not. Just getting in, then, is all that really matters; but "getting in," at a top ranked university is unbelievably competitive, requiring thousands of hours of intense preparation.

The set of ideas which support *gakureki* were put in place in the latter part of the nineteenth century, soon after Japan threw off its system of hereditary selection of leaders. Officials of the new regime wanted young men trained in the ways of the Western world, but they were not ready to include ordinary people in a system of preparation for leadership. Early modern higher education in Japan was for the children of the former hereditary elite. At that time, there was no higher secondary school system, and while theoretically anyone could take and pass the entrance examinations, only the elite class could afford the special tutoring required in order to prepare for the exams. Except for a few random geniuses from farm or worker families, early in the twentieth century, university students were more often the product of well-to-do family circumstances.

Gradually, secondary schools spread across the country, and by the 1920s, people from all walks of life were receiving the kinds of preparatory education that made them realistic candidates for passing university entrance examinations. Slowly, Japan began to replace its hereditary elite with an elite based more on academic merit, or at least the kind of merit inherent in memorizing the huge amounts of factual material necessary for passing the examinations into reputable universities. In Japan, the habit was developed early—and that habit has never really been broken—of considering people in leadership roles as being naturally the graduates of a few elite universities, and further, of thinking of those people as inherently superior to every one else.

It needs to be pointed out that Japanese universities, at least the top fifteen or twenty, the ones that really count, are part of a widely agreed-upon ranking. Americans recognize the high ranking of Harvard, Stanford, the University of California, Berkeley, and several others as among the best institutions in the country, but not everyone would list them in the same order. Here, there is only a broad category of top schools, ranked differently by different people for different reasons. In

Japan, the top ten or so institutions are pretty much in the same order in everyone's mind.

If a student can get into one of the top five or six, he (and perhaps even she, if she is willing to run the risk of sacrificing the chance for normal marriage and family life) will be virtually guaranteed of what is considered in Japan to be an elite career; that is, a secure job with a top corporation or public agency. Such jobs offer much more prestige and usually higher pay than jobs available to people who graduate from lesser institutions. If he (and less likely in this case, she) is somehow one of those few hundred walking encyclopedias who each year pass the exam for the one institution at the pinnacle of Japan's education pyramid, the University of Tokyo, the payoff is not merely an elite career, but the real opportunity for leadership status in whatever organization he blesses with his presence.

Graduates from the University of Tokyo, *Tōdai* 東大, as the Japanese like to call it, (abbreviated from *Tōkyō Daigaku* 東京大学) dominate at the top in every important part of Japanese life. For example, there have been twenty-eight prime ministers since the end of World War II; twelve of them have been Todai graduates; in fact, ten came from the same department, the Law Department of Todai. (Law in Japan is an undergraduate major concerned mainly with business law.) In one study we conducted a few years ago, of the top three executive officers of the 75 largest corporations and banks in Japan, fully sixty percent were Todai graduates. By comparison, only a bit more than four percent of CEOs and other top governing board members of the largest 500 corporations in the United States are from top ranked universities such as Harvard, Yale, Princeton, Berkeley or Stanford. It is hardly any wonder, then, that the scramble to enter the top universities is so ferocious: If you pass the entrance exam for Todai, your chance of success is not merely good, it is just about guaranteed.

Scores on the examinations are not merely the most important determinant of who gets in, they are the only determinant. Extra-curricular activities, athletic prowess, the stature and accomplishments of one's parents, even high school grades, all have no bearing at all on who gets into a university. Students take the examinations anonymously, identified to readers of the examinations by assigned number only, and they either pass or fail—that's it. The taking of the entrance examinations each spring by young Japanese who want to enter college, *juken* 受験, as it is called in Japanese, reaches the level of national obsession. It is the subject of all kinds of newspaper and magazine articles, which feature topics such as examination questions from past exams, and it is one of the most frequent topics of conversation, especially among college hopefuls.

As you read this, you are probably thinking to yourself that the idea behind *gakureki* does not make a whole lot of sense. Imagine if, in the United States, there were a tradition of unofficially reserving half of all top government and business positions to, say, graduates of Harvard. Waste of mountains of talent from other sources is only the most obvious weakness in such a system. The Japanese themselves seem to be very much aware of the self-imposed burden represented by *gakureki*. There is always a great deal of criticism of the system in every kind of media, and there is always talk about somehow doing away with it, but there does not seem to be any way for an acceptable alternative to *gakureki* to develop, and the system is still very much alive in contemporary Japan.

One of the greatest contrasts between university life in the U.S. and Japan is the timing of celebration. Universities and colleges in this country have entrance ceremonies, but only students attend, many students are transfers, and the ceremony is not considered very significant. Graduation, on the other hand, is a great occasion for U.S. college students, signifying the end of a long period of struggle and accomplishment. Parents attend when they can; there are tears of joy, cameras and parties. In Japan, it is just the opposite. Graduation, since it has been guaranteed to happen on time, is not a big deal. There is a ceremony, but there are no parents, and perhaps a third of students don't even show up. But the entrance ceremony in Japan is a grand affair, with the president of the institution welcoming students to a new identity they will carry all of their lives. Parents always attend; this is the time of tears of joy, cameras and parties.

EXAMINATION HELL

There is so much pressure put on young people, on men more than women, to get ready for college entrance exams, that the whole process is often referred to as "examination hell," *shiken jigoku* 試験地獄 in Japanese.* It is not hard to understand why. Passing the entrance examinations to a good university is the only route to the most highly honored success, so it was natural that focus on these examinations spilled over from the ordinary school system into a system of private schools which supplement the regular curriculum. These supplemental schools, called *juku* 塾, range in size and formality from not real schools at all, but just a room in someone's home where some private tutoring is carried out, to elaborate plants that are actually bigger than some public schools. Their sole purpose is to prepare students for college entrance examinations.

More than half of all senior high school students in Japan, a good portion of junior high students, and even some elementary school pupils attend *juku* at least at some point in their student careers. Students often attend *juku* two evenings a week, plus Saturday afternoon (Japanese have regular school on Saturday morning, and the Saturday *juku* session follows three and a half hours of ordinary school). A sizable minority attend some kind of *juku* class every single day of the week. *juku* are not inexpensive, and they are not much fun; none that we know of offer any recreation or social functions of any kind. *juku* are pure academic grind.

Some students who take and fail to pass the examination to the university they want to enter will sort of drop out of society, studying virtually all their waking hours for the entire year, until the time for the examination to be taken again the following Spring. There is a label for these kinds of students, they are called *ronin* 浪人. If you remember from the chapter on feudal warfare, that was the word used in feudal Japan to identify samurai without any clan to fight for—kind of homeless warriors. Today, *ronin* are school-less students. Academic *ronin* sometimes

---

* There is nothing equivalent to the Western theological concept of "hell" in Shinto or Buddhism. Jigoku in Japanese refers to what we might term "hellish" circumstances.

A young man is congratulated by his family for passing the entrance exam for Waseda University. His future is not quite as secure as those who get into Todai, but he will graduate on time and likely find a good job.

live in small apartments near the university. They will try again when the time for the exam rolls around again. They usually have little social life, spending virtually every day and even most evenings in the university library, studying.

That kind of pressure on a certain percentage of Japanese pre-college youth takes its toll. Many Japanese study so hard that they fail to develop socials skills and ways of coping with the world outside the home. Each year, literally tens of thousands of elementary and secondary school age children acquire a neurotic symptom the Japanese call *tōkōkyohi* 登校 拒否, literally "refusal to attend school." It is not that they are terrified of the school itself or of the people there; Japanese school teachers at all levels, together with all other school personnel, seem to be among the kindest and most patient people anywhere. That kind of neurosis is the only way some young Japanese imagine they can escape the intense pressure of *gakureki*.

Pressure to succeed in entering a reputable university has moved backward down the age ladder during the past forty years or so, so that the pressure really begins to build up at a very early age for children. Many mothers of young Japanese children only three or four years old have already begun a strategy of special tutoring for their children, so that they will have a better chance to qualify for special preschool. This, they believe, will get the children started on the long road to a highly ranked college.

JAPANESE UNIVERSITIES

A higher percentage of Japanese graduate from colleges and universities than in the United States—about 38 percent for Japan versus about 30 percent for the U.S. However, it would not lead to a fair comparative assessment of higher education in the two societies if we let the above statement stand at that. In Japan, most of that academic intensity comes to a screeching halt the minute a student passes the entrance examination and begins life as a college student.

To put it bluntly, most Japanese students at even the best universities in the land do not learn very much while at college. With a few exceptions, such as programs in engineering at selected universities, Japanese undergraduates (as stated above, very few go on to graduate school) have a rather easy time of it. Curricula are not very demanding; most classes run for a full year, from early April to the next March, but they have only one 90 minute meeting per week, which comes to about thirty-five hours for each class for the entire year. Compare that to the average American university classes, which normally meet around forty hours each in a single term. And while Japanese university students generally enroll in more classes in a given year than a typical American student, they actually need complete only about the same number of classes as American students in order to move to the next year level. No wonder, then, that Japanese students usually enter a university fresh out of high school, almost never transfer to another institution (if they did they would have to start all over as freshmen), stay in lock-step order—freshman, sophomore, junior, and senior in yearly succession—and almost always graduate in exactly four years. You see, then, that there is some relief from the severe demands of student life in the Japanese university system.

The average Japanese of pre-college age is perfectly aware that he or she is not likely to join the *gakureki* elite. As already stated, almost forty percent of graduating seniors actually go to college. Most end up in private institutions, only a few of which have rankings high enough to give them special advantages. Speaking bluntly once more, we should point out that most of the private, non-elite universities in Japan deserve their reputation of mediocrity. Even at the elite schools, most students don't take academic life very seriously, as we have already pointed out. Non-elite higher education in Japan suffers the added burden of very poor ratios of students to faculty, resulting in huge class sizes of often hundreds of students.

If there is any serious learning going on in most Japanese university classes (except for engineering and some other applied subjects), the Japanese are very good at concealing it. Most professors seem to sort of go through the motions of teaching, often delivering what American students would consider numbingly boring material, while student attendance is quite low and interest in class work minimal. Grades (which are always passing grades) are frequently based on written reports, something like take-home exams, which are often so general and undemanding in

Entrance Ceremony for Waseda University. Only about 4,000 students are actually being accepted as freshmen, but all family members and friends are among the 10,000 or so who are there.

nature as to actually insult the intelligence and academic background of the students.

Until the recession of the mid-1990s, these graduates from non-distinct private colleges and universities were able to get white-collar jobs in the corporate world with companies below the level of the elite track. Recently, the Japanese have had to follow the pattern in other industrial nations of reducing the number of salaried employees to economize during difficult times, and it has become more difficult for graduates of non-elite institutions to land good jobs.

Research carried on by university faculty does not play such an important role in the development of technology as it does in other nations. While there are some exceptions where technological breakthrough has occurred in university laboratories, most research and development that ends up helping Japanese industry is done by the corporations themselves.

Education in Japan, then, while it has served Japan well and is in many ways the envy of the world, is not without its problems. Japan has one of the highest literacy rates in the world in spite of a writing system that is certainly among the world's most difficult to master.

In the next chapter, we explore something which, perhaps more than any other social factor, differentiates Japanese from Americans. It is the institution of religion.

Chapter 12
Religion

Although the analogy may seem a bit silly, trying to impart to Westerners the way religion fits into Japanese society is a little like trying to explain to a group of fish what life is like in the environment of land-bound creatures—with Americans being the fish and the Japanese the land-bound creatures. The point behind the analogy is that it may be hard for American students to comprehend a society in which religion is not an important part of the cultural psyche. Western and Middle Eastern societies, the places which have influenced our thinking and understanding of life and reality the most, have, in a psychological and philosophical sense, been swimming in a religious framework for more than a thousand years.

Consider the history of the Western world: In the Middle Ages, tens of thousands of people were put to death for minor deviations in the way they practiced Christianity. In fact, a near fanatic strictness of application of religious hegemony over individuals continued in Spain until well into the nineteenth century.* Of course, much has changed since then, but it has proven difficult to completely shed the deep and ubiquitous role played by religion.

The Japanese never had that kind of experience. They never lived in a culture in which God and religion towered over them, pronouncing what was right and wrong or good and evil, watching and judging their every thought and, indeed, their every impulse.

---

* The Spanish Inquisition, founded in 1481, was not formally abolished until 1834.

We of the West, whether we are personally committed to any particular religion or not, are saturated with religion through our history, our culture, and our language. While the f-word has come to be extremely common, religious reference is still ubiquitous in the use of "strong" language. When Americans are angry ("God damn it!"), surprised ("for heaven's sake!") or ("Oh my God!"), disdainful ("for God's sake!"), mean spirited ("go to hell!"), or hopeful ("God willing"), religious references come easily into use. It would be rare to go through a single day without hearing utterances similar to those. Even in Russia, ruled by a Marxist regime for seventy-odd years under an official policy of atheism, the phrase *bozhe moi!*, "(oh) my God!," never fell out of usage. The Japanese, of course, have their version of strong language. However, interestingly, none of it refers in any way to sex or religion.

Religious references can even be a part of the legal system: In some states, if a natural disaster is deemed, "an act of God," insurance companies may not be legally liable for financial compensation to policy holders. All these references in common speech are just the shadow effect of the overall pervasiveness of religion in the life of Western and Middle Eastern societies.

There is no doubt that Western industrial societies, especially those outside of the United States, have drifted to a considerable extent away from religion as a central part of the mental life of the majority of citizens. But even today, about 90 percent of Americans have some sort of belief in a monotheistic God. It will likely come as a surprise to Americans to hear that in Japan, the percentage holding those kinds of beliefs would be close to zero. There is religion in Japan all right, but it impacts the population there very differently from the way it impacts Americans and people in many other societies.

THE ROLE OF RELIGION IN JAPANESE LIFE

To people whose ideas concerning religion are influenced by the religions most accessible to Europeans and Americans—Christianity, Judaism, and Islam—there is a tendency to see religion as the matrix of morality and good behavior. The term "righteous" for example, can mean simply very religious, or it can also mean upright and moral in a non-religious sense. Historically, the two concepts have been closely linked in the Western mind. The connection between religion and ethics is not universal, however. As pointed out in the earlier chapter relating to general cultural themes, in Japan there is little, if any, link between religion and morality, ethics or standards of right behavior. It must be especially puzzling to hear of this in light of the amazingly low rate of crime in modern Japan. If you think that a society must use religion to keep people in line, well, Japan proves that you are wrong. Japanese society is very orderly, but social order in Japan stems mostly from obligations to people as described in chapter 9, not from religion.

Even a brief description of religion in Japan would not be complete without mentioning something of the extremely modest role religion actually plays in the mental life of the average Japanese person. There are two overriding characteristics of religion in Japan that seem to be polar opposites, but which nonetheless are both true: On the one hand, Japanese are as loyal to the rituals of their traditional religions as any people in the world. A large portion of the population would never think of failing to show respect for their religion by failing to visit a temple or shrine during one of the three days of the New Year's celebration on January 1ˢᵗ, 2ⁿᵈ or 3ʳᵈ of each year. Yet those same people usually label themselves as *mushinronsha* 無信論者, literally, "non-believer." These people don't actually believe that their religion has any ultimate meaning, but they enthusiastically engage in it anyway. I know that may seem strange to you, but it is true nonetheless.

The kind of emotional engagement and deep commitment one often sees among religious people in other societies is, to a great degree, absent in the religious life of Japan. There is very little that is analogous to devoting one's life to God, or to Jesus or to Allah, in the Japanese experience. Even the clergy in Japan relate to their work more like technicians than as guides to some deep spiritual truth. Priests in Japan provide a service that is needed for various events; they learn how to apply the rituals and operate the ceremonies. In their personal lives, they are, and are expected to be, people with attitudes and life styles and personal habits not really very distinguished from anyone else's. Japanese don't invite members of the clergy into their homes for dinner the way Americans often do. But if they ever did, it is likely that they would be treated like any other guest, without a sense that language and manners should be carefully controlled in the presence of a person with a special holy calling.

In the many ways we can measure religious activity or commitment, *religiosity* as sociologists call it—church attendance, belief in a God, belief in an afterlife, respect for religious commandments, and other aspects of religious life—Japanese people are among the least religious people in the world. In a comparison with a sample of other societies, we see that Japanese take religion far less seriously than do people in other places.

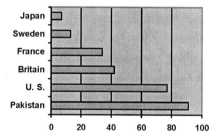

Percentage of population answering "yes" to the question "Is religion important in your daily life?"†

It is far from a perfect analogy, but one way to describe the way most Japanese relate to religion would be to compare it with the celebration of Halloween in the West. Halloween has survived through many centuries and shows little sign of dying out. Generation after generation of Americans and Europeans get involved in Halloween in various and changing ways; it's something people participate in because of tradition and because it can be fun. It is part of our cultural heritage, something many people look forward to and for which a considerable amount of

† Shapiro, Andrew L. World Values Survey. Vintage. 2005.

money and effort is spent. But it certainly is not something anyone would think of as a major focus of life, or even something to take very seriously at all. When living in a place such as India or China where Halloween is not celebrated, most Americans probably don't miss it very much. Although religion is certainly more pervasive and important in Japan than Halloween is in the West, the degree of psychological commitment is somewhat similar.

Religious rituals dot the calendar and can be witnessed throughout the year in every part of the land. However, the average Japanese participates in religious ceremonies and rituals in a way that to Americans would appear rather casual, without any sense that they are of any deep importance. Just like Americans who don't miss Halloween very much when caught during that season in other places, Japanese don't appear to have any feeling of loss concerning the religious elements of their society when traveling or living outside of Japan. There are Buddhist temples in several American cities where Japanese nationals and their families live while on foreign working assignments. Most of the Japanese-appearing people who attend services in places like that are Japanese-Americans, who as Americans, tend to take religion more seriously.

MAJOR RELIGIOUS INSTITUTIONS

The two major religions in Japan are normally identified as the native religion of *Shinto* 神道, and a version of the religion of Buddhism, *bukkyō* 仏教 in Japanese, originally imported from China. At least, these are the two overt religions in the society, the ones with conspicuous physical and behavioral elements, the ones with formal priesthoods, buildings, and property—all the trappings of religions recognized around the world. But before we explore these two fundamental institutions of Japan, we should reveal something about a less obvious religious influence in the country. This religion has no priesthood, no temples or other edifices (well, hardly any), and is usually not even appreciated as an integral part of Japanese culture by the people who live there. It is what we call Confucianism, what in Japanese is known as *jukyō* 儒教, "teachings of the scholars."

Confucianism came to Japan as Japan first began importing elements of Chinese civilization in the third and fourth centuries A.D. Within two or three hundred years, by the sixth century, it was overshadowed as a formal religion by Chinese Buddhism, a religion more spectacular in presentation, and attractive because it was accepted as carrying with it elements of magical power. Confucianism never went away, however; it continued to work its influence in the Japanese mind and the way they behave.

Confucianism is sometimes defined as a philosophy instead of an actual religion. One reason for this is that there is no god in Confucianism; in fact, there is no supernaturalism of any kind.[‡] As developed by the Chinese, it is more of an outline for a harmonious society and for harmonious and effective living for individuals and families. It emphasizes strict ethical rules and a social order based on obligations and two-way loyalty, both up and down social hierarchies. There is not actual worship in Confucianism, but rather ideas of correct thinking and correct behavior. Social ritual and proper observance of etiquette are important components of the system.

One part of Confucianism puts emphasis on correct behavior and that seems to have resulted in what the Japanese refer to as *kinben* 勤勉, or *kinbensei* 勤勉生; it is usually rendered in English as "diligence," but it is a concept with considerably more profound overall cultural affect than what is usually imparted by that English term. If you ever work with Japanese, you will come to understand the true affect of *kinbensei*. We don't think there is much reason to believe that Japanese people enjoy their leisure time any less than Americans or people of any other society. But when they turn their attention to any task, there is a tendency toward intenseness of focus that seems to be a kind of national trait. Conversation, humor, and distraction are blocked out. As with all characterizations, it is not true in every case, but while at work, Japanese can easily acquire a seriousness, an attention to detail, and an immunity to boredom, that is

---

[‡] The same thing could be said of Buddhism, although in popular usage, some magic is associated with that religion.

more pronounced than for any people we have ever witnessed. Having said this, however, one should be cautious in attributing these qualities completely to Confucianism. It is likely that some of these characteristics are a blend of native cultural themes, helped along by a compatible and encouraging philosophy.

Even though Buddhism became a far more formal part of Japanese life early on, Buddhism itself was in some ways influenced by an undercurrent of Confucianist thought. One can see this in the theme of secularism throughout Japanese recorded history. Unlike Renaissance Europe, where science and religion were natural enemies and science had to fight to get its principles accepted, in Japan, as modern science arrived in the nineteenth century, there was never religious resistance to any of the revelations of secular knowledge.

Confucianism received a great boost, elevating it virtually to the level of one of Japan's formal religions, during the Edo Period. Leaders of the Tokugawa regime were attracted to a type of updated Confucianism that had been popular among the elite in Sung 宋 Dynasty China (960–1278 AD). That philosophy stressed discipline, respect for authority, duty, loyalty and other qualities the Tokugawa wished to establish as an outline for the society they ruled. Samurai routinely studied Confucian philosophy, and a Confucian academy in Edo was the first formal institution of higher learning in the country. When Meiji leaders needed a base on which to build a new Western-style center of higher education, it was not so difficult to simply transfer the Confucian Academy into what came to be Tokyo University. It was originally set up at the beginning of the Meiji period to train government officials in Confucian-style dedication to the new nation.

Eventually, the modernizers of Meiji came to disdain all the old pre-modern features of Edo Japan. For the leaders of the new state, Confucianism represented the past, part of the old Japan, which they were determined to replace. These men were much more interested in Shinto, something purely Japanese, which they wanted to get the population to rally around as a symbol of national unity. All formal references to Confucianism were dropped; only the very Confucian Imperial Rescript on Education, read each morning at all primary and secondary schools for many years before World War II, remained as a part of the old Confucian system.

From that time, around the 1880s, Confucianism has mostly worked under the surface, not as part of the formal religious environment. For a description of the formal environment, we turn to the two formally institutionalized religions.

CO-RELIGIONS

A casual visitor to Japan would likely conclude that it is a deeply religious place. Signs of religious practice and belief are everywhere, from large and well maintained religious structures in the biggest cities, to neighborhood shrines and temples. Even in the deepest countryside, one frequently comes across tiny alters and religious statues. In some cases, these are relatively far from any dwelling or settlement.

One of the first things a visitor to Japan is likely to notice is the architecture of Buddhist temples and Shinto shrines. They stand out so much because, in addition to being virtually everywhere Japanese people live, they usually are the only traditional buildings—the kind of physical evidence people who grow up in Western societies associate with Asia— still found in contemporary Japan. Costumes and rituals connected with the people who preside at these places, while in some respects similar to scenes in other parts of Asia, are quite distinct from anything usually found in the West.

One aspect of religion in Japan that could easily confuse foreigners is the relationship between the two religions. A recent travel brochure described Japan as having two major religions, Buddhism and Shinto. While true, that statement in the brochure could be extremely misleading because it fails to point out a characteristic which sets Japan off from most of the rest of the world. Normally, if a society has more than one religious orientation, people are associated with one or the other.

If someone, for example, pointed out that the two major religions of India are Hinduism and Islam, it would be accurate to imagine that the two religions have historically divided people into separate communities and that the two groups have been rivals and even bitter enemies on occasion. But this is not the case in Japan: Buddhism and Shinto are not rival religions; people do not belong to one or the other. Individuals in Japan, actually over ninety-five percent of the adult population, have, for well over a thousand years, embraced the two completely separate religions at the same time, using one for some purposes and the other for other purposes.

Buddhism and Shinto both constitute what sociologists usually categorize as a church. The term signifies a religious tradition widely accepted as legitimate, with a considerable history and stable organizational and theological features. In Japan, these two religions have divided up religious chores. Shinto handles things like weddings, christening, and blessings for success in various enterprises, while a main duty for Buddhism is taking care of the dead through funerals and memorials at certain intervals after death. Buddhism also has its own system of blessings and good luck rituals, but even when the work of the two overlap, there has been a remarkable lack of any sense of competition between the two throughout Japanese history.

Public places where rituals take place—Buddhist temples, *o-tera* お寺 in Japanese, and Shinto *jinja* 神社, normally rendered into English as "shrines,"—are found in every neighborhood, attended at various times of the year by the same people. Today, temples and shrines are mostly supported by money donations given each year from local residents, and most receive enough funds for adequate maintenance and staffing. In many parts of rural Japan, the two religions share the same grounds, with both a temple and a shrine standing side by side.

SHINTO

The Shinto religion is by far the older of the two. It is native to Japan and has only token representation in any other nation. Shinto grew out of a particular type of ancient nature worship and animism in which local spirits, usually identified with animals, together with physical objects in the landscape, were imbued with relative degrees of a type of supernatural power which the Japanese call *kami* 神. An alternate

reading of the Chinese character for *kami* is *shin*, and the label *Shinto* 神
道, means simply the way of *kami,* or as some would translate, "the use
of *kami.*" In its original form, Shinto is quite like the type of animism
practiced by many primitive tribes in various parts of the world. Things
in the natural landscape are given the quality of holiness, or in other
words, much of Shinto is a kind of nature worship. In addition to parts of
nature, there are various spirits or small-case gods which can help people
or, sometimes, cause trouble.

A rural setting where jinja and o-tera sit side-by-side.

Shinto has always been closely associated with the agricultural cycle,
and even today, the Emperor, who plays the role of the high priest of
Shinto, transplants a few strands of rice sprouts in a Shinto ceremony
each spring, symbolizing the beginning of the rice-planting season. When
Buddhism arrived, as that religion was more theological and not directed
much at natural features, Japanese people gradually incorporated new

Chinese rituals and practices into their lives, while not giving up the nature worship they had so long lived with.

There was a time, as suggested above, when Shinto was elevated to the official national religion, with government support and the imposition of a large organizational structure of ranked shrines throughout the nation. This began in the 1880s and 1890s, and it continued in various degrees from that time right up to the end of World War II. The new leaders of Japan were desperate to form a strong national identification among all the Japanese people as the country ended its feudal period and opened its doors to the outside world.

The men who came to power at that time were convinced that the nation needed to be tied tightly together with national institutions, such as the Emperor, and a national religion, in order to build a strong sense of identity with the state. Buddhism, of course, with its obvious foreign origin, was difficult to make serve in this regard, so Shinto was the religion chosen for this role.

The Shinto religion was sort of reinvented at that time into a complex network with official government sponsorship. Some new theology was hastily put together for Shinto, most of which was designed to instill pride of nation. Some of this new Shinto-based nationalism was openly racist and glorified Japan's acts of aggression and imperialism in Asia. Primarily for that reason, during the U.S. occupation of Japan following defeat in the war, national Shinto was completely dismantled and Shinto went back to being what it was before the late nineteenth century—basically a community religious institution divided into very loose networks, without sponsorship or financial help from the national government.

BUDDHISM

The Buddhist religion came to Japan from China during the period of intense borrowing of all things Chinese. For a few hundred years, Buddhism remained mainly a system of magic and blessing for the elite classes; in fact, for a while, it never got much outside the capital; it expanded first to Nara and later to Kyoto, when Kyoto became the capital in 794. Buddhism is a world religion, and there are certain overriding aspects of the faith which tie Japan together in a very loose way with other Buddhist countries in East and Southeast Asia. Religion, however, has to fit any society it is taken into, and as the Japanese are particularly good at domesticating foreign cultural imports, it was not long before a distinctly Japanese version of Buddhism began to develop.

Around the eighth century, while still mainly a religion for aristocrats, two main Japanese branches of the religion were formed. One was called Tendai 天台 and the other, Shingon 真言; the latter is still an important part of Japanese Buddhism today.

Slowly, Buddhist teachings seeped down into the lives of common people; by the tenth century, Buddhist temples could be found in all parts of Japan, even in the larger peasant villages. In the twelfth and thirteenth centuries, three new popular Buddhist movements swept Japan: Pure Land Buddhism (*Jōdo Shū*浄土宗 in Japanese), *Nichiren Shū* 日蓮宗 and *Zen* 禅. Formation of other branches of the religion and splintering off of older organizations has produced something like the case with Protestantism in the U.S.—many separate groups with subtle differences in theory and practice, but with no one group ever reaching a position of dominance over all the others. All the while, Shinto continued to be an important part of both official ceremony surrounding the Emperor and the everyday affairs of ordinary people.

FUNCTIONS OF BUDDHISM

As already suggested above, an important duty of Buddhism, and frankly, the source of most of its income, has centered on taking care of the dead. Funerals are the most prominent part of the Buddhist system of rituals, but taking care of the dead in Japan goes beyond simply performing funerals. After people die, a series of memorial services are held at various intervals, which must be performed by official ordained priests. For most branches of Buddhism in Japan, these services begin forty-nine days following the funeral and continue at three years, seven years, and up to ten years after the death, providing there are still family and friends around to arrange and pay for them.

In previous times, Japanese buried their dead, but for many decades, all Japanese (except for the Emperor and his immediate family) by law must be cremated. A few days following death, the bereaved family and friends meet at the family temple to share a simple meal and reminisce over the life of the person whose funeral will be held the following day. In some cases, the unembalmed body is viewed during this ceremony through a small window in the wooden box holding the body. It is still customary to provide a place at the table for the departed, signified with a bowl of rice with chopsticks stuck in from the top.

The next day, with usually a somewhat larger group on hand, priests will begin the actual funeral ritual, which consists mainly of sutra chanting that continues on for about an hour; the sutras are approximations of Sanskrit texts, and no one in the audience has any understanding of their meaning. During the chanting, all participants in the funereal approach an alter and toss into a large bowl a small amount of incense. Following all the chanting and incense transfer, the entire party repairs to the crematorium to wait around while the body goes through the actual cremation process. An hour or so later, when what is left of the cremated bones cool off, family and friends pick small pieces of charred bones, with two people using separate pairs of chopsticks grabbing a single piece together and placing it in a special urn. The urn containing the remains is then either deposited in the family stone cemetery monument or placed in an honored space within the home of one of the survivors. (Two ritual ingredients of funeral rites, sticking a set of chopsticks into the center of a bowl of rice and holding a single item at the same time with two sets of chopsticks, have become so associated with funerals that all children in Japan are taught never to engage in either of these two acts at the dinner table.)

With the exception of funerals and memorials after death, there has never been anything like mass, a sermon, or a church service in Japan, in either of their religions. People relate to both religions mainly in a private way, by pausing at the alters of temples and shrines and engaging in very personal rituals of respect. There are, on the other hand, literally hundreds of festivals centering on both temples and shrines, with virtually every neighborhood in the land having its own festival of whatever size at an allotted time during the year. A few of these festivals, such as the Nebuta Festival in the city of Aomori, in extreme northern Japan, and the Hakata Dontaku in Fukuoka, in northern Kyushu, have become popular tourist attractions, for which millions of dollars are spent in preparation.

A little over one percent of Japanese are professed Christians. Christians in Japan have had more influence than their small numbers would suggest; two of the nation's post-war prime ministers have been Christians. At one time in the 16th century, the Christian population reached as high as perhaps five percent. However, in spite of intense work by thousands of dedicated foreign missionaries, the percentage of Christians has not increased appreciably over the past hundred years.

SECTS AND CULTS IN JAPAN TODAY

A sect is defined as a type of religious group that stands out somewhat from the rest; its religious practices have broken away from those of established churches and run counter in some way to the traditions of a given society. It is as a sect, of course, that most major world religions began, including Christianity, original Indian Buddhism, and the various branches of Japanese Buddhism identified above. Contemporary Japan, just as most modern nations, has been the birthplace of many new religious movements over the past several centuries, though most have either died out or remained relatively small on the national religious map. During the past few decades a few sects, while not very strong in numbers, have displayed an impressive facility for raising money, per-suading devotees to turn over their property to the organization and, in the process, accumulating hundreds of millions of dollars in assets.

One sect in particular grew in the post war period to achieve the status of a major religious organization, with ties to an important political party. This sect is called *Sōka Gakkai* 創価学会, "value creating association" in Japanese, while abroad, it is often known as Nichiren Shoshu, reflect-ing its self-styled association to Nichiren, a well-known theologian of the thirteenth century. Sōka Gakkai encourages much more emotional involvement in religion than ordinary Buddhism or Shinto, and in the

1950s, it was a dramatically expanding organization which formed its own political party, the Kōmeitō, 公明党 or "clean government party." The growth curve of Sōka Gakkai eventually slowed and even stopped, but although ties between the religious body and the political party have been officially banned as unconstitutional, it remains a powerful organization, with just under ten percent of the religious affiliation of the nation.

A cult, as you probably know, is a sect-like group that harbors beliefs and follows practices that are even less widely accepted by the society at large. Because of the controversial character of their beliefs and practices, cult members tend to be isolated from the rest of society, and in some cases, the isolation involves complete physical separation. Isolated as they are, cult members are vulnerable to extremist ideas and often come to have complete faith in a charismatic leader, no matter how strange his or her ideas might seem to an outsider. We cannot leave this discussion of religion in Japan without mentioning something about one of the most spectacular cults to emerge anywhere in the 20th century.

THE AUM SHINRIKYŌ

Japan is a relatively orderly and dependable place. It has, for example, the lowest crime rate of any of the larger industrial nations; in recent history, people there have gone about their daily business without any need to fear an encounter with anyone or anything that could harm them in any way. The country has its share of calamities, but these are almost always brought on by nature—things like typhoons, earthquakes, and rainy seasons without enough rain for the farmers. Citizens of Japan have long had a tendency to feel that as long as they stayed home, that is to say, stayed in Japan, they would be able to trust the people and institutions around them to keep them safe and protected.

That rather remarkable sense of security in the routines of ordinary life was suddenly shattered, at least temporarily, on March 20, 1995, when small bottles of the deadly gas *sarin* were released simultaneously in cars on three of Tokyo's busiest subway lines during rush hour. Only eleven people were killed, but over five thousand were injured enough to require medical treatment. A month and a half later, on May 5, two canisters of highly poisonous cyanide gas attached to a timing device were discovered and disarmed by security forces in a toilet area of Shinjuku station—a gateway to the western suburbs of Tokyo and one of the busiest train stations in the world. Police investigators estimated that there was enough cyanide in the canisters to kill at least 10,000 people.

Stunned and initially baffled, authorities slowly began to trace the two incidents to a religious cult called *Aum Shinrikyō* アウム真理教. (*Shinrikyō* translates to something like, "true knowledge," or "true way." Aum is a sound used in Hindu and Tibetan Buddhist chanting and usually spelled "oum" in English.)

The Aum Shinrikyō cult had membership of less than five thousand people in Japan, only a few hundred of whom were full-time, live-in devotees, and a few hundred more in, of all places, Russia. It was founded by an enigmatic figure, legally blind, who called himself Shoko Asahara—a brilliant student while in university and a person with a highly charismatic personality. Like more than a dozen such groups that have sprung up in Japan over the past fifty years, Aum Shinrikyō was highly secretive and demanded complete devotion from followers. What set Aum Shinrikyō apart from the others was its ability to attract highly educated people with technical skills—in some cases, graduates from the most prestigious universities in the country.

A few followers of the cult eventually cooperated with police, and the stories they told were utterly fantastic, sounding more like scenarios from a James Bond movie than like anything in real life. Some former members told of bizarre schemes to bomb Tokyo with lethal gas, killing most of its population, and then hold the rest of the country hostage, in order to actually take control of the nation. Not all of the allegations were ever proven, but it was made clear that the cult had a large poison gas factory at the foot of Mt. Fuji and that delivery systems of those gases were in the process of being manufactured there. It also came to light that more than twenty people were murdered by the cult, including a lawyer trying to help parents retrieve children from the cult and seven rural residents, who were killed the previous June, when the cult engaged in practice sessions of releasing poison gas.

The arrest and trial of Shoko Asahara and the other leaders of the cult mesmerized the nation, receiving higher television ratings than even the death and funeral of the Showa Emperor in 1989. Never has a man been hated by so many Japanese. Court proceedings in Japan often continue over longer periods than almost anywhere else in the world. Finally, ten years after he was arrested, Asahara was sentenced to death; he was finally executed in 2005.

People in Japan are certainly not alone in their occasional vulnerability to cults, which promise emotional fulfillment and the achievement of some lofty purpose. Cults have been part of the life of all modern societies, in recent decades as well as throughout history. And we must remind ourselves that as dangerous as Aum Shinrikyō appeared to be, a few thousand individuals is a very tiny representation of the Japanese population. It is true, on the other hand, that standard religious practices in Japan offer very little of any sense of purpose or meaning; people sometimes turn to commitment to some sort of extremist cause, whether in politics or in a new quasi religious movement, as the only available outlet for devotion. It is, therefore, not actually so very surprising that, while all are small in numbers of members, there are over a thousand religious sects and cults in contemporary Japan.

MAGIC AND DIVINATION IN CONTEMPORARY JAPAN

A foreigner from a Western society cannot live in Japan for very long without realizing that there is more obvious popular magic and divination than he or she is used to at home. All societies incorporate magical practices, both within and outside of established religion, in order to attempt to influence the outcome of events beyond human control. The yearning to understand and control events is a major reason why religious practices develop in human societies. Praying, for example, from a strictly technical standpoint, is a type of applied magic when used to attempt to cause something to happen or not to happen.

Attitudes toward divination and fortune-telling in Japan differ significantly from those in most Western countries. In the U.S., for example, it was something of a minor scandal when it was revealed that while living in the White House from 1981 until 1989, Nancy Reagan routinely consulted an astrologer, with the implication that some of what the astrologer told her could have affected decisions made by her husband, the president. It would be difficult to imagine something like that causing so much negative attention in Japan. Regular sessions with fortunetellers are so common for people of all walks of life in Japan that it would be unusual to find that someone making an important decision had not consulted a fortuneteller, including the executives of Japan's biggest corporations.

In the West, the Church in the Middle Ages incorporated some aspects of popular magic, but it banned all other forms of magic and divination as the work of the devil. Even today, the amount of non-religious magic and divination practiced by average people in Western societies is limited to just a few forms, with astrology being the most popular. The Japanese never experienced a similar purge of popular magic and divination, so, as one might imagine, there are more forms of them around for everyone to see, and they play a more prominent role in the lives of people there.

Currently, the Japanese use the same Gregorian calendar as that used in all modern societies. On many of the calendars hanging in homes and offices all over Japan is a categorization of each day of every month as very propitious (a good day for marriages and other important events), somewhat propitious (ok for some important events), or unpropitious (a bad day to plan events). Wedding halls are very expensive to rent on propitious days, and while the same halls could be rented at a fraction of that cost on unpropitious days, there are few takers.

Hardly a single building is ever erected in Japan, from office buildings to private residences to warehouses, without first consulting a system of geomancy—divination which establishes the most favorable place for entrances, toilets, kitchens, and other features of the structure. This kind of divination, known to many Americans by its Chinese name, *fang shuei,* is called *hō gaku* 方学 in Japanese (the same characters are used in both languages). This, along with many other aids in reaching decisions, is not officially part of Buddhism or Shinto. It is part of a multi-billion dollar industry that relies on private practitioners who study and practice as sort of divination counselors.

The percentage of Japanese who consult with fortunetellers is significantly higher than for people in other industrial societies. It would be difficult to come up with an exact figure—Japanese have come to be a bit sensitive about reporting their involvement with various forms of divination—but a good indication can be had by comparing the advertisements for fortune telling services in the yellow pages of telephone directories for major cities. There are several entries advertising fortunetelling services in the yellow page directory for Los Angeles, taking up about a quarter of a page. For Tokyo, the yellow pages section of the telephone directory currently (2009) lists 440 fortunetelling establishments; a few of them have

This crowd is visiting Tokyo's Meiji Shrine on one of the three days of the New Year's celebration. Two or three million people will visit this shrine on those three days, and another six or seven million will visit other shrines and temples in the city. It is so crowded that it takes over an hour to simply work one's way up to the shrine's alter to throw in a few coins. Most of the people in the crowd, if asked, would likely declare that they have little or no religious belief, yet as uncomfortable as it is to be there, there they are.

very large ads—a half-page long—and the entire section of fortunetelling ads runs on for nine pages! Even all the people who pay for the ads in the telephone directory represent only a segment of the fortuneteller population. Several times that many are part-time fortunetellers and do not advertise publicly for fear of attracting the attention of Japan's national income tax authorities.

So then, in conclusion, while religion fulfills certain social needs in human societies, and these needs in a very general way are similar throughout the world, the ways religion fulfills its functions differ in important ways. Westerners are used to a single all powerful God; to the notions that religions are exclusive and that a person can be associated with only one at a time; and to the ideas of religious ethics and commandments.

In the three previous chapters, we briefly examined the three basic institutions: Family, education and religion. Next, we will take a look at how official power functions in Japan, followed by the closely related subject of the economy.

Chapter 13
Politics and Government

Western Europe, North America, Australia and New Zealand share a lot with Japan. All are mature technocratic industrial societies, and all have well established and stable systems of representative democracy. Japan has had a functioning system of representative democracy since the early 1920s, with only a relatively short interim of military control of government for about five years, until defeat in World War II. After experiencing a hundred pages of this book, it should not be surprising for you to read here that there are differences between Japan and the U.S. and other Western societies in the way democracy plays out.

Of course, just as in the U.S. and elsewhere, popular representative government in Japan is to an extent compromised by wealth and power. In some cases, the will of the populace is circumvented by those with special influence over government. There is no society in which this is not the case, but again, these things take on a Japanese twist.

Japan operates under what is called the "parliamentary" system of government. Canada, Britain, and most democratic systems follow that pattern. France and the United States are among the few industrial societies which have a separate executive branch of government, independent of the legislature. The parliamentary system was adopted by the Japanese as it modernized in the Meiji Period, and the Occupation did not force them to alter it.

Japan has an elected parliament, the *kokugikai* 国儀会 (called the "Diet" in English), with two separate houses, an upper house, the not-so-important House of Councillors, *sangi-in* 参議院, and the all-important lower house, or House of Representatives, *shūgi-in* 衆義院, which is much like the British Parliament. Although Japan is smaller than the U.S. by population, Japan has more legislators: 480 in the lower house and 242 in the upper house, for a total of 722, versus 535 for the total of both houses of congress in the U.S. As in Britain, the lower house in Japan is by far the most powerful. Originally, the lower house was set up as a body of representatives from the "common people," and the upper house, as in Britain, was reserved for the titled aristocracy. This was the case up until the end of World War II. Today, the upper house operates mainly as a debating society; it can exert some influence when controversial issues arise, but it is the lower house that actually passes the laws and presides over the national budget.

The Prime Minister and all the members of his or her cabinet sit in parliament, and just as in Britain or other parliamentary systems, they are often forced into debate on the floor of the legislature when important questions arise. When there is disagreement, the debate can be quite feisty. Parliamentary debate is one time when the polite and good mannered Japanese sometimes turn overtly critical or even nasty. Parliamentary debate in Japan is broadcast on national television, and if you listen closely when the PM or cabinet members answer questions from the floor, you can sometimes here remarks from the opposition such as *usotsuki* 嘘つき "liar! "*dorobō* 泥坊 "thief!" *baka* 馬鹿 "idiot!" which are picked up by the microphones and come over clearly on the audio.

Several writers about politics and economics in Japan have referred to an "iron triangle" of power. The three elements of the triangle are the elected government, the governmental ministries, and the world of big business. These three are somewhat more coordinated there than in the U.S. We will describe the first member of the triangle a little here and discuss the role of the ministries a little later. We will have much more to say about the third member, big business, in the following chapter.

As we will see below, elected officials have less direct overall power in Japan due to the enormous influence of Japan's ministry bureaucracy. But elections certainly do have meaning, and the Japanese people do vote politicians out of office from time to time. In some ways, Japanese people have more functional democracy than in the United States: For example, a much greater percentage of the population actually bothers to vote (usually 70 to 80 percent versus the 50 percent or less in the United States). The sights and sounds of politics are impossible to avoid during election season. Posters are everywhere, and very loud sound trucks moving through the streets of towns and cities all day around election times, blasting out political slogans and the names of politicians seeking votes, give one the feeling that elections are quite important in Japan. However, even more so than in the United States, most important decisions in Japan only involve popular will to a limited degree.

With Japan's defeat and occupation after World War II, the old Meiji Constitution was thrown out. General MacArthur ordered a small staff of surprised and inexperienced Americans to write the new constitution for the Japanese in English (he ordered them to complete the task within one week), which was then translated and forced upon Japanese politicians. This is the constitution Japan has to this day; it is full of awkward phrases in Japanese, due to its origin in a foreign language.

Like the standard parliamentary system of government found all over Europe, the prime minister is elected by the members of the lower house of parliament. If one political party does not have a majority of the members of that house, it must form a coalition with smaller parties to get enough members to "form a government," which is to say, elect a prime minister who can then select the cabinet ministers to head the major agencies of government.

POLITICS IN JAPAN

In the 1950s, two political parties, the *Jiyū Tō* 自由党 "Liberal Party," and *Minsei Tō* 民政党 "Democratic Party" merged to form the *Jimin Tō* 自民党 "Liberal Democratic Party," usually abbreviated to LDP in English. That party, the LDP, has dominated the political life of Japan for almost all of the time since. It is somewhat similar to the Republican Party in the U.S. in that it has tended to be pronouncedly pro-business, although, due to the Japanese tendency toward consensus and conciliation, the LDP has backed many quite liberal policies, such as socialized medicine.

There have been 24 prime ministers since 1955; for 54 years until 2010, all but three were head of the LDP.

It appeared a few years ago that the LDP was breaking up. Some new parties were formed as members defected. But by the early years of the 21st century, it made a measure of return to dominance, and it appeared that in terms of political power, such as it is in Japan, the country had returned to what it had been for a very long time, an LDP one-party system.

It may be too early to tell as this is written, but all that may have changed late in 2009. Recession had infected the Japanese economy, as it did the economies of all industrial nations. While Japan had suffered financial downturns before, this time it was accompanied by a host of nagging problems: Soaring school costs, record unemployment, deflation, and an aging and shrinking population. All this left families fearful of what the future held. For a long time, the people seemed to think that the LDP had done a good enough job of providing peace and prosperity, but sentiment rather suddenly turned against it, and Japan was ripe for political change. A brand new political party was formed by deserters from the LDP, together with people who had not been in politics previously. It was named the *Nihon Minshu To* "Democratic Party of Japan" (日本民主党), with former LDP member Hatoyama Yukio (鳩山由紀夫) as its leader. In stunning fashion, the election of August 30, 2009, swept the LDP from its powerful majority, with the JDP capturing 308 of the 480 seats in the crucial lower house, while the LDP kept a mere 119. It was the worst defeat for a governing party in Japanese history.

If we are to believe the Japanese media, this was, "not an election, it was a revolution." There were all kinds of editorials the day after the election proclaiming that two party democracy had finally come to Japan. JDP leaders were full of announcements of a new day for Japan, with a completely new political style and a radically new agenda.

There are some interesting parallels between the cycle of events involving Hatoyama Yukio and those of Barack Obama: Both rode a deepening loss of faith in government to easy victories. Both hoisted the banner of change as their main rallying cry. Both seemed to offer a significant challenge to existing policies and institutions. Both have led administrations that have been established for more than a year and a half, and both have found it much harder to exert change than most people imagined. As in the United States, rhetoric about change in Japan has been a lot easier than bringing it to fruition.

MINISTRY BUREAUCRATS

The Japanese have a phrase, *kanryō seiji* 官僚政治, "government by bureaucrat." By that, they recognize the huge role played by the ministries in Japanese life. Ministry members are not elected, and there is no limit to how long they may serve. While both those conditions apply to the U.S., what is different is the fact that many, if not most, important laws have actually been written by those bureaucrats, who pass them on to the Diet for formal vote.

Compared with presidents of the U.S., prime ministers in Japan play a much more modest role. Although Japan has been a "one party" system for most of the time since World War II, the Liberal Democratic Party is not a unified organization like one-party systems in other nations. It is divided into factions, *habatsu* 派閥 in Japanese. These factions function almost like miniature parties, and there is a great deal of struggle between them to get their leaders appointed as prime minister. This has worked to limit the term of office of prime ministers and thus limit any chance to institute a coherent program of administration. Since the end of the war, there have been twelve U.S. presidents; during that same period, the office of prime minister has been filled twenty-nine separate times, and only one individual ever served in that office more than five years.

A numerical fact furthers the message here: When a new president of the United States takes office, he and his administration can appoint over 2,000 top government bureaucratic officials, all answerable to the president. When a new Japanese prime minister takes office, he can appoint only about 20 such people: The others are already in place in the form of career ministry bureaucrats who cannot be hired or fired by the prime minister.

Even more important, in another big contrast to the United States, Japanese politicians lack sufficient staff to gather information and write legislation, and in most cases, they have far less knowledge and experience about important issues than the ministry elite. As mentioned above, most legislation that passes the Diet every year is written by, and promoted by, these unelected ministry officials. Further, the way these laws are written gives ministry bureaucrats extensive leeway in interpreting laws through "administrative guidance." And in any case, the ministry officials issue administration ordinances, guidelines of how laws are to be interpreted, which outnumber the actual laws passed in the Diet by 9 to 1.

The point was humorously made in a political cartoon we saw a few years ago. Two policemen are seen standing across the street from the Diet building in front of another building, which most Japanese would recognize as the Diet member's office quarters. Scurrying in the background are what appear to be civil disaster workers carrying stretchers with bodies on them. One policeman says, "What a tragedy that the gas leak caused all the Diet members to be found dead at their desks." The other policeman adds, "Yes, but great luck that the gas leak was confined to that one building so that the normal running of government is not affected."

The cartoonist exaggerated quite a bit, but it is easy to see what point he was trying to make about the Japanese system, at least up to the immediate present. The government ministries have throughout Japan's modern life played a considerably more important role in the way Japan is run than have elected parliament members. Much of what is done by government in Japan has been done by these unelected officials, who have few restraints over them from the elected side of government. These people are career civil servants who started their jobs soon after college graduation and worked their way into top ministry positions by their 50s, and sometimes earlier.

Government by bureaucrat seemed to work pretty well as Japan modernized and then rebuilt its economy after the war. The bureaucrats did not have to stand for re-election and could therefore be completely objective in dealing with issues. It should also be added that in spite of their modest pay by the standards of business, there have been very few scandals and cases of corruption among Japan's leading ministries.

However, whether it is a good thing or a bad thing, there are definite signs that *kanryō seiji* may be about to come to a screeching halt. Mr. Hatoyama, the new Prime Minister, has declared war on the whole system. A completely new set of policies aimed at greatly curbing the power of the ministries has recently been put into place. If the Prime Minister gets his way, politicians will have more influence over legislation and the application of laws than is now the case. Mr. Hatoyama is attempting to wrestle the all-important national budget from the Ministry of Finance and to require policies of ministries to pass political scrutiny.

Up to now, in the main ministries, such as METI (Ministry of Economy, Trade and Industry), Ministry of Finance, and Ministry of Foreign Affairs, etc., the top minister is not the most powerful person in the organization. Rather, it is the administrative vice minister of each agency who is most powerful. The minister has been a political appointee, much like cabinet secretaries in the United States, but more like a figurehead, with much less actual influence. Politically appointed ministry heads stay with the agency only for an average of about two years. Being an appointed minister is a type of political exposure for a later run at the Prime Minister role. The administrative vice minister, on the other hand, is a career bureaucrat, is very well educated and experienced, and has been with the agency for his (seldom, but occasionally, her) whole career since graduating from Tokyo University or another prestigious institution. The administrative vice ministers in Japan, up to now, have been very powerful individuals, independent, as we have said, from elected politics, and complete specialists in their areas of concern.

Under reforms initiated by Mr. Hatoyama, the balance of decision making in the ministries would revert far more to the actual appointed ministers, with less power remaining with the vice ministers. Some of the reforms have already been put into place, but several others are still in the debating stage. In 2009, it appeared that the most extreme aspects of *kanryō seiji* were about to come to a screeching halt. Mr. Hatoyama, the new Prime Minister, declared war on the whole system. A completely new set of policies aimed at greatly curbing the power of the ministries began to be put into place. The Prime Minister wanted to create a system in which politicians would have more influence over legislation and the application of laws than has been the case. Mr. Hatoyama attempted to wrestle the all-important national budget from the Ministry of Finance and to require policies of ministries to pass political scrutiny.

The fate of these reforms was dealt a great blow when, suddenly, in May of 2010, Hatoyama Yukio suddenly resigned as prime minister, largely as a result of his disappointment and failure to deal effectively with the question of U.S. air bases on the island of Okinawa. Some of his toning down of the power of the ministries may survive his passing, but it is too early to tell.

JAPANESE POLITICIANS

However, even prior to the reforms championed by former Prime Minister Hatoyama, the Diet and those politicians in top positions in the Diet were certainly not powerless. Among other things, laws must be passed—even if mostly written by ministry officials—and tax revenues must be allocated. But the post-War Japanese political elite can be best described as playing a supportive role for the corporate and ministry elite, and as we have already said, the political elite are only a weak third member of the "iron triangle" of elites in Japan today.

From the late 1980s, however, the political elite have become even weaker, due to several major corruption scandals within the political ranks and a growing sense of mistrust by the public. Before 1993, and going back to 1955, the political elites from one political party—the Liberal Democratic Party (LDP)—dominated Japanese politics, winning every national election in that almost-40-year period. As we saw above, that seems to have come to an end.

ELITE UNITY

Since World War II, cooperation, coordination and unity have become even more common among the top levels of power in Japan. There are several powerful means of unity which bring the Japanese elite together far more than elites of the United States or Europe today. Among these means are the exchange of personnel across elite groups, old school ties, intermarriage, and to a much lesser extent, social clubs.

The extensive practice of *amakudari* 天下り is an important means of elite interlock and unity. It means, literally, "descent from heaven." *Amakudari* refers to the common early retirement of powerful ministry officials, who then move "down" to top corporate positions. Each year, for the past three decades or so, up to 200 individuals who were members of the bureaucratic elite left their government positions for new corporate positions in companies that were regulated by the very ministry from which these individuals "retired."

Amakudari Officials in the Top 100 Corporations

From Ministry of Finance	151
From METI	118
From Ministry of Development	74
From Ministry of Transportation	65
From Bureau of the Environment	40
From Postal Service	34
From Bureau of Defense	33

Source: Kerbo and McKinstry. *Who Rules Japan?* Praeger, 1995.

Another key means of elite unity, old school ties, is centered on the nature of the Japanese educational system. A small number of universities in Japan are considered most prestigious and are most important to enter for gaining elite status later—with Tokyo University, or Todai for short, by far the most important. It is very difficult to pass the examination to get into Tokyo University, which also means that the elite members thus selected are certainly among the brightest in Japan and, therefore, given more legitimacy once they are in elite positions. But it also means that friendship ties formed while at Tokyo University will be carried on throughout their lives, creating extensive elite unity. Some of the graduates will go to Sony, some to Toyota, some to Sumitomo Bank, and still others to places such as the Ministry of Finance, METI, and the Foreign Ministry. But where ever they go, these old school ties will keep them unified and working together.

With respect to the bureaucratic elite, a 2006 study showed that 59 percent of all recent graduates entering the "fast track" to top ministry positions were Todai graduates. Virtually all of the heads of the most powerful ministries (administrative vice ministers) were Todai graduates, although that is beginning to change somewhat now. In the most influential government ministry of all, the Finance Ministry, Todai graduates still dominate.

Among the corporate elite, we find the same pattern. In the study cited above, we found that of the 154 "top industrial elite," 45 percent were Todai graduates. In the powerful big business organization, Keidanren, 6 of the 8 chairmen since 1946 have been Todai graduates. Looking at the top three executive offices in each of the top ten banks in Japan, 19 of the 30 are Todai graduates, with the same pattern found in all types of industries in Japan. For the political elite, we find much the same pattern, especially for top LDP members and prime ministers.

It is not simply having attended Todai, and especially the Law Department at Todai, that is important: Because of the Japanese system of age ranking, people of the same age reach the very top of all types of elite positions at about the same time in Japan. This means that people in top positions in corporations, the ministry, and politics at any one point in time were most likely classmates or even roommates when they were college students. But there are still other means of unity.

Finally, one rather unique means of unity can be described with the following example: Six of the post-War prime ministers, about a dozen corporate elites, several ministry elite, and even the late Showa Emperor's brother and sister have something in common besides being among the inner circle of elites—they were all directly related through marriage. There is a common practice of intermarriage among the Japanese elite, which creates powerful family alliances called *keibatsu* 経閥. Some Japanese social scientists presenting data on such family alliances claim that about 40 *keibatsu*, or extended families, dominate the Japanese corporate economy and government.

The means of creating these *keibatsu* family links are also interesting. There are private groups and individuals, along with relatives, who specialize in match-making among elite families. And much more than in the rest of the Japanese population, the elite families use the old tradition of arranged marriages to form such family alliances or marry their off-spring to influential people. One practice today is for such match makers to identify and introduce to elite families the "up and coming" young men in the powerful ministries.

There are even brochures identifying such young men, meant for the eyes of interested elite families. An arranged marriage with one of these men can have very useful benefits when the man moves to the top of the ministry in later years, or when he retires early to join the company of his in-laws, using the ministry ties of his earlier years. If one of these wealthy families needs an heir to take over family leadership and has no sons, they can always create what is called a *yoshi* 養子, a traditional system of formal adoption of a son-in-law. The young man assumes the family name of his bride and is, in every legal sense, heir to family enterprises.

Like all nations in that magical circle of what the United Nations categorizes as "developed," a kind of euphemism for wealthy, Japan has a democratic form of government. But each country has its own unique history and its own special cultural features. As we have seen, democracy in Japan does not follow very closely a pattern familiar to residents of the United States. But except for the short five-year period of military domination, Japan in the modern era has had a system of government which has served the nation rather well, and which by and large meets the needs of the population.

As with all modern political and governmental systems in the major nations of the world, the Japanese system stumbles along, functioning more or less adequately, but with many blemishes. Democracy is seldom pretty in the way it plays out in any society. Certainly, the ideals of "government of the people" are compromised in Japan, as they are in the U.S. and elsewhere. The Japanese had a taste of non-democratic government from 1940 to 1945. In our many years of dealing with the Japanese, we have known only a very few who indicate any desire to return to that.

SPECIAL INTERESTS AND MONEY POLITICS

Perhaps even more than most other democratic societies today, it takes money to get elected and reelected in Japan—lots of money. With the possible exception of Italy, it can be said that money has corrupted democracy in Japan more than in any other major industrial nation. Between 1955 and 2003, one study found that some 90 percent of LDP campaign funds have come from large corporations.

A result of all this is that election to the Diet can bring money—again, lots of it. While Japanese parliamentary members are legally paid only about $160,000 per year, they can end up being very rich. A revealing survey of the wealth of Diet members, required for the first time by a law that went into effect in 2003, provides a rough estimate of their assets. Diet members, including those from both the upper and lower houses, averaged something like $1,200,000 per member. For LDP members alone, the average was $2.1 million per member, with LDP politicians accounting for three quarters of all assets of Diet members.

Still, politicians do not get into the Diet without enough votes from the people. As a result, when it comes time for national elections, most voters in Japan have been conditioned to think of what politicians can do for their local benefit. Herein comes the root of what Americans call "pork-barrel" politics—politicians are evaluated by voters by how many bridges, roads, libraries, civic centers, etc., etc., have been forthcoming, not on ideology, and not on pressing national or world issues. And we should add here that politicians in Japan are not much affected by their involvement in scandals: Some have been reelected again and again, even after their implication in outrageous financial corruption, because, in spite of what outsiders might think of them, they could deliver the goods to local voters.

LOCAL GOVERNMENT

The central Japanese government located in Tokyo is much more powerful in the everyday lives of people than the one located in Washington D.C. is for Americans. But, even with governmental power quite centralized and with most important decision-making reserved for the national governmental bodies, local government does play some role in management of problems on the local level. Things such as roads, bridges, and school buildings are built and managed by local governments. There are 47 prefectures in Japan, something like smaller versions of U.S. States, which are headed by the equivalent of an American state governor. In addition to the prefectures, there are four special districts similar to Washington D. C. in the U.S.* There are also 200 city governments in Japan, with a city council and a mayor as in the United States.

There are, however, some big differences when these local governments are compared to those in the United States. As already noted, they have much less power and independence. Most of what these local politicians can and cannot do is determined by the national government in Tokyo. Local governments can hire teachers, but what is taught is regulated by the national Ministry of Education. Also, the courts and police are run by the national government. The most important limitation on local government influence, however, comes from the control of finances. The vast majority of taxes collected in Japan are collected by the central government, and the money needed to run public schools and build bridges in local areas, along with almost everything else, is then given back, according to need, to the local governments and local agencies. If the central government does not like what is being done in local areas, the money is cut off.

In the next Chapter, we begin a brief exploration of the Japanese economy, which, even more than in the U.S., is inextricably welded to national politics. In the 1950s and 60s, Japan pulled off what many people called the "economic miracle" of not only re-establishing itself

---

* The four special districts include the entire island of Hokkaidō (the dō (道) in Hokkaidō), the two metropolitan districts of Osaka and Kyoto, administered as *fu* 府, and Tokyo, as *to* 都, "capital."

as a major industrial society, but of eventually exceeding the per capita industrial output of the nation that defeated it in WWII. That was quite a feat, and although nowadays people naturally think of China as the economic miracle of Asia, Japan's climb to economic prominence, not once but twice within a century, is worth knowing about.

Chapter 14
The Japanese Economy

Today, when most people think of the economy of Asia, they naturally turn their attention to China. And rightly so. The speed of Chinese economic development over the past two decades has been spectacular, far greater than almost anyone had predicted. China now produces more cars and trucks than either the U.S. or Japan. It seems like almost anything you buy these days is "made in China." But Japan is and will be a powerful economic force in the world. If we look critically at domestic economies of entire societies, the way people actually live their lives, we cannot avoid the fact that China, while powerful in economics and military, has huge problems in providing for all its citizens. In this regard, it is helpful to put a few things in perspective.

Due to its enormous export industry, China has amassed a giant amount of capital, coming from all parts of the world. That country's investments in the economy of the U.S. helps keep our economy afloat. As a major player in the world economy, that, coupled with its military capacity, has propelled China to the forefront of international prominence.

Recent Chinese accomplishments have impressed us, as they have impressed everyone else, and in no way do we wish to diminish them. Looking at the two economies, however, that of China and that of Japan, only Japan is a mature industrial economy, while China, for all its recent growth, is still a developing nation, even by Chinese definition. This is so because of the inability of prosperity to reach a large percentage of the population. There are now probably more Chinese millionaires than there are in Japan; but keep in mind that there are over *eleven times* more people in China. As dynamic as China's economic growth is, an overriding problem for China is *distribution* of wealth. Over ninety percent of Japanese are categorized as middle class by world standards, with a comparatively high standard of living. In the eastern part of China, especially along the coast, a large middle class has grown as large as that of the United States. Shanghai has more buildings of fifty stories or higher than there are in all of Japan.

However, there is another part of China: 300 million Chinese live in the western regions of the country, a place where private vehicle ownership is rare, medical services are skimpy and often only semi-professional, and where the average income is just barely enough for a family to get by. There is more industry in the west now, but such things as access to higher education, foreign travel, and high quality consumer goods are still in the future for most residents of that part of China. While the per capita annual *gross domestic product* (GDP) for China as a whole has doubled over the past fifteen years to just under $12,000, the comparable figure in Japan is around $38,000.

So while we should recognize that China will continue to fulfill its destiny as a great economic force in the world, the notion that Japan has or will somehow fade into obscurity is not at all a realistic assumption. For many decades, Japan will remain one of the wealthiest and most productive nations, a place with one of the highest standards of living.

THE BUSINESS WORLD BEFORE WW II, THE ZAIBATSU

Although Japan developed its industrial economy much more recently than the other industrial nations, it was the first Asian country to become an industrial society. In 1868, when a rebellious army of samurai and peasant soldiers from southern Japan marched into what is now Tokyo, the revolution, or what the Japanese call *meiji ishin* 明治維新 "The Meiji Restoration," had finally come. As we have seen, the primary concern of the new Meiji Government was the threat of either European or American colonization and subsequent economic exploitation. To prevent this type of colonization, the new political elites wanted to arm themselves with the fruits of Western industrialization, and they wanted it fast. As they correctly ascertained, only a powerful economy, and a strong military of their own, would bring them security and eventual equal treatment from the Western powers.

As Chapter Seven explained, the Japanese first sent many of their best and brightest to Europe and America during the late 1800s to study the institutions of the West; these scholars later reported back as to what could best work for Japan. They especially liked and copied many aspects of Bismarck's Germany. They set about to create a capitalist industrial economy, skipping many stages of the more gradual development that had occurred in the West.

In the beginning, the new government started its own industries, especially when it was judged that these industries were most important for rapid industrialization. However, the government officials running these businesses, almost all ex-samurai, turned out to be rather poor businessmen. After running up losses by operating inefficient companies, the government decided to sell these government-run industries to private individuals and groups. Few Japanese, of course, had the money or access to government loans for such purchases. But some of the old merchant families had enough money, as did many former daimyō and samurai who were given government compensation after losing their old positions after 1868.

This transfer of major industrial control from government to private owners created a class of wealthy families called the *zaibatsu* 財閥, which soon came to almost completely dominate the Japanese economy in the pre-World War II era. These powerful families created many types of corporations in different industries. The biggest of these old *zaibatsu* include many corporate names well known today, such as Mitsui 光井, Mitsubishi 三菱, Yasuda 安田 (later changed to Fuji 富士), and Sumitomo 住友.

In some cases, the government granted them exclusive rights to certain economic activity, as with Mitsui's first role as banker to the new government. A result of all this was a great concentration of wealth and economic power with just a few family-run cartels, the *zaibatsu*. Before World War II, just the top 10 *zaibatsu* families in Japan controlled about

75 percent of all corporate assets. Today, Japanese workers have many advantages, but before the war, exploitation of workers was extreme.

Comparing economic circumstances throughout the industrialized world today, we find that Japan is less stratified than most, with the overwhelming majority considering themselves to be "middle class." Ironically, before WWII, Japan was one of the most highly stratified. While the income gap between corporate elites and workers has grown recently, it is still only about 17 to 1 compared to before the War, when it was well over 300 to 1. Zaibatsu families lived lives like royalty, with mansions in many parts of Japan and chalets in Switzerland. There was small middle class, but most Japanese people lived lives of relative poverty. Parents sometimes sold their daughters into prostitution in order to survive economically. In the countryside, taxes took about 35 percent of the crop, and rents paid to landowners usually took another 50 percent. There were many peasant revolts and violent urban strikes during the 50 years that preceded World War II, all violently suppressed. At that time, Japan was certainly not the country of harmony, relative equality, and cooperation that is often depicted today.

Defeat in the war pretty much ended *zaibatsu* dominance, at least the way it existed to that time. Before the end of World War II, the Mitsui family was the richest in Japan; indeed, it was one of the world's most wealthy. Then, soon after the end of World War II, on October 8, 1945, two trucks under U.S. Army escort pulled up at the Mitsui headquarters in Tokyo. The drivers got out, and with the help of some Mitsui employees, they loaded onto the trucks some forty-two wooden cases containing $281 million in Mitsui securities: Soon, the securities were gone, and with them the Mitsui *zaibatsu*.

THE STRUCTURE OF JAPANESE BUSINESS—KEIRETSU

But Japanese are not Americans. The idea of individual financial and industrial enterprises operating in a completely independent environment just does not make sense to the Japanese. Slowly, groups of corporations began to form teams of industrial cooperation. Although some of them carried the same names as the former *zaibatsu*, the post-war groupings are structured and operate very differently than the pre-war *zaibatsu*. There no longer is a single family at the center. The old *zaibatsu* each had affiliation with a particular political party. In a way, the new groupings are more flexible and stronger because they relate to the entire governmental structure rather than to just a single party. These new groupings are called *keiretsu* 経列. It is the *keiretsu* groupings that form the essence of the Japanese economic might today, and they create several of the key features of the Japanese economy. As we have said before, Japan is a nation of groups, and corporations are no exception.

Six *keiretsu* dominate the Japanese economy: They are Mitsubishi, Mitsui, Sumitomo, Fuji, Daiichi Kangyo, and Sanwa. These *keiretsu*, groups of corporations, are not as tightly held together as were the *zaibatsu*. While the *keiretsu* stand at the top of Japan's economic pyramid, Japan's economy since the war is far more spread out, and the *keiretsu* do not control nearly as much of the total economy as did the pre-war *zaibatsu*. At the end of World War II, 70 percent of corporate stock in Japan was family owned. Today, most stock is owned by other corporations—that is, the corporations own each other. It has been said that today Japan is a capitalist society with few true capitalists.

Depending upon whose definition is followed, these big 6 together contain from 187 to 193 main corporations, accounting for about 15 percent of all corporate assets, including 40 percent of all banking assets, 53 percent of all insurance assets, and 53 percent of the real estate business.

But in some ways, the *keiretsu* continue the tradition of group cooperation. For example, they help each other, trade with each other, exchange personnel, and work together as lobby organizations for mutual interests. If one company is in trouble, for example, others in the *keiretsu* will help it through the rough times. The CEO of each company within a *keiretsu* is the member of the "presidents club" of that *keiretsu*. The club operates to restrain the behavior of other executives in the group. If wage demands of one executive within the *keiretsu* become excessive, or if performance lags, the others in the *keiretsu* will act to discipline that person for the good and survival of the whole group—a practice which normally does not happen in other industrial systems.

Japan's economy has been called a "dual economy" because there are two quite different degrees of work environments, corresponding to two degrees of size and power of enterprises. These separate worlds of the Japanese economic picture should be kept in mind when we hear stories of workers with "lifetime employment" and extensive worker benefits, such as company housing, in Japanese corporations. These things do exist in Japan, but they are primarily for the 30 percent of Japanese workers in the core sector of the dual economy, sectors I and II below, the big corporations of the largest *keiretsu*.

Below is a kind of schema of the way Japanese companies are arranged: Vertically, from most powerful at the top to smallest and least financially secure at the bottom.

I
Large, highly capitalized *keiretsu* companies with 4,000 to 50,000 employees. This level represents about 30% of the Japanese work force. Many worker benefits.
II
Sub-Elite companies. 300 to 4,000 employees. Includes large retail companies and other large enterprises, but smaller than for category I. About 20% of the Japanese work force. Some worker benefits.
III
Small businesses with 20 to 300 employees. Thousands of small companies in manufacturing, service and retail businesses. About 30% of the workforce. No worker benefits.
IV
Family run enterprises with very small work forces of 2 to 20 employees. Far more of these than in other industrial societies. About 20% of Japanese workers work in these tiny establishments, with little worker security, in often unsafe environments.

Category I consists of all of the giant corporations you are familiar with: Sony, Honda, Canon, Hitachi, Bridgestone, Nintendo, etc. These are most powerful companies in the largest *keiretsu*. They make hefty profits even during economic downturns. They are completely international, selling products on every continent. It also includes enterprises you probably don't know much about; the giant utility companies, construction giants, and huge shipping companies.

Category II businesses would also include some companies that sell products in the U.S. Seiko, Brother, and Minolta are in this category; they are big, well capitalized companies in slightly smaller *keiretsu*. These companies offer some of the worker benefits you may have heard about, but they have not proven as secure as places of employment as the ones in category I.

Category III firms are part of the lower half of the dual economy. These organizations are undercapitalized and have a rather shaky record of survival. They often lay employees off and offer virtually none of the famous worker benefits. These companies are likely to be providers of products and services to category I and II companies and are outrageously exploited by them. The pay is modest and the security dubious.

Category IV are the "mom and pop" little retail establishments. These are the small confection and toy stores that dot every Japanese community. Occasionally they involve some assembly activity, but whatever they do, they operate on a shoestring budget, often with extended family as the only employees.

This is the reason for the label of "dual economy." The worlds of categories I and II, above the heavy line, are completely different from the bottom categories. The top two categories have financial weight, security, government cooperation, and enviable conditions for workers. The bottom two categories have none of these things; they exist in a completely separate economic environment.

It is easy to see why many Japanese study so hard. Poor Americans have a difficult time at graduation time. Who should they go to work for? Big blue chip companies sometime offer good jobs, but they are not necessarily the best choice. Small firms often offer better advancement opportunities and more flexible work environments. For Japanese, there is not much of a dilemma in this regard. Typically, one simply takes a job with an employer the same rank as one's university. Universities are ranked in Japan by category. There are about fifteen universities ranked in the highest category; another twenty or thirty in the next highest category, and so on. This may be loosely the case in the U.S. as well, but it does not impinge on the type of job one gets to the extent it does in Japan. There, top government and private enterprises hire exclusively from the top ranked universities. Category II enterprises hire from slightly lower ranked schools.

Category I jobs are universally judged in Japan to be the most desirable. They give the most prestige, pay the most, and offer all of the wonderful worker benefits people keeping hearing about. To work as a white collar worker for one of the companies of a major *keiretsu*, especially the parent company, is to reach the pinnacle of the world of what the Japanese call *sarariman*, the white collar office/management employee.

KEIDANREN

Some years ago the phrase "Japan Inc." was used in a negative way to indicate the unfair way Japanese business was tied tightly to its government, in a unified attempt to compete with and overcome businesses in Europe and America. While this idea underestimates the amount of competition within Japan itself, there is some truth to it. The former MITI, now called METI, (Ministry of Economy, Trade and Industry) *keizaisangyōshō* 経済産業省, has, and still does to an extent, guide Japanese industry toward the best international competitive posture, providing major corporations with a great deal of industrial intelligence.

But rather than some form of paternal dictator to the Japanese economy, the ministries in Japan are simply players of a team. The captain of that team is an organization called *Keidanren* 経団連. There is nothing exactly like the *Keidanren* in any other industrial nation. It translates to something like "The Federation of Economic Organizations," but that doesn't really describe its function. *Keidanren* works to coordinate all aspects of Japan's financial, productive, trade and even to an extent, governmental processes. The chairman of *Keidanren* is generally considered the most powerful man in Japan. He is usually chosen from one of the most profitable corporations in the country. *Keidanren* does not work toward, or even attempt to eliminate, industrial competition. What it does is to monitor all aspects of the economy so that competition, which the Japanese recognize as necessary, does not go so far that it damages the overall health of the economy.

There are about 1,000 member of *Keidanren* who meet regularly in a large building in downtown Tokyo. Membership is supposed to be secret, but anyone familiar with the country can easily figure out who most of the members are. Some members are non-voting ex-officio such as the Prime Minister and the heads of all major ministries. Voting members include heads of all six major *keiretsu,* together with CEOs of most important companies within them. The *Keidanren* coordinates the activities of the all important ministries with the leading elected officials, in a way which can be outlined with the following graph. Notice how interconnected are the four centers of power and influence, and these lines of interconnectedness do not exaggerate the level of coordination between them.

Due to the role and function of the *Keidanren*, the overall power structure in Japan is far more integrated and coordinated than in any other capitalist system. So while Japan is definitely a market driven capitalist state, the way it is nurtured and managed as an organized whole is reminiscent in some ways of the political/economic policies of the former Soviet Union.

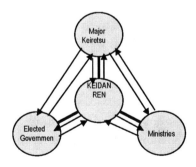

Obviously *Keidanren*, for all the advantage of having such a powerful coordinating agency looking over the economy, has not always been successful in preventing economic downturn. Real estate values got out of hand in the late 1980s as property in the city of Tokyo came to be of greater monetary worth than the real property value of the entire United States. A huge amount of money was borrowed using these inflated property values as collateral. When these highly inflated values began to collapse, as the *Keidanren* probably should have anticipated, many banks were left with a mountain of uncollectible loans. This created a great economic hole, which the Japanese have only recently climbed out of. And again, *Keidanren* was blindsided, as was almost everyone else, by the enormous world-wide effect of the U.S. financial collapse in 2008. The speed at which they will climb out of this latest economic hole is yet to be determined, but their prognosis is at least as bright as that of the U.S. or Europe.

WORKER-EMPLOYER RELATIONS

A great deal has been written over the past thirty years concerning how Japanese workers relate to their jobs and how employers there treat their workers. In 1982, a Japanese-American professor wrote a book called *Theory Z*. That book described the way Japanese employers took a very conservative approach to hiring new employees because of the traditional obligations toward workers. Observers have described employees identifying with the places where they work with almost family-like loyalty. It is a fact that many, probably most, white collar employees of Japanese corporations are more committed in terms of time to their place of work than to their own families. Ouchi went on to explain that workers were almost never laid off and had access to an impressive array of services, such as company owned resorts, highly subsidized housing, and even counseling and spouse-hunting services.

Some observers have gone so far as to indicate the difference between the worker/employer relationship in Japan versus the same relationship in the West with a food shopping analogy: In an open air market, someone who seeks to buy onions can approach a merchant selling onions, and if the shopper likes the quality, and if he or she approves of the price, then the sale can take place. However, the shopper is not normally obliged to buy onions from any particular merchant, and if he or she finds the same quality onions elsewhere at a better price, it is likely that that is where the shopper will purchase onions. If, for some reason, the merchant doesn't want to sell onions on that day, he is not obliged to do so.

With some exceptions, that is sort of the spirit of the Western worker/employer type of relationship. A worker offers his or her time, ability, experience, or whatever for sale. The employer, if he needs that person's work, in a sense *buys* the work. But the employer is not obligated to buy the person's work, and may stop buying it. The worker is usually free to sell his or her work to another buyer if offered a better price. Now, of course the analogy is certainly not a perfect one. Labor unions can and do intervene to prevent workers from getting fired, and in fact, workers in some American and European situations have related to their work places precisely the way Japanese workers are supposed to.

On the other hand, the great majority of workers in Western countries relate to employers in pragmatic and utilitarian terms. Employers, for their part, do not seem to feel guilty in terminating the services of any number of workers when there is financial advantage in doing so. Some of this same type of relationship can be seen in Japan today, but there is an element of Japanese history which influences the employment environment in another direction.

It is simplistic and completely overstated to suggest that workers in Japan consider their work place in the same way they think about kinship relations. But it is quite true that employers in that country are pressured by tradition to consider workers, to the extent that they are able to do so, almost like members of an extended family.

Many people feel that part of this "family orientation" surrounding the Japanese worker/employer relationship stems from experiences in which the concept of family was, in a legal sense, actually the case. As the merchant and manufacturing class grew to have so much economic power during the Edo regime, the *bakufu* began to worry that those very rich merchants and manufacturers could threaten the dominant position of the warrior caste. Rules limiting the number of unrelated workers were meant to put a damper on the size and wealth of these enterprises. The chapter on Edo Japan explained how workers were simply adopted as family members to get around the ruling. Both authors once met the owner of a *sake* brewery in the city of Nara, who told them that the family business which began around 1810 had, by the 1850s, over twenty workers carrying the owner's family name. Except for a few actual relatives who worked at the business, the rest were all adopted into the family as adults.

It has always been a puzzle as to why the *bakufu* would make a rule and then allow such a simple way of circumventing it. Why not just make it illegal to adopt adults, or at least severely limit the number of adult adoptions by a single family? They had complete power in Japan, and adoptions would have had to be registered with local *bakufu* officials, which would have given them an easy way to control the situation. We have no good answer for this. One possibility is that certain members of the *bakufu* figured that keeping manufacturing and trade enterprises so small would inhibit the provision of things that members of the warrior class needed, or at least wanted. They may have concluded that it was less trouble to allow the subterfuge then to rescind the rule.

We don't think the practice ever involved more than a relatively small portion of Japanese workers in the Edo Period, but small percentages of a population can sometimes make a profound impact on a culture. Consider the pioneer experience in America, cited as responsible for the emphasis on independence and self-reliance in American life. During the early 19th century, as the pioneers settled in the plains, hundreds of thousands of Europeans were populating American cities along the East Coast. The total pioneer population probably never amounted to more than five percent of the total number of Americans.

It is, of course, difficult to document just how strong the tradition of adopted workers was in creating Japanese attitudes toward the workplace. But consider this: These workers could not be fired, and they could be relied on under almost any circumstances. Owners were responsible for their total welfare, not just for their pay. Identification with the establishment by the people who worked there was, of course, fundamental and absolute. That was literally one's family. It is likely that at least some of this feeling has carried over into worker/employer relations in the modern period. Perhaps all Japanese employers would prefer to have this kind of worker environment; most simply can't afford it.

It must be pointed out that some of this two-way loyalty has been eroding over the past twenty or thirty years. A few companies, faced with severe financial difficulties, have resorted to the American practice of simply laying off workers to help the "bottom line," rather than trying to shift them to *keiretsu* sister companies. In some cases, there were just not sister company jobs available. Workers, for their part, are not as universally committed to their employers as in previous generations. One study indicated that almost 20 percent of workers under 35 years of age have changed jobs at least once since the beginning of the century. Most of what was described above as characteristic of worker/management relations still holds true, but not to the guaranteed extent as before.

WEALTH AND INCOME INEQUALITIES IN POST-WAR JAPAN

The people who run the largest private enterprises in Japan are, in almost all cases, far less wealthy than their counterparts in the U.S. Japanese executives and board members of the biggest companies are corporate bureaucrats rather than rich capitalists. Their salaries are modest compared with salaries in other capitalist countries, and after retirement, their life styles are not so set apart from other people, with fabulous residences and great personal fortunes. The first author once resided for a time in an apartment a few buildings away from the private house of a retired CEO of the Seiko Corporation. His house, albeit a little larger than most, was not that much distinguished from the others in the neighborhood.* On a modest professor's salary, one would never have the resources to live anywhere near a retired CEO of a large American corporation.

At the end of World War II, Japan lay in ruins, with a large part of the population living on the brink of starvation. Production was less than 20 percent of what it had been just 5 years before. Not only did World War II destroy lives and property, but it also destroyed social structures.

---

* Of course, for starters, retired CEOs of U.S. firms would never live in neighborhoods that contain apartments.

And it set the stage for rebuilding a society that could now be different in many ways.

The mountainous wealth of the old *zaibatsu* families left a bitter taste in the mouths of many Japanese after the war. The top echelon of wealth and power was swept away, at least in economic terms. What remained were those who had worked for the *zaibatsu* and who had the knowledge and expertise to run corporations. These men were not wealthy, and in fact, they never had a chance to accumulate anything close to *zaibatsu*-style wealth. In this way, Japan had a chance to begin again with a new economic elite, one that did not consider great wealth its birthright.

There has been a continuation of this trend, a kind of new tradition of bureaucratic leadership replacing capitalist ownership. There are interesting restraints on income at the top of Japan's economy, not seen in other wealthy societies. The feeling of being part of the homogeneous group tends to make top industrial leaders reluctant to ask for big salary increases. It is not just corporate executives, however, who have had restraints on wage demands: It was the devastation brought on by World War II that helped create a feeling of unity through common misery, making people self-conscious of excessive wage demands.

The first of the changes came rather dramatically. After the stock ownership of the other top *zaibatsu* families was taken, the "Law of the Termination of *Zaibatsu*" of 1948 resulted in a simple government confiscation of most of the remaining large accumulations of private wealth. With family control out of the way and much lower wealth inequalities after the war, Japan was able to avoid the typical capitalist wealth gap between the top and bottom of the economy. This continued for a long time, well until the 1980s. Even as this is written in 2010, there is still less wealth and income disparity in Japan than in all capitalist nations, with the exception of Sweden and Finland. It is true, however, that since the mid-1980s that gap has begun to grow, and while it is still far less pronounced than in the United States, wealth inequality has risen as an issue in Japanese politics.

Japanese workers have relatively high incomes compared to the other major industrial nations, while the top Japanese executives, as already established, earn much less in salary than one might expect. In the United

States, the situation is just the opposite: Workers, especially in the service sector, are not paid much by the standards of industrial societies, while top executives are often paid several times the salary of the President of the United States.

While incomes of the bottom 20 percent of Japanese workers have been falling in the last 10 years, and while the poverty rate has been going up in recent years due to Japan's long economic slump, income inequality and poverty in Japan are still much lower than in the United States. Data from the United Nations *Human Development Report* for 2009 indicate that the income gap between the average income of the richest 10 percent and the average income of the bottom 10 percent is about 16 to 1 in the United States, while for Japan, it is only a little over 4 to 1.

A great boost to Japan's reorganization as a more egalitarian society came with the extensive land reform ordered by the American Occupation in 1946. In rural areas, these changes had especially beneficial results for peasants and farmers, who received land and support from the government, eliminating the long standing inequality between rural and urban areas. Since that time, farmers have become relatively well off in Japan.

WORK AND UNIONS IN JAPAN

The Japanese work place is in the process of change since the down turn of Japan's powerful economy in the first half of the 1990s. Also, there has been much distorted information about Japanese management styles and work in Japan in recent years. "Life-time employment" does exist in Japan, but only for about 30 percent of employees, who work for the biggest corporations in Japan's dual economy.

Japanese work longer hours than the people of any other major industrial nation, except perhaps the United States. At an average of about two thousand hours per worker per year, Japan and the United States are almost tied. As a comparison, German workers put in about 1,400 hours per year.

While the number of hours worked each year is coming down in Japan, tradition sometimes gets in the way. It is not so much that Japanese workers are forced to work such long hours, but that dedication to the company and co-workers makes Japanese people feel guilty if they do not stay in the office late or give up some of their vacation time. One large Japanese bank, for example, started a policy of requiring lights to be turned off after a certain hour at night one day a week.

The hard work and company devotion in Japan cannot be well understood unless we remember the greater importance of the group in Japan compared to the United States. Nor can other aspects of the Japanese workplace be well understood without this focus on the group. For example, one study of the 7 leading capitalist nations asked managers if long term employees should be fired if their performance suddenly went down: The highest response of yes was in the United States at 77 percent, while only 33 percent in Japan said yes.

In Japan, they in fact have a special "position" and word to describe low performing workers, but workers they are unwilling to fire—*madogi-wazoku* 窓際族, based on the English term "window dressing." After the boss and co-workers give up on trying to improve the performance of the person, they are just sort of left alone, not fired or laid off, but tolerated as low performers. With a long recession in the 1990s and 2000s, and new competition from a revitalized U.S. economy and China, Japan is slowly changing this practice; some Japanese companies are starting to lay-off workers for the first time.

Finally, in this context, we can mention the standard Japanese promotion policies, which Americans usually find surprising. While again, there has been some modification of this policy in recent years, traditionally, and even today for the most part, all employees are promoted together according to age, not in terms of some specific achievement criteria. The first question from Americans is usually, "how can they motivate anyone to work hard if there is no special incentive?" Again, we must remember the importance of the group, in this case the work group, in Japan: The Japanese view is that rewarding one person over others can cause disharmony. On the other hand, rewarding the group as a whole for achievement creates more unity and improves group performance.

One might conclude that there would be no need for unions in such a healthy relationship between workers and employers. There are unions, and they play an important role. The first thing to note about unions in Japan is that many unions in Japan are company unions, in contrast to, say, the United Auto Workers in the United States, which represents workers across many companies.

In the U.S. experience, when someone says "a company union," this usually implies that the union is controlled by the company and has no real power. It is true that there is usually less bold confrontation between management and labor in Japan, but not because unions are powerless. Because the Japanese idea of worker-management confrontation is somewhat different from that of other societies, they more often see teamwork rather than an adversary relationship as making up worker/management relations. This may, in large part, be corporate ideology at work, but the unions in Japan can at times push management rather hard in protecting their interests.

While most people who work full-time in Japan belong to company unions, about ten percent of Japanese workers, mainly those who work in public transportation, are organized into municipal, or in some cases even national unions. As a holdover from the leftist movement of the Occupation period, some public transportation and other government blue collar workers are even today organized into nation-wide labor organizations. The most powerful of these is the *Nihon Rōdōsō Gassō Rengokai* 日本労働組合総連合会 "The Japan Association of Allied Labor Federations." These unions go on strike every year or so in the spring, in something called the "spring wage offensive" *shunto* 春闘. But these "strikes" are a far cry from the strikes common today in other societies. Japanese are, after all, Japanese. City-wide and nation-wide strikes are held to "make a point" with the voting public, and not to start a kind of small war with government agencies, as is often the case in Italy and other European countries. With a typical regard for public welfare, they are announced in advance, usually last for only a few hours, and are scheduled to cause minimum inconvenience to the public.

What can be said in conclusion to this brief foray into Japan's economic circumstances? Well, it is true that Japan does not stand out as the economic miracle worker it did in the 1980s. It had its own bank crisis, which seriously damaged economic growth for a decade. It has a growing shortage of blue collar workers and doesn't seem to know how to deal with that while accommodating public attitudes towards immigration.[†] The wealth gap in Japan will probably continue to grow somewhat; greed is extremely difficult to counter in any society. But when we step back and contemplate the Japanese economy in broad strokes, almost any objective observer would conclude that for sixty years or so, it has worked remarkably well. The income gap, although rising, is comparatively low, poverty continues to be lower than in the United States, workers are well paid, unemployment has been kept quite low, and Japan has been able to afford excellent services to its citizens—health, education, security, etc.

It is interesting to note that the United States, the wealthiest country in the world, often struggles to provide that level of service. The comparison is not entirely fair: It is far easier for the Japanese to get the population to pull together on any social issue, due to its homogeneity. Japan did not import slaves, it did not have millions of diverse immigrants for two centuries, and it does not share a continent with a developing country.

Economics has not burdened the Japanese with some of the economic hardships found in many other societies. However, from both the native perspective and viewed from the outside, Japan does certainly have nagging problems. In the following chapter, we take a look at some of those problems.

---

† This problem will be reviewed in some detail in the final chapter, *Facing the Future.*

Chapter 15
Problems and Prospects

B ack in the 1980s and 90s, there appeared a flood of books written by Americans and Europeans about Japan, with titles such as "Japan As Number One" and "The Japanese Miracle." It was almost as if Japan had discovered how to create a more perfect society and to somehow avoid many of the calamitous issues here at home. Certainly, there is much to be admired about Japan: It has low rates of divorce, crime, unemployment (even with recent increases, still far below U.S. and European levels), poverty, AIDS, and teenage pregnancy (only 1 percent of births are to teenage mothers, compared to 20 percent in the U.S.); there are almost no guns, very little drug use, and high rates of positive things like literacy and high school completion. The Japanese even live about five years longer, on average, than Americans.

So what can we possibly have to say about the subject of social problems that will cover a whole chapter in a little book on Japanese society? For one thing, the perception of social problems can be quite subjective. What is a calamity to the Japanese would be in some cases a wonderful outcome to Americans. Japanese media recently suggested that with the gunning down of the Mayor of Nagasaki in broad daylight in April of 2007, the country was starting to be just as dangerous as the U.S. Newspapers went on to lament that in the previous year of 2006, there were 52 gun homicides in Japan out of a total of 980 homicides nationwide.

The comparison is painful: For each of the past several years, the number of homicides in the U.S. has hovered around 13,000, over 7,000 of which involved firearms. Even considering that Japan's population is less than half that of the U.S., Japan has a very long way to go to be "as dangerous." Perhaps more importantly for our discussion here, there is, unfortunately for the Japanese, a down side to what Americans see as the low rate of social problems in Japan. For one thing, Japan is changing, and some of these standard social problems are becoming more worrisome to the Japanese, even if the levels of these problems are still much below those of other societies. But, in addition to this, many of the reasons for Japan's low rate of social problems would themselves be seen as social problems elsewhere. Some of the above, extremely flattering, descriptions of Japan do come at a price.

An example of this has to do with crime statistics. In large part, crime is low because the police keep a close watch on all households in the nation; the divorce rate is low, in part, because women have few acceptable alternatives to staying married.

As we have already seen, many cultural values certainly differ between countries such as Japan and the United States, and these values set the stage for what we see as good or bad. For example, sexual discrimination in the Japanese work place, and even sexual harassment, are only now becoming defined as significant social problems in Japan, as women have become more organized and able to make the nation recognize these situations as problems.

A SHRINKING AND AGING POPULATION

With the world bursting at the seams as the number of humans approaches seven billion, and as many societies struggle to feed exploding populations, a few nations—Japan and most European nations—face a counter reality, trying to keep the number of their citizens from *declining!* Anyone crammed into a subway under the streets of Tokyo at rush hour might not think this would be such a bad trend; fewer people mean more space and less crowding. But a shrinking and aging population presents its own problems, especially frightening to a nation like Japan, with such heavy obligations toward its citizens.

In 2005, Japan's population stood at 127,628,000. As of October 2009, it had shrunk to 127,541,000. That might not seem like a huge decline, but keep in mind that modern economics, together with a whole range of social planning in contemporary societies, is based on the assumption of *growth*—growth in the number of consumers and growth in the number of tax-paying workers. When this does not happen, a whole new reality sets in.

Not only are there fewer Japanese than in the recent past, but the profile of the population is changing dramatically—it is getting older. How to take care of so many old people and how to pay the bill for taking care of them is staring Japan right in the face. Traditionally, as people reached old age, custom dictated that they would be cared for by their grown children, as discussed in the chapter on family. That system worked well enough in rural Japan, when there were always several adult children around. However, two important trends have sabotaged this tradition: The first of these trends was the rapid urbanization of the country since 1950. Seventy percent of the population now lives in urban areas. As you read earlier, there was not much space for the rapid growth of cities; consequently, urban residence units in Japan are the smallest of all the countries in the industrialized world. The traditional three-generation household has become more and more difficult to arrange for most of the country.

The other trend is the plummeting birth rate. Since the 1950s, the average number of children born to Japanese women has continued to fall and stands now at 1.36. In order to replace those lost to the population each year, a rate of 2.13 children per couple is required, which is the rate for the United States.

Many Japanese women enjoy their single life a great deal, with some actually looking at marriage and motherhood as unwanted drudgery. They tend to marry later—the average age of marriage is now close to twenty-seven for women—and once married, they are wary of having more than one or two children. Small residence units and the exceptionally high cost of sending children through school are factors adding to this trend. Over time this will, and even has already to an extent, resulted in too many old people who have to be cared for by public expense, and too few workers paying taxes to support them. Those old people are also hanging around longer than the old people of any nation on earth. Current life expectancy for women stands at 86.06 years, and for men at

79.29 years.* The government estimates that by 2050, the ratio of active workers to retired people 65 and older will be 2 workers to contribute for each three retirees!†

Japan, like other industrialized societies (with of course the exception of the United States), cares for the medical needs of its population through a type of socialized medicine. Patients pay ten percent of total care costs, with the wealthiest paying somewhat more and the government paying the rest. The system works quite well, with Japanese receiving among the best medical service in the world. The national life expectancy verifies that fact. But it is an expensive system (though costing less per person than what the United States pays), and as the population continues to age, it's getting more and more costly. Estimates for 2010 put the figure of government health care costs at the equivalent of about $327 billion for that year alone.‡ When economists ponder that figure, stretching over a decade or more and growing all the time, the question of sustainability becomes very real.§

If you read this as an American, especially if informed that there is usually a labor shortage in Japan for some industries, you might be wondering why the Japanese government does not apply the obvious solution to the problem—that of encouraging the immigration into the country of a generation of younger workers. But cultures have their "hang-ups." The idea of allowing large numbers of non-Japanese into Japan is something like the subject of hand gun ownership in the United States. Most of the world cannot understand the American insistence on so much gun ownership and consider it a horrible, self-defeating neurosis. But the attitude of a large number of Americans, perhaps a majority, toward gun ownership is not likely to change significantly in the foreseeable future. And so it is with attitudes toward immigration in Japan.

---

* Tokyo: Ministry of Interior and Communication. "Population Estimates, Monthly Report." Sept. 1, 2009.

† Japan Times, Oct. 1, 2009.

‡ However, even though the U.S. does not have a comprehensive national health system, overall health costs in the U.S., at about 3.2 trillion dollars, are over seven times those of Japan.

§ www.demographicwinter.com. 508.

There is currently a larger percentage of people not of the Japanese race residing within the population now than ever before. But it is still minuscule for what we could call an open society, where people would be free to come, and even stay and work under certain circumstances. Foreign workers have never much surpassed one percent of the total population, and the idea of granting permanent residence to substantial numbers of non-Japanese would be about as politically feasible as asking all Americans to turn in their guns to the government.

Small numbers of foreigners, especially well educated ones, have not been a big problem for the Japanese people. But massive immigration, especially where it would likely come from, the poorest countries of Southeast Asia, is so repugnant to the majority of the population that it could not even come up for serious political discussion.

School expenses have recently become somewhat politicized, and some observers believe that a contributing factor in the success of the Japan Democratic Party over the Liberal Democratic Party in the August 2009 elections was the generous (about $375) grant it promised young mothers of school-age children per month if that party took power in the national legislature. The grant was projected as a government sponsored measure to increase the birth rate. Sociologists both within and outside Japan are skeptical.

CRIME

Yes, compared to all other advanced industrial societies, and especially the United States, the streets are safer in Japan. White-collar crime by corporations is a different matter, and politicians are as likely to be corrupt as in other industrialized countries. Comparing crime statistics for traditional street crimes (robbery, rape, etc.) across national borders is a tricky business due to differing measures and effectiveness in collecting crime figures. But when it comes to comparing traditional crime rates between Japan and the United States, even if they were off by several percentage points, the contrasts would still be staggering. In a typical year, the United States has from 5 to more than 100 times the amount of crime found in Japan, depending on the type of crime. Crime has gone up slightly in the last couple of decades, but there have been nothing like the levels experienced in the United States.

Japan has very strict gun control. Only a few hundred private individuals in the entire nation—specially licensed security officers, a few body guards, etc.—can legally possess hand guns and keep them in their residences. Some hunters may store hunting rifles with the police, but hand guns in the hands of ordinary citizens are strictly prohibited. A lot of Americans wouldn't like to live without being able to own guns, but the effect on crime statistics is unquestionable. Committing a store robbery with a knife, for example, requires much clumsy effort, and therefore is less often tried. True, some organized crime members in Japan get guns, but it is not easy to do, and the mere possession of a hand gun is a frequent reason for imprisonment of organized crime figures.

Annual Murders per 100,000 population 1990–2000

United States	9.4
Canada	5.5
France	4.6
Germany	4.2
England	2.0
Japan	1.2

Source: UN Demographic Year Book, 2004

Percent of Population Victimized by a Crime per 100,000 Population 1990–2000

United States	28.8
Canada	28.1
Germany	21.9
France	19.4
England	19.4
Japan	9.3

Source: UN Demographic Year Book, 2004

THE CRIMINAL JUSTICE SYSTEM

Japanese police are well trained; a college degree is usually required, and they are highly respected by the Japanese population, rather than feared. However, the Japanese police also have the ability to do many things not accepted in the United States. For example, in every Japanese community, and in local neighborhoods in the large cities such as Tokyo and Osaka, there are hundreds of small police boxes called *kōban* 交番. These are always manned by one or more police officers in the daytime and evening hours, and in busy areas, usually for the complete twenty-four hours. These police officers keep close watch on the comings and goings of everyone in the neighborhood, and they are required by law to check homes regularly to keep up their records on who lives in the house, and such things as occupations and all other important records about the people in the household.

All people living in Japan must register with the local government when they move into the area. Failure to do this results in a knock on the door early one morning by a police officer in his regular uniform, with his gun at his side and clipboard in hand. This can be a bit of a shock to a foreigner living in Japan who is not familiar with local customs.

What this means is that when a crime is committed in the neighborhood, the police usually have some ideas about who to talk to and look for; or, at least, their good relations with the people of the community allow for many eyes watching to report things. A result is that the arrest rates per 100 offenses in Japan are about 95 percent for murder (about 70 percent for the US) to 80 percent for robbery (25 percent for the US).

Once a suspect is arrested for a crime, the comparison to the U.S. criminal justice system becomes even more stark. Japanese police can hold a suspect for interrogation for up to 23 days with no access to a lawyer. When suspects are brought to trial, 99 percent are convicted by a panel of 3 judges (there are no jury trials in Japan),⁵ with over 80 percent convicted using signed confessions, obtained during police interrogations. As one might suspect, there have been many cases of people convicted

---

⁵ Though in 2008, Japan instituted a kind of jury system with private citizens sitting as more like advisors to these judges.

of crimes they did not commit, with some in prison for decades before the fact was discovered. People both inside and outside Japan, such as Amnesty International, have been increasingly critical of these aspects of the Japanese criminal justice system.

After a person is convicted of a crime, however, the United States and Japan differ in the other direction. Few convicted criminals in Japan are given prison time, with Japan having one of the lowest per capita prison populations in the world, compared to the United States's highest. In Japan, it is assumed that the shame of conviction, along with the low chance of getting a good job and, after release, the continued constant watch by the local police, are enough to deal with the problem. For those sent to prison, however, the treatment is tough: There is almost no freedom, with very rigid rules regulating all aspects of life behind bars. Japanese prisons, however, do better at realistic job training than institutions in the U.S. There are executions in Japan, though fewer than in the United States, and with a different philosophy: Death sentences are reported in Japan, but there is no publicity when the execution is finally carried out.

ORGANIZED CRIME

At least as much as the notorious mafia in the United States, and likely much more, Japan has a bigger than life image of the *yakuza*, the Japanese version of organized crime. Like the U.S. mafia, the *yakuza* are well organized into separate families and are involved in many kinds of illegal activities, from drug trafficking and prostitution to extortion. They even seem to look like the Hollywood version of American gangsters, with dark suites and black ties, and with big American cars, which are very rare in Japan and are often called "gangster cars" when seen on Japanese streets. The complete body tattooing, which is common among the yakuza, though, does not fit the American mafia image.

There are, however, many significant differences, some primarily matters of degree. For one thing, the yakuza are much less violent. We have both came close to a rather rare event in Japan: In one case a hit man, out to get a rival gang member, using an old hand gun to do his business, missed completely, managing only to put a couple of holes in the bullet train as it came to a stop at the station. Your first author was just arriving at the station at the time and actually heard the shots. Within minutes, there were about fifty policemen all over the area. They later captured the culprit, which seemed to surprise no one. In 2007, your second author was living in Sendai, north of Tokyo, when hit men killed two people in the apartment just down the street. Again, the hit men were arrested within 24 hours.

The *yakuza* started as professional gamblers and racketeering organizations in the Edo Period. They were often seen much like Robin Hood figures in times of trouble, sometimes acting on the behalf of peasants. Because of this history, today the *yakuza* continue to have a somewhat romantic image for some people. While their activities have always been focused on the illegal, there has been a kind of code of honor; they see themselves as something like the old samurai, being careful to avoid causing trouble for ordinary citizens.

The Japanese national police office reports about 3,000 groups of *yakuza*, with about 80,000 members in Japan. Recently, these groups have been moving into more complex forms of legal and illegal business activities and making considerable money in the over-heated real estate market of the 1980s. Many of the scandals involving savings and loan banks going broke in the mid-1990s due to bad real estate loans and political corruption in the late 1980s and early 1990s involved *yakuza* groups.

BŌSŌZOKU: YOUTH GANGS

While Japan is relatively free of most serious types of street crime, there is certainly no absence of many kinds of less serious deviance. An important example in recent years has been the disruptions and trouble caused by youth "gangs." An image of LA street gangs and drive-by shootings, however, is not part of the Japanese scene: More typical are rowdy street parties and motorcycle races, with engines revved up as loud as possible, at say, 3 a.m., in neighborhoods where people are trying to sleep. The chief activists in this type of deviance are motor cycle gangs called *bōsōzoku* 暴

走賊, made up of young people in their teens or early 20s who are clearly defined as losers in Japanese society. These are the young people who have not tested well enough to get into the good high schools that prepare young people for college, or even well enough to get into good technical high schools leading to well paying working-class jobs.

The Japanese society is a tough place for these young people, with no second or third chances in an educational system very different from the United States. Their *bōsōzoku* activities are a form of rebellion against this society that has shut them out of legitimate opportunities to succeed. At the same time, however, *bōsōzoku* membership can be a means of achievement, as many theories of youth gangs in the United States have suggested. A high percentage of the organized crime figures in Japan, the *yakuza*, are recruited from these youth gangs (a kind of alternative means of social mobility and opportunity).

WORK AND STRESS

That great asset of the capacity for diligent concentration and hard work which has brought Japan so much success in the world can have a down side. It is possible, even likely, that many Japanese work too hard. There is a rather common term in contemporary Japan that probably will never have a popular equivalent in the U.S. It is *karōshi* 過労死, or death by overwork. It describes the premature death of usually men, due to exhaustion from too many hours of work over too long a period.

Among the advanced industrial nations, Japanese people work longer hours than anyone. As noted in the previous chapter, the average hours worked per year range from over 2,000 for Japanese people to, as stated earlier, about 1,400 for Germans. But these are officially reported hours and the averages. Many Japanese white collar workers are at work many more hours than this. The problem of over-work in general is considered serious enough that the Japanese government has mounted an ad campaign in recent years telling people to stop working so many hours. There have been posters in trains asking everyone to please take all of their vacation time, which most full-time male workers seldom do. Government offices have been closed Saturdays in recent years, and some corporations are actually *requiring* their office employees to stop work at least one day a week by 6 pm, in some cases cutting off electricity to the building to force them out.

The pressure of the group to work hard remains strong, and to make the company seem to fall in line with national demands to reduce working hours, the figures at the office level can be manipulated a little.

While *karōshi* no doubt is real, with estimates as high as 10,000 deaths per year, it is not the only problem of over-work. With fathers going to work before their children wake up and getting home at 9 or 10 at night, many children are being raised with very little fatherly contact. Most Japanese social scientists expect that such fatherly neglect must be taking its toll on children, especially young boys, who are often lacking a strong male role model. A recent survey of 3,000 children in Germany, Japan, and the United States found that Japanese children had the lowest respect for their fathers, much lower than in the United States.[**]

There is also the problem of expanding the domestic economy: Japan cannot forever keep its economy going only by exporting goods to other countries like the United States. It must have increased domestic consumption, and that requires some time off from work in order to shop and buy things. The entertainment industry in Japan must concentrate on a young audience—people with less money to spend than, say, men in their thirties and forties. Many of life's pleasures for working-age men in other countries are simply not available for Japanese men during their working years. Many of them play golf on weekends, but closer scrutiny reveals that golf more times than not involves the work group or the hosting of business clients—a kind of extension of work.

It is not surprising that the Japanese motion picture industry turns out movies almost exclusively aimed at teenagers and college-age viewers. There were some great movie directors in Japan's past, but almost no artists of international renown have received recognition in recent years. Japanese travel the world over, and one cannot go to any tourist destination without encountering Japanese travelers. You may not have noticed that almost all of them are people of retirement age. Young pre-married

---

[**] Los Angeles Times, July 6, 1993.

Japanese and those over age 60 feed Japan's travel industry. The rest are too busy working.

BULLYING

One of the most publicized problems of recent years, and one that Japanese people seem always to be asking Western social scientists to share some possible wisdom about, is bullying. Quite simply, this is where groups of school children, otherwise decent and obedient children, gang up on some poor boy or girl with physical and more commonly, psychological harassment, until the victim will no longer attend school, or in extreme cases, commits suicide. The Japanese newspapers of late seem full of cases of children who have committed suicide, leaving behind heart wrenching suicide notes saying they can't take the bullying any longer. The Japanese Ministry of Education claims that bullying has gone up 2.6 times from 1995 to 2005, with 56,000 cases reported, though very few have caused deaths.

There is a flip-side to a high degree of unity and homogeneity for a society. Extensive in-group unity almost always creates less tolerance for diversity or even slight differences.

Bad as this seems, a little perspective is useful. The Japanese Ministry of Education recently reported that over 6 suicides in a fifteen-month period were due to bullying. When we look at the statistics, the suicide rate of those aged 10 to 17 is actually slightly higher in the U.S. than in Japan. And there has never been anything remotely like the spectacular shootings in American schools over the past few years. Even though there is much less violence than in schools in the United States, the Japanese public has a somewhat higher expectation of school discipline and compliance for its youth, and parents there probably are just as concerned about school violence as are American parents.

SEX AND THE SEX INDUSTRY

Defining sexual behavior and sexual attitudes across cultural boundaries can be tricky and can easily lead to ethnocentric conclusions. What is sexual deviance in one place is normal behavior in another. On the other hand, there are aspects of this subject that a very large percentage of Japanese themselves would indeed interpret as a social problem.

Considering the seriousness with which Japanese people seem to approach their work and the strength of the family system, Americans who have never been to Japan might assume Japanese people to be very modest, even prudish about sex. The assumption is quite wrong.

More like Europeans than Americans, Japanese people tend to be less "uptight" about matters of sex and sexual deviance. Homosexuality is not a big issue, and pornography is quite open: Vending machines on many street corners of Tokyo sell sexually explicit magazines. It is not uncommon to see large ads showing young women, very provocatively clad, holding a featured product in magazines and on billboards.

Perhaps more startling to foreigners are the sexually explicit comic books called *manga* 漫画, which are read openly by men on commuter trains and subways all over Japan. *Manga* started out as diversion for children, but since World War II, they have evolved into several types; a few are definitely not appropriate for very young readers. Some of these *manga*, in fact, have violent themes of rape, bondage, and brutality against women, which in the minds of many Japanese have crossed the threshold of decency, occasionally causing outcries against them in the Japanese mass media.

All of these sexually explicit magazines, as well as movies, however, are covered by one basic censorship rule in Japan: No pubic hair can be shown. Beyond that, it's pretty much whatever readers want. Somewhat to the amusement of most foreign residents of Japan, there are employees of *manga* publishers' import houses for magazines who spend their days marking out the pubic hair with black markers.

Another interesting aspect to the subject of sex in Japan are "love hotels"—hundreds of them all over large cities. Even small towns of any size have at least a few. "Love hotels" are simply hotels where couples pay for a room by two-hour time segments, with many sexually oriented devices and features supplied in the rooms. These places are all quite openly advertised as love hotels with purple lights outside and suggestive names such as "Love Haven," "Blue Pleasure," etc. Many have special entrances so that customers can quickly enter and even hide their car behind a curtain in the driveway. There are other countries, of course, that have such love hotels, but in no other country are there so many, so openly displayed for what they are.

Thailand, for example, noted for its sex industry, is actually more modest about sex in some ways, and their love hotels are much more difficult to identify from a distance. One reason for the demand for such numbers of love hotels in Japan, however, is understandable given crowed housing conditions, where few young people have cars or even apartments away from their parents before getting married. Remember that Japanese tend to marry later than Americans and are often still unmarried in their late 20s or even early 30s.

Prostitution in Japan is illegal, but also quite open. Virtually all cities have their brothel sections. Ads for house calls or hotel calls by these ladies are typically plastered all over phone booths and other public places in certain parts of cities, as well as handed out to men on busy street corners.

We have dwelled upon the extent of sexual openness in Japan to make an additional point: The American assumption tends to be that when sex is openly displayed as it is in Japan, there will be extensive sexual deviance of the worst kind as a result. In other words, rape, rampant teenage sexual activity, and teenage pregnancy would be associated with loose controls on the open show of sex in the society. As much of the social science research shows, and as Japan makes clear, the above assumptions are again proven wrong.

Crime statistics indicate that rape is relatively rare. What is even more remarkable, however, is that for the most part, the openness toward sex in Japan has not led to extensive sexual promiscuity among Japanese teenagers. It is impossible for young girls and boys to escape viewing such explicit sexual activity, and some of it can even be seen on the regular television channels. But for many years, studies have shown Japanese teenagers to have slightly (but only slightly) less involvement with sexual activity than Americans of their age.

There has been a long history of casual views toward sex and nudity in Japan. It was only with increasing Western contact and influence about 100 years ago that Japan became uncomfortable with such practices as same sex public baths. Prostitution has been quite accepted through most of Japanese history, to the point that a couple of hundred years ago, much like theater and movie reviews in newspapers today, one could find reviews of individual prostitutes and brothels in openly published magazines.

Japan, however, is changing. And while rape and other sexually related violent attacks remain relatively rare, other kinds of sexual deviance and crime seem to be increasing. One form, passively tolerated for years, called *chikan* 痴漢, has recently come to the attention of authorities and the media. *Chikan* refers to both the act and the men involved in fondling women in crowded trains. One survey found that 70 percent of high school girls have been victims, but only 2 percent of these cases were reported to police. What is so striking to outsiders, and Japanese as well, is how this activity is so organized. There are videos on how to do it and even a magazine aimed at *chikan* participants.

Despite all we have said above, there is evidence that some young people are also changing, becoming more sexually active, and becoming involved in what most Japanese define as deviant types of activities. Throughout history, it seems, most societies have had their generational conflicts, with older adults saying that the young are no longer as hard working and moral. Such complaints have been heard for at least a couple of decades in Japan, but recently, there may be some grounds for these complaints.

With respect to our current subject, national surveys indicate that young Japanese women in their 20s, for example, are becoming more sexually active and delaying marriage as long as possible. And for the past ten years, Japanese newspapers were filled with a new activity called "telephone sex clubs." There are estimated to be over 2,000 of these clubs in Japan. These telephone clubs operate by charging men about $40 to sit in a booth waiting for calls from a teenage girl in response to the widespread ads. Only a small percentage of Japanese girls have gone farther than just calling once and talking to the men for a few minutes, but girls who agree to have sex with these men usually get about $1,000.

SUICIDE

As most people are aware, suicide has a long tradition in Japanese society. In samurai culture, suicide was an honorable, even required, way of accepting defeat or failure, or of taking oneself out of a situation to benefit the larger group. In one of the classic tales of the Edo Period, *The Forty-Seven Ronin*, known in Japanese as *chūshingura* 忠臣蔵 "tale of the loyal retainers," samurai avenge the death of their feudal lord; then, to maintain their honor after the forbidden act of revenge, they commit mass suicide. In real life, after defeat in battle, the samurai defending the feudal domain, retainers, and even close relatives, were expected to atone for their shame by committing suicide. At the death of Emperor Meiji, several of his closest aids committed suicide. And of course, more recently, there were the famous *kamikaze* fighter pilots of World War II, who flew planes loaded with TNT into American war ships in desperate efforts to turn the tide of the war.

There remain some elements of this tradition of ritual suicide in Japanese society today—but only some. During 1989, for example, the manager of one of the most winning professional baseball teams in Japan committed suicide after a losing season. More recently, the director of a nuclear power plant committed suicide when it was found that his company covered up a leak of radioactive steam, as did the public school official in one large school district who was in charge of school lunches in the summer of 1996, after a food poisoning outbreak made thousands ill. During political scandals, there have been recent cases of trusted aids committing suicide to protect their bosses.

But such extreme measures are now rare. More common is the practice of resignation to take responsibility for an agency's mistake or failure. Corporate scandals often lead to the resignation of the top executive who had no real responsibility for the scandal, as with the CEO of Japan Airlines after a crash killed over 500 people in 1985. Government officials may resign to apologize and take public responsibility for an accident or mistake, as did the head of Japan's Self Defense Force when a submarine struck a fishing boat and killed several fishermen in 1988. It can be rather tough at the top in Japan, though it must be said that suicide is no longer seen as appropriate in those situations.

Suicide crops up consistently when examining Japanese history. This has given rise to the idea, common even within Japan itself, that the Japanese are the most suicide-prone people on earth. But when we examine comparative suicide rates today, we find that Japan is only slightly above average when calculating the number of suicides per 100,000 population, and nowhere near the rates of the suicide leaders of Finland and Austria. And when we look within certain categories of the population, there are some surprises. Many Americans think, after learning of the great pressures placed upon Japanese children to get into a good university during "examination hell," and many Japanese themselves assume, that Japanese teenagers should have a very high rate of suicide. Indeed, every year after these exam results are announced, there are front page news stories about a couple of teenagers throwing themselves in front of a train after failing the exam. But though the Japanese rate of teenage suicide was among the highest in the 1950s, it has gone down considerably since then, and it is relatively low today. And, as mentioned earlier, when we look at the actual figures, the U.S. teenage suicide rate has, in several recent years, been higher than for Japan.

Comparative Suicides per 100,000 Population 1990–2000

Finland	27.6
Austria	24.3
France	20.3
Belgium	19.3
China	17.6
Germany	16.6
Japan	**15.6**
Sweden	15.6
Canada	13.0
United States	**12.2**
Netherlands	10.5
South Korea	9.4
England	8.0
Italy	7.8
Spain	9.3

Source: UN Demographic Year Book, 2006

In Japan, blame and frustration is less likely to be projected outwardly to others in the group and more likely to be projected inward, to the self. In recent years, the United States has been called a "nation of victims:" Whatever is wrong, it is someone else's fault. In contrast to that tendency, when Japanese become frustrated or angry, they more often turn on themselves rather than lashing out at others.

There are other things that worry Japanese, aside from those that constitute social problems. Some of these problems face all advanced societies. We'll take a look at a few of these in our last chapter.

Chapter 16
Facing the Future

K eeping pace with the unfolding of events in societies in any part of the world can be a humbling experience. Experts who spend their entire careers investigating various cultural, political and economic trends are sometimes caught completely off guard in the face of cataclysmic events. Many expert observers felt that the Soviet Union was weakening as the world entered the final quarter of the twentieth century. However, almost no one foresaw its sudden and complete collapse in 1991. So, being thus forewarned, we will take a chance at monitoring a few trends in Japanese life that, while not certain, appear very likely to continue.

Let's begin by proclaiming that in spite of its normal range of nagging problems, Japan will continue to be what it has been for some time, a world leader in technological development, a modern prosperous democratic society, a place with one of the highest standards of living for the bulk of its citizens in the world, an economic leader among nations, and an equal partner with the geopolitical power brokers.

To "count Japan out" is to fail to comprehend the context of its accomplishments. When we consider Japan becoming an industrial nation with a prosperous and well adjusted population, it is indeed impressive when we look at the advantages held by other nations. The United States, for example, supplies a portion of its own petroleum. Its farmland covers an area larger than the farmland of any other nation, and food products are one of its main exports. With generous deposits of coal, iron, and many other minerals, it grew to prosperity for the first 100 years of its existence without even the need for large-scale international trade. It has a large population, but it is blessed with a great deal of room to distribute that population.

When we look at Japan, we see a quite different set of circumstances: Japan is extremely deficient in natural resources. Petroleum, metals of all types, and every other ingredient necessary for industrial production must be entirely imported. Only 15 percent of the total land area is suitable for agriculture. Japan imports more than half of its food supply. Because most of the country is so mountainous, a population 40 percent of that of the U.S. must squeeze, for living space, into an area of arable land about the size of New Jersey.

There is an important message we can gather from this. It is that what has brought Japan economic prosperity does not lay in the ground—it is found in a more difficult place to see and measure. Japan's leverage into membership among the richest countries of the world is buried deeply in its culture. It has several manifestations; perhaps the easiest to recognize is the capacity for concentrated hard work. It is not universal in Japan, of course; no cultural feature ever is. We personally have known a few decidedly lazy Japanese. But the old principle, "anything worth doing is worth doing well," is deeply ingrained in the Japanese psyche.

"Work," and that word has more shades of meaning than is usually assumed, is not just something one does for money in most cases in Japan. Many Americas and many people all over the world find their work absorbing and pleasurable. And perhaps the notion that Japanese find pleasure in work is not an accurate description. It is not so much that people enjoy their work so much in Japan, but rather that they get so integrated into it. Any kind of sloppiness, even casualness, concerning a task done by a Japanese person is rare to see.

JAPAN'S "ME GENERATION"

Whether the older Japanese generation like it or not, however, the problem of overwork described in the previous chapter may have solutions on the horizon. According to older Japanese, young people there are becoming more self-centered, less willing to sacrifice for the group, and much more concerned with leisure time activities. According to the way the older generation sees it, Japanese teenagers show "less respect for parents and teachers" and are less likely to follow the value orientations of the older generation. In other words, the old methods of inducing conformity, so successful with earlier generations of Japanese, may indeed be weakening.

Opinion polls consistently back up these observations, as do observations obtained by simply walking around Japan today. A few Japanese young people can be seen with colored hair (forbidden by most schools in the past), punk rock clothing styles, and other signs of youth rebellion that are contrary to the values of their parents. Some Japanese, in fact, have begun calling this "the American disease." In the West, especially in America, young people most always had independence and at least a mild form of rebellion against the values of their elders. In fact, in contrast to Japan, the process of growing up in America can almost be defined as a process of becoming independent from parents. With the affluence of modern Japan, and more media influence from the Western industrialized nations, especially the United States, Japan is adopting some of these characteristics.

Some Japanese worry about whether the younger generation has any values at all. Japanese people were not only shocked at the *Aum Shinrikyō*, which, as you know, tried to kill many Japanese in a gas attack in the Tokyo subway system a few years ago, but also were shocked by the fact, as mentioned in chapter 12, that so many of Japan's best and brightest youth, such as top graduates from Tokyo University, had been attracted to the cult. We have noted that there are some 1,500 small religious cults operating just at the foot of the famous Mt. Fuji alone. The mid-1990s brought a flood of news commentaries about the lost and alienated Japanese young people. A general theme is that the older generations were taught to value hard work to achieve material success. Japanese young people have material success: Other values, it is said, have not been forthcoming to give young people purpose and meaning in life.

While attitudes of what the Japanese call the "me generation" are noticeable, many foreign residents of Japan, bringing as they do a somewhat wider view of the phenomenon into play, see it as normal, even inevitable social process. After all, many other cultures have had that kind of orientation of their young population throughout modern history and have survived and even thrived.

In our opinion, rebellion in Japan is often more a degree of posing than any kind danger to social order. For example, young people with long hair and black leather, punk clothing can be seen dancing in public around Tokyo's large Yoyogi Park every Sunday afternoon. However, a large percentage of these "youth rebels" will make it home in the evening in time to complete their homework.

Japanese worry about an evolving drug problem. Drugs certainly can be found in some of the disco areas of Tokyo, and according to magazine accounts, four or five percent of housewives abuse tranquilizers. But the scale of drug abuse is quite small by international comparison.

Some critics in Japan seem to fear that the country will fall victim to some of the problems that other industrial societies have experienced: Laziness, mindless self-obsession, youthful boredom, isolationism, etc. Some call this the "rich nation disease." But, of course, it is a kind of luxury that such a problem even is conceived of in a country that only fifty or sixty years ago dealt with widespread poverty. Now, the debate can turn to how the first Asian nation to achieve extensive prosperity for the masses will deal with the "rich nation's disease."

Japan is reaching maturity. It started its process of industrialization less than 150 years ago, and much of it was delayed or reversed by World War II. The 1980s was the first time a large majority of Japanese ever experienced affluence. Affluence, it is often said, is one of the biggest stimulants for change: People live longer; there is a decline in the birth rate as there are more options in life and children become more expensive; and there is less motivation to work so hard when people are well off and do not have to worry about living in the streets and facing starvation, as did some of Japan's population in the 1940s and early 1950s.

China and South Korea are currently experiencing the pressures of change associated with economic development much more intensively than Japan has for a long time. When economies change, social values change with them. Perhaps this will be after all, as many people predicted decades ago, the Asian century. Japan has longer experience with the physical and social realities of development than the other two, and however serious its problems seem at the time, its influence and role in Asia will undoubtedly be significant.

REDISCOVERING ASIA

It may seem strange to Europeans and Americans to read that Japan is recently becoming more interested in Asia. After all, isn't Japan part of Asia? By geography, race, history, and culture, Japan is unquestionably Asian. In some interesting ways, however, the country has stood outside the image of a typical Asian nation.

We can see this fact more clearly when we compare Japan with the nations of Europe: Those nations have not always, or one might even say, have not usually, gotten along well, but nonetheless, they share a great deal. For the most part, they share the same race, the same core religion, and the same linguistic family, and they have had a more or less continuous historical interaction for most of the past 2000 years. All that makes Europe seem like a kind of natural cultural region. Europe is home to unique cultural expressions of course, but consider this: France, Spain, Greece, England, the various states of Germany, Sweden, Russia, Belgium, Denmark, and Bulgaria have had kings and queens who were part of a giant interrelated family tree!

In spite of the fact that Japan got virtually all of its original elements of civilization from China, Japan traditionally has never been part of something conceived of as "Asia" to the extent that, say, England has been part of Europe. There is not enough space here to go into all of the reasons for this, but here are a few: It was pointed out in the very first chapter of this book that Japan, while situated in East Asia, was far enough away from the mainland to develop cultural traits not connected or related to those of mainland Asian societies. And boy, are the Japanese ever aware of this. There are few, if any, people on earth who are so focused on how they are different from other people as the Japanese.

As you now know, Japan was almost completely isolated from the outside world for two and a half centuries. This is not ancient history; that isolation ended only about 140 years ago. Being by themselves for such a long time had the effect of rendering any contemporary cultures, including Asian cultures, extremely foreign. The extremist samurai who resented any outsiders treading on what they considered the sacred soil of Japan in the late nineteenth century did not make exceptions for Chinese or Koreans. All non-Japanese to them were equally foreign.

In a desperate attempt to stave off the powerful forces of the West, Japan self-consciously elected to follow a Western course. Japan's development as a modern industrial economy drew virtually nothing from any Asian source. As the country turned its back on Asia, it did so not only in a material sense, but in a philosophical and psychological sense as well. 1500 years in the past, the Japanese admired everything Chinese. But as Japan began to industrialize, Japanese had the image in their minds of fellow Asians as backward, even uncivilized. In the two wars with China, Japanese soldiers referred to the enemy as *changoro* ちゃんごろ, something like "chinks." We have already witnessed in chapter two what disdain Japan showed toward its Korean colonial subjects.

Japanese military behavior in Asia during World War II was often abominable, and the majority of adult Japanese were at least partly aware of this. In spite of that, however, a strong feeling of superiority over other Asians definitely survived Japan's defeat. As the Japanese re-industrialized in the years following that war, the rest of East Asia lagged behind. Significant gaps in economic development are commonly the gist of ethnocentrism.

There are all kinds of evidence of the relatively low regard Japan long held toward fellow Asian cultures. Language study is certainly one of them. In schools and universities, the Japanese have long studied foreign languages. English is a required subject, as much a part of the curriculum as mathematics. Many students choose to study a second foreign language, and the choices have for most of the twentieth century been French, German, and Spanish. Chinese came in a distant fourth, and the Korean language was barely studied at all outside of Korean communities in Japan.

As the Japanese population crept toward a high level of per capita affluence in the 1960s, like their co-class compatriots in Europe and America, they became addicted to foreign travel. It is interesting to monitor where they went. The U.S. and Europe were their favorite destinations, followed by Hong Kong (a British colony at the time) and Guam (a U.S. territory).* China was, of course, closed to tourism until the 1970s, but South Korea was not closed and was by far the shortest distance away of any foreign nation. Lots of Korean/Japanese visited Korea, but quite few Japanese with no Korean ancestors, outside of business travelers, ever were motivated to go there.

The flowering of technological sophistication by the Japanese a hundred years ago taught the world a lesson—*material progress is not connected to race or ethnicity*. Interestingly, the Japanese had to learn that lesson by themselves. South Korea, traditionally an agricultural economy, slowly began to industrialize in the 1960s. By the 1980s, Koreans began to produce high quality export products. As the critiques of these products were more and more positive, Japan began to realize that it had a competitor on its hands. Slowly, a kind of image transformation occurred for many Japanese. If Korea could do these things, then perhaps Koreans were worthy of being taken more seriously. It was an imperceptible transformation, but suddenly in 2002, something proved that it had happened.

It took the form of Japanese acceptance of, and positive reaction to, a Korean media production. The production was a long 20-episode television drama; Americans might call it a soap opera. In English, it is known as *Winter Sonata*, the story of a young Korean man who becomes successful in the United States and eventually returns to Korea. It was very popular in South Korea, and a Japanese television executive decided to dub it in Japanese and take a chance by showing it in Japan. It immediately became an explosive hit. In 2003, when the lead actor, Bae Yong Joon, visited Japan, he was mobbed by young women like any American or European rock star. One cannot help but wonder whether twenty years earlier, there would have been any interest in the drama, or whether a Korean actor would have been interesting to the Japanese public at all.

That was only the beginning of something called *kanryū*乾流, "the Korean flood." Not only were things Korean now perfectly acceptable, especially for young people, everything Korean was suddenly super cool.

---

* *Japan Times*, January 29, 2006.

The popular Korean singer Dong Ban Shin Gi, singing both in Korean and a kind of phonetic Japanese, quickly made it to the top of the charts. More television dramas followed. By 2009, there had been no less than 42 television programs produced in Korea and shown in Japan.

Korea was also discovered as a place to visit. From 1998 to 2007, Japanese tourism to Korea, including family members of all ages, increased fourfold.† On the governmental level as well, Koreans were being accepted as equal partners in Asia. After decades of delay, finally on February 11, 2010, the Japanese government issued a formal apology for the occupation and colonization of Korea. It is interesting to contemplate that this was not seen as necessary in the past. Now, it was.

Japan's other East Asian neighbor is also experiencing an image make-over. It is not so much the technological sophistication of China that has impressed Japan. (Many of the high-end products produced there are still made under foreign patents.) It is the sheer wealth of that nation, especially the large number of wealthy Chinese tourists increasingly ar-riving at Narita airport, the gateway to Tokyo. As with Korea, China, too, is coming to be viewed with greater respect. This is most evident in foreign language study. From a handful a few years ago, by 2007 there were 530 secondary schools in Japan that offered courses in Mandarin Chinese. By that time, over 18,000 students had formally studied the language—twice as many as for French and four times the number of students who had studied German.‡

In Japan, academic study of foreign language strongly emphasizes reading and translating. The spoken version of a foreign language is not paid much attention to in school. For that reason, people who wish to develop spoken competency must enroll in what Japanese call *kaiwa gakkō* 会話学校 "conversation school." These are private schools, usually conducting classes in evenings and on weekends. It is a large industry; there are over a thousand conversation schools in the country. Since the end of the war, over 90 percent of conversation schools taught spoken

---

† 週間朝日 *Shūkan Asahi*, July 22, 2009.

‡ Jcast ニュス．ビジネッス＆メデアウオッチ, *Jcast News. Business & Media Watch* Oct. 16, 2009.

English almost exclusively. However, about five years ago, spoken Chinese began to catch on, and now almost half of the students in conversation schools study Mandarin. The main reason for this is that jobs that require Chinese have multiplied rapidly. Various service personnel, especially, are discovering that Chinese can be more useful in dealing with costumers and clients than English.

As soon as China opened its doors to tourism in the late 1970s, Japanese were among the most frequent visitors. But for twenty-five years, by far the largest number of Japanese tourists ended up in places like Paris, Rome, California, New York City, and Sydney. Interest in visiting China has grown dramatically recently. In 2005, for the first time since World War II, a larger number of Japanese tourists visited China than the U.S., and the trend has continued.§

So the Japanese are in a sense re-discovering that they are a part of Asia, and more importantly, that Asia is not so bad a place to be a part of. In the future, all three of these cultures will likely be more integrated in economic terms, and that can lead to other kinds of integration. Japan must still overcome bitter memories of its behavior toward China and Korea during the first half of the twentieth century. Both those countries keep some of the memories alive through their school systems. No one expects a European Union style "Asian Union" anytime soon, but certainly Japan will show increasing interest in other Asian societies as equal partners.

COMING TO GRIPS WITH IMMIGRATION

In an earlier chapter, we made the comparison between the attitude toward gun ownership in the United States and the attitude of most Japanese toward immigration. The point we were making was that due to entrenched attitudes in both situations, these things are pretty much closed to significant change. But there is an important difference between the two realities. Many people are of the opinion that there are too many guns in the U.S. and that a more reasonable society would see to it that

---

§   Ibid.

such easy availability was curbed. But what if it never is? Don't be too concerned. The U.S., with all its guns, will still get by for the foreseeable future. So many guns cause a lot of problems, but this society will muddle through with or without them.

The subject of immigration into Japan, however, is not like that. It's not that it would be nice to have more immigration. The problem is much more serious: Given the very low birth rate and aging population, *unless Japan can manage to overcome its aversion to large-scale immigration, its very survival as a leading industrial society is in jeopardy!*

It was mentioned previously in this book that Japan's death rate exceeds its birth rate, so that the population is starting to decline. In 1990, Japan was the seventh most populous nation; today, twenty years later, it stands at number ten and dropping. The age of the population is increasing as well. Other countries in Europe face this problem, but their immigration policies makes it possible to absorb enough foreigners to offset declining numbers of people. Japan, as you must know by now, has had a deep aversion to that kind of liberal immigration policy. It must somehow change its attitude.

A United Nations study estimates that in order to sustain Japan's economic prosperity, it will need 17 million foreign workers by 2050, or about 600,000 immigrants of working age each year until then. Compare that with the reality of the past twenty-five years, during which only one million foreign workers—total—have gained residence status during that entire period.

Governments in open societies must pander somewhat to popular opinion. Sometimes, such pandering results in policies which are supposed to address a problem, but which are completely useless and occasionally even counterproductive. For example, a policy a few years ago was launched to allow three thousand Chinese immigrants per year. But to forestall public criticism, it was stipulated that the Chinese immigrants must all be college trained, with professional status. Exactly the kind of workers Japan does not need. Another program was launched to allow 1,000 Filipino nurses to enter and achieve residency each year. But they all had to pass a difficult Japanese language course to become eligible, and over 90 percent of them could not do so.

Various guest worker programs were begun in the 1980s, but guest worker programs never work very well anywhere, and Japanese experience was no exception. A few hundred workers each year were brought in from Bangladesh, Pakistan, India and of all places, Uruguay. They were to stay for two years, but without Japanese language ability, they could only carry out the most basic tasks. Many overstayed their visas and became illegal, causing a great headache to Japan's law enforcement agencies.

A really significant program of importation of workers began in 1998, when over 300,000 Brazilians of Japanese ancestry were persuaded to resettle in Japan, presumably permanently. We wrote a little about this earlier, describing how naive Japanese officials were in assuming that because most of them were racially Japanese, they would fit in with the society smoothly. The Brazilians did not spread out through the country, but congregated in just a few cities. Hamamatsu, a city of about 50,000, 200 miles southwest of Tokyo, currently is home to 18,000 of these Brazilian-Japanese.

There came to be so much friction between the Brazilian immigrants and their Japanese neighbors that in 2005, the local government in Hamamatsu offered to pay all expenses for any individual or family who would move back to Brazil with the stipulation that they never return! Only a few hundred took the deal.

But there is hope. The long held resistance to the issue of immigration is showing signs of weakening. As you read this, the dyke against immigration is slowly beginning to spring holes. If nothing would change in Japan's current, very strict, immigration standards, experts keep reporting that by 2050, Japan's work force would be reduced by one third. That fact and its implications on funding care for the aged is finally reaching the consciousness of the bulk of the population. It is now a truism in Japan that something has to be done, and there is no "something" without greatly increased immigration.

One positive development has been that the subject of immigration is no longer taboo for public discussion. The Chairman of Sony, Nakatani Iwao, caused quite a stir in 2009 when he was quoted in a magazine article as calling for Japan to immediately begin a program of mass immigration.

Even before that, in the summer of 2008, eighty Diet members in the lower house made public their recommendation that the percentage of immigrant workers in Japan be increased from its present 1 percent to 10 percent by 2020.

The last bastion of opposition, and the most difficult to overcome, is the population itself. Japanese in general just do not like to live around foreigners. A few are OK, but masses of foreigners living in their communities is something that most still find unacceptable. Public opinion does seem to be softening just a bit. *Mainichi Shimbun*毎日新聞, one of Japan's leading newspapers, is interested in this subject and periodically conducts surveys of attitudes toward immigration. In the year 2000, 83 percent of a sample of Japanese adults responded that they were either strongly or somewhat strongly against mass immigration. In 2009, the percentage had fallen to 71 percent—still a hefty majority, but at least moving in the right direction.

Objective reality would seem to show that Japan really does not have a choice in the matter. It will not be easy; the Japanese have never had to contend with that kind of social diversity. The government will have to proceed with stealth-like caution. It will have to face down a great deal of public opposition. Programs have to be realistic and practical to be effective as long-term solutions. One problem has always been that the government insists on Japanese-language competency in approving resident visas. If the future need for immigrants is to be met, or even come close to being met, that is not a realistic requirement. Can you imagine the logistical difficulty of teaching half a million immigrants coming to the country each year to speak and write Japanese within a short time? The American experience should be instructive. First generation immigrants will be only semi-fluent and largely illiterate in the national language. But that problem will pass in time.

Perhaps the most negative result of greatly expanded immigration when it comes, as it must, will be the establishment, for a long time, of a two-tiered society. Many of those of the first, and even second generation and beyond, will tend to form an underclass. They will be poor by the standards of the country, less educated in the Japanese way, and able to participate in the national life only to a limited degree. This situation may persist and become a permanent social problem. But even that is better than losing the country's industrial base.

The Emperor once asked the Japanese people to "endure the unendurable." They did so and not only survived, but built a better society than existed before. Japan will not remain exactly the kind of society that it is today, but we predict that adjustments will be made, attitudes will mollify, and the country will continue to survive and prosper.